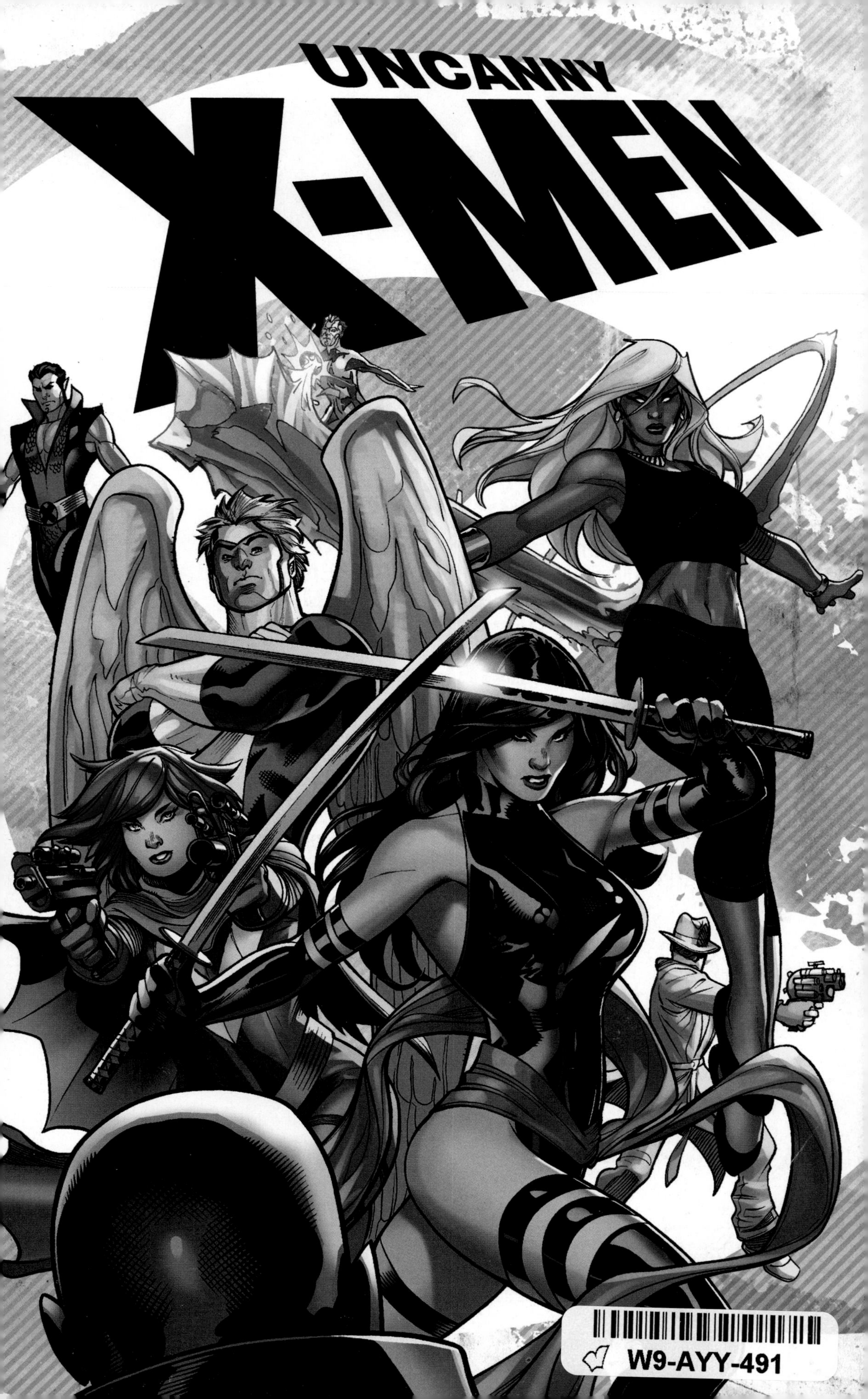
UNCANNY
X-MEN

UNCANNY X-MEN

BREAKING POINT

Writer: **KIERON GILLEN**

ISSUE #534.1

Pencils: **CARLOS PACHECO**
Inks: **CAM SMITH** with **DAN GREEN** & **NATHAN LEE**
Colors: **FRANK D'ARMATA**
Cover Art: **CARLOS PACHECO, CAM SMITH** & **SOTOCOLOR**

ISSUES #535-538

Pencils: **TERRY DODSON**
Inks: **RACHEL DODSON**
Colorist: **JUSTIN PONSOR**
Cover Art: **TERRY DODSON** & **RACHEL DODSON**

ISSUE #539

Artist: **IBRAIM ROBERSON**
Colorist: **JIM CHARALAMPIDIS**
Cover Art: **SIMONE BIANCHI**

Letterer: **VIRTUAL CALLIGRAPHY'S JOE CARAMAGNA**
Assistant Editor: **JORDAN D. WHITE**
Associate Editor: **DANIEL KETCHUM**
Editor: **NICK LOWE**

Collection Editor: Jennifer Grünwald • Editorial Assistants: James Emmett & Joe Hochstein
Assistant Editors: Alex Starbuck & Nelson Ribeiro • Editor, Special Projects: Mark D. Beazley
Senior Editor, Special Projects: Jeff Youngquist • Senior Vice President of Sales: David Gabriel
SVP of Brand Planning & Communications: Michael Pasciullo

Editor in Chief: Axel Alonso • Chief Creative Officer: Joe Quesada • Publisher: Dan Buckley • Executive Producer: Alan Fine

UNCANNY X-MEN: BREAKING POINT. Contains material originally published in magazine form as UNCANNY X-MEN #534.1 and #535-539. First printing 2011. ISBN# 978-0-7851-5226-2. Published by MARVEL WORLDWI
INC., a subsidiary of MARVEL ENTERTAINMENT, LLC. OFFICE OF PUBLICATION: 135 West 50th Street, New York, NY 10020. Copyright © 2011 Marvel Characters, Inc. All rights reserved. $16.99 per copy in the U.S. and $1
in Canada (GST #R127032852); Canadian Agreement #40668537. All characters featured in this issue and the distinctive names and likenesses thereof, and all related indicia are trademarks of Marvel Characters, Inc
similarity between any of the names, characters, persons, and/or institutions in this magazine with those of any living or dead person or institution is intended, and any such similarity which may exist is purely coincide
Printed in the U.S.A. ALAN FINE, EVP - Office of the President, Marvel Worldwide, Inc. and EVP & CMO Marvel Characters B.V.; DAN BUCKLEY, Publisher & President - Print, Animation & Digital Divisions; JOE QUESADA, C
Creative Officer; JIM SOKOLOWSKI, Chief Operating Officer; DAVID BOGART, SVP of Business Affairs & Talent Management; TOM BREVOORT, SVP of Publishing; C.B. CEBULSKI, SVP of Creator & Content Development; D
GABRIEL, SVP of Publishing Sales & Circulation; MICHAEL PASCIULLO, SVP of Brand Planning & Communications; JIM O'KEEFE, VP of Operations & Logistics; DAN CARR, Executive Director of Publishing Technology; S
CRESPI, Editorial Operations Manager; ALEX MORALES, Publishing Operations Manager; STAN LEE, Chairman Emeritus. For information regarding advertising in Marvel Comics or on Marvel.com, please contact John D
SVP Integrated Sales and Marketing, at jdokes@marvel.com. For Marvel subscription inquiries, please call 800-217-9158. **Manufactured between 8/11/2011 and 8/30/2011 by QUAD/GRAPHICS, DUBUQUE, IA.**

10 9 8 7 6 5 4 3 2 1

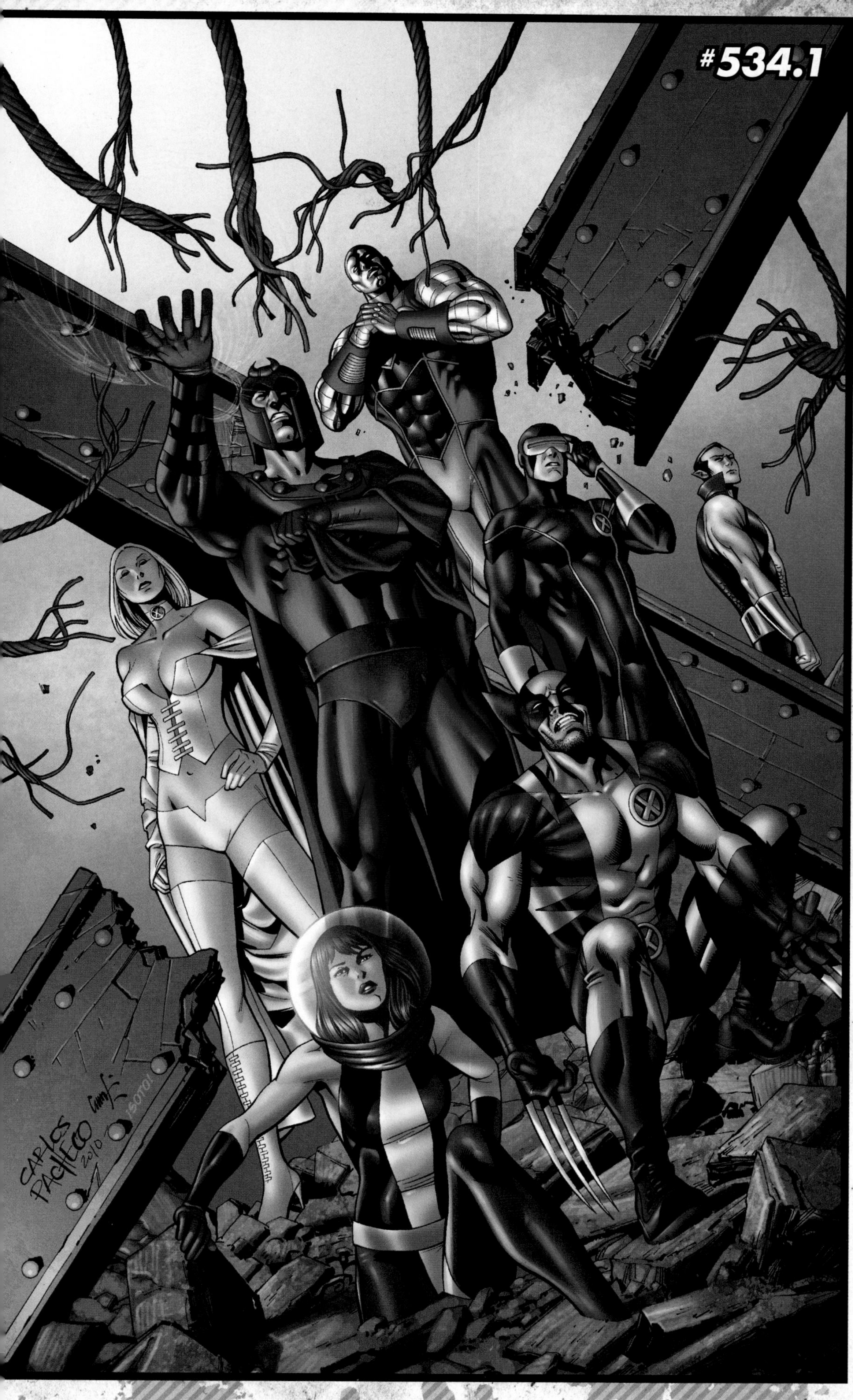
#534.1
CARLOS PACHECO 2010

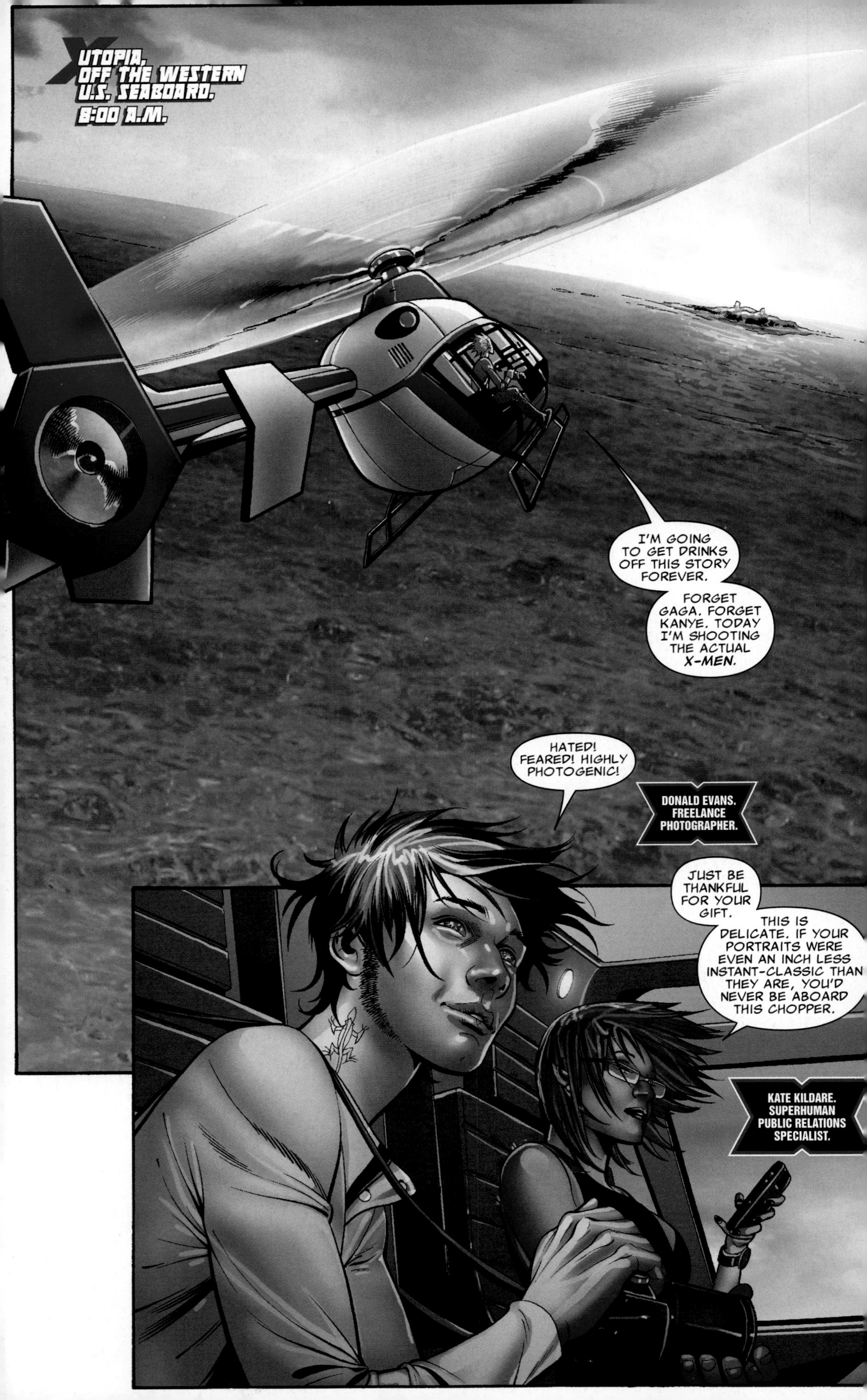
UTOPIA, OFF THE WESTERN U.S. SEABOARD.
8:00 A.M.
I'M GOING TO GET DRINKS OFF THIS STORY FOREVER.
FORGET GAGA. FORGET KANYE. TODAY I'M SHOOTING THE ACTUAL X-MEN.
HATED! FEARED! HIGHLY PHOTOGENIC!
DONALD EVANS. FREELANCE PHOTOGRAPHER.
JUST BE THANKFUL FOR YOUR GIFT.
THIS IS DELICATE. IF YOUR PORTRAITS WERE EVEN AN INCH LESS INSTANT-CLASSIC THAN THEY ARE, YOU'D NEVER BE ABOARD THIS CHOPPER.
KATE KILDARE. SUPERHUMAN PUBLIC RELATIONS SPECIALIST.

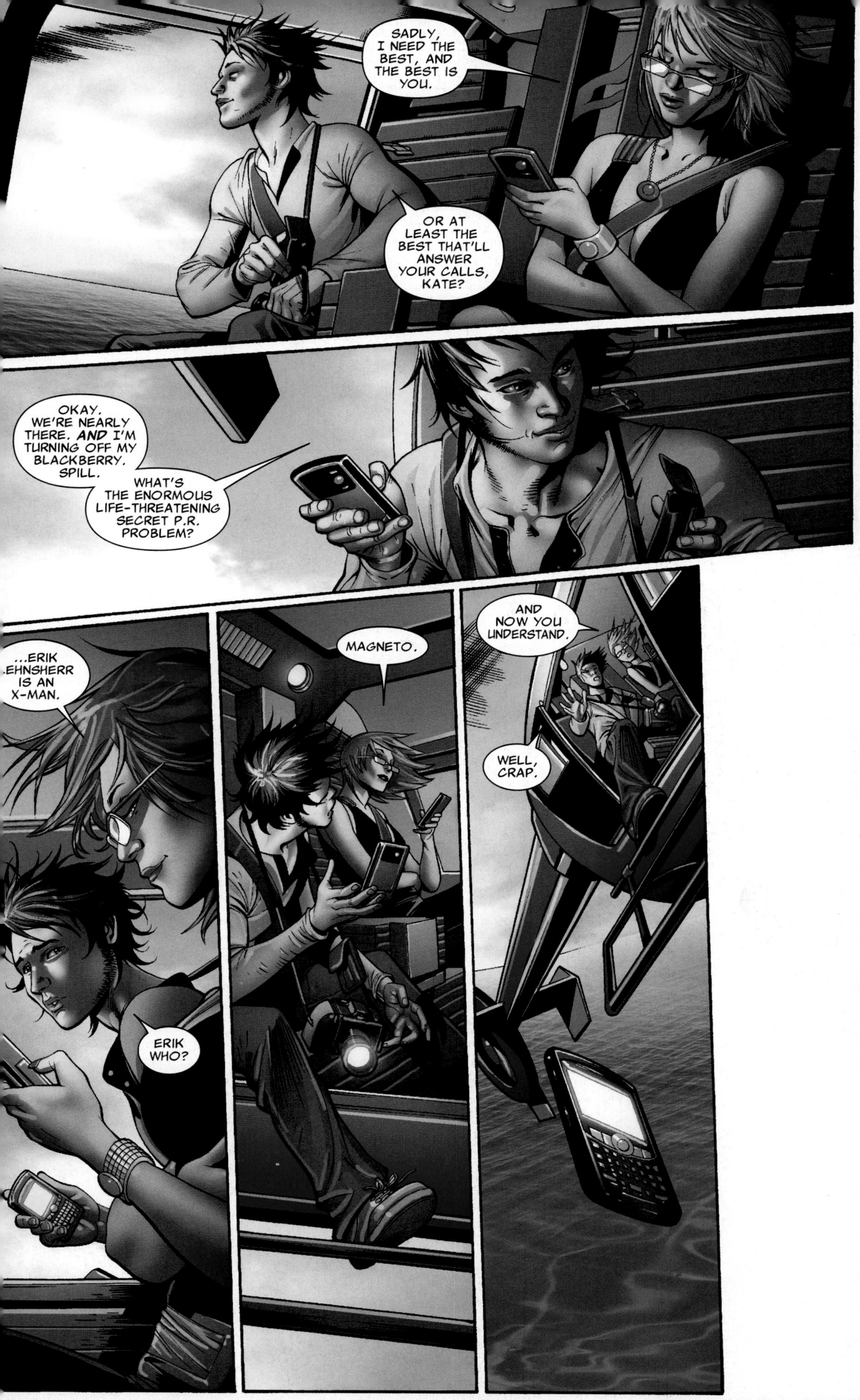
SADLY, I NEED THE BEST, AND THE BEST IS YOU.
OR AT LEAST THE BEST THAT'LL ANSWER YOUR CALLS, KATE?
OKAY. WE'RE NEARLY THERE. AND I'M TURNING OFF MY BLACKBERRY. SPILL.
WHAT'S THE ENORMOUS LIFE-THREATENING SECRET P.R. PROBLEM?
...ERIK LEHNSHERR IS AN X-MAN.
ERIK WHO?
MAGNETO.
AND NOW YOU UNDERSTAND.
WELL, CRAP.

BORN DIFFERENT WITH AMAZING SUPER-POWERS, THESE MUTANTS CAME TOGETHER TO PROTECT THOSE THAT HATE AND FEAR THEM. NOW, THEY HAVE DRAWN TOGETHER, LIVING ON THE ISLAND OF UTOPIA OFF THE COAST OF SAN FRANCISCO. THEY ARE...THE UNCANNY X-MEN.

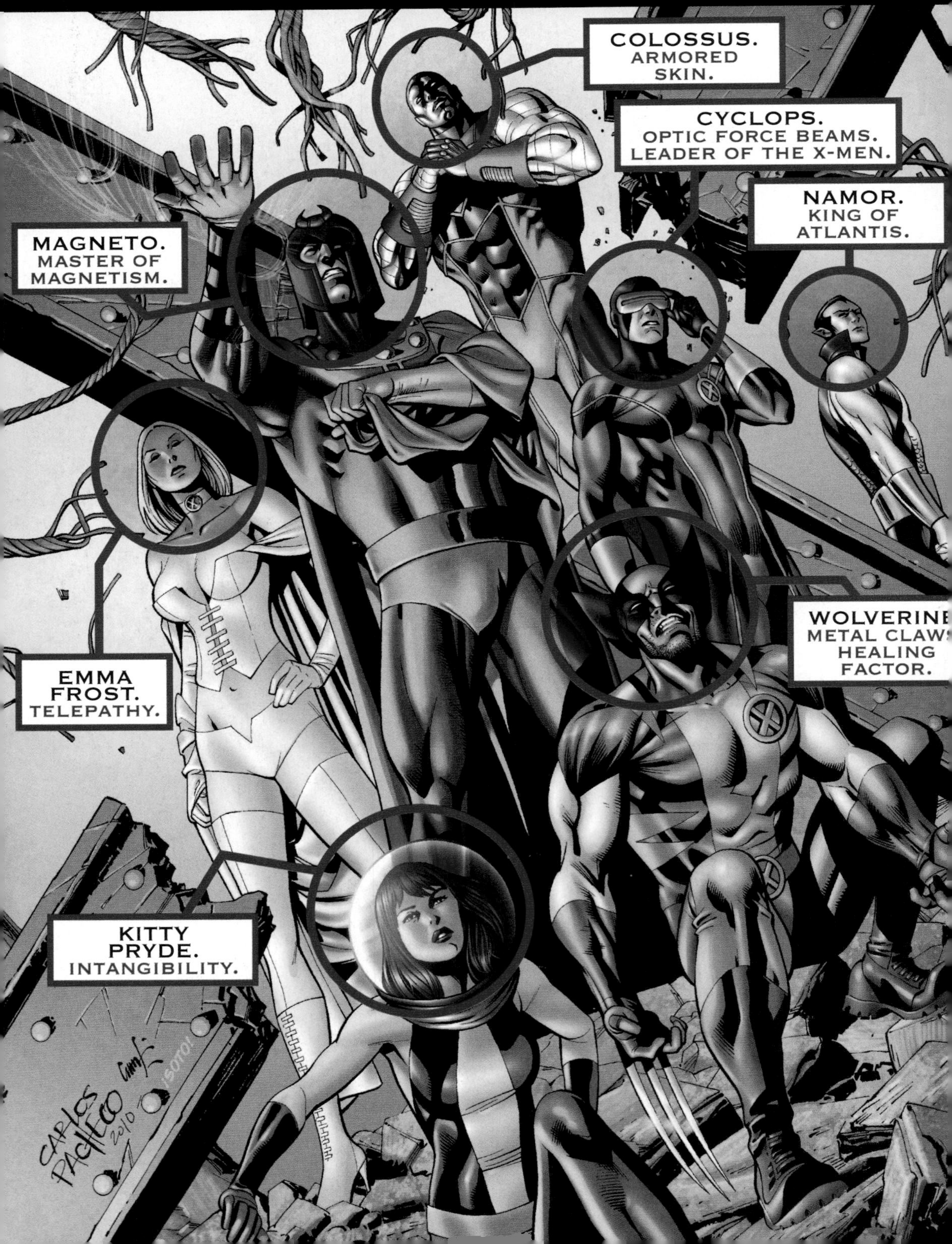
COLOSSUS. ARMORED SKIN.
CYCLOPS. OPTIC FORCE BEAMS. LEADER OF THE X-MEN.
NAMOR. KING OF ATLANTIS.
MAGNETO. MASTER OF MAGNETISM.
WOLVERINE METAL CLAWS HEALING FACTOR.
EMMA FROST. TELEPATHY.
KITTY PRYDE. INTANGIBILITY.
CARLOS PACHECO 2010

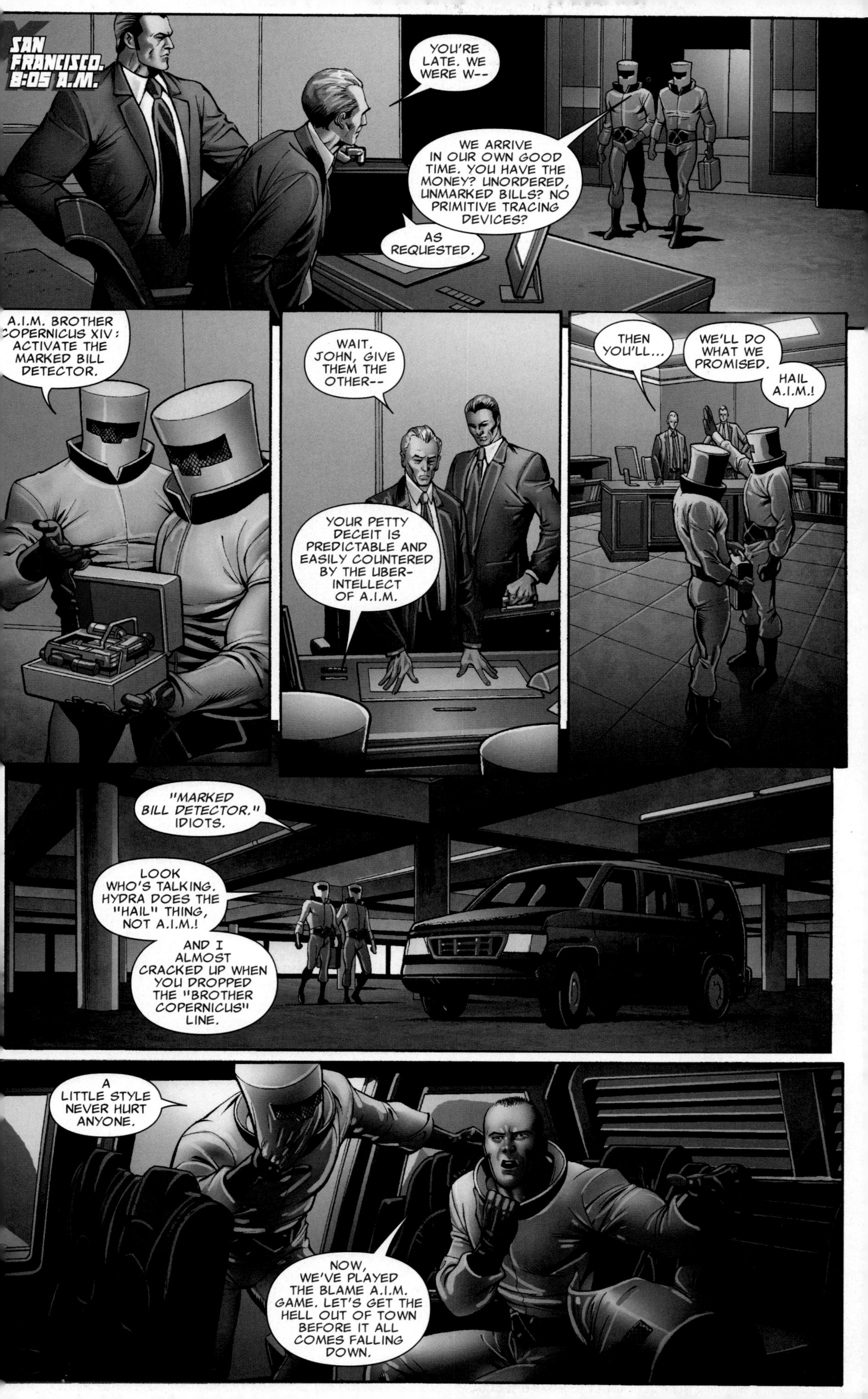
SAN FRANCISCO. 8:05 A.M.
YOU'RE LATE. WE WERE W--
WE ARRIVE IN OUR OWN GOOD TIME. YOU HAVE THE MONEY? UNORDERED, UNMARKED BILLS? NO PRIMITIVE TRACING DEVICES?
AS REQUESTED.
A.I.M. BROTHER COPERNICUS XIV: ACTIVATE THE MARKED BILL DETECTOR.
WAIT. JOHN, GIVE THEM THE OTHER--
YOUR PETTY DECEIT IS PREDICTABLE AND EASILY COUNTERED BY THE UBER-INTELLECT OF A.I.M.
THEN YOU'LL...
WE'LL DO WHAT WE PROMISED.
HAIL A.I.M.!
"MARKED BILL DETECTOR." IDIOTS.
LOOK WHO'S TALKING. HYDRA DOES THE "HAIL" THING, NOT A.I.M.!
AND I ALMOST CRACKED UP WHEN YOU DROPPED THE "BROTHER COPERNICUS" LINE.
A LITTLE STYLE NEVER HURT ANYONE.
NOW, WE'VE PLAYED THE BLAME A.I.M. GAME. LET'S GET THE HELL OUT OF TOWN BEFORE IT ALL COMES FALLING DOWN.

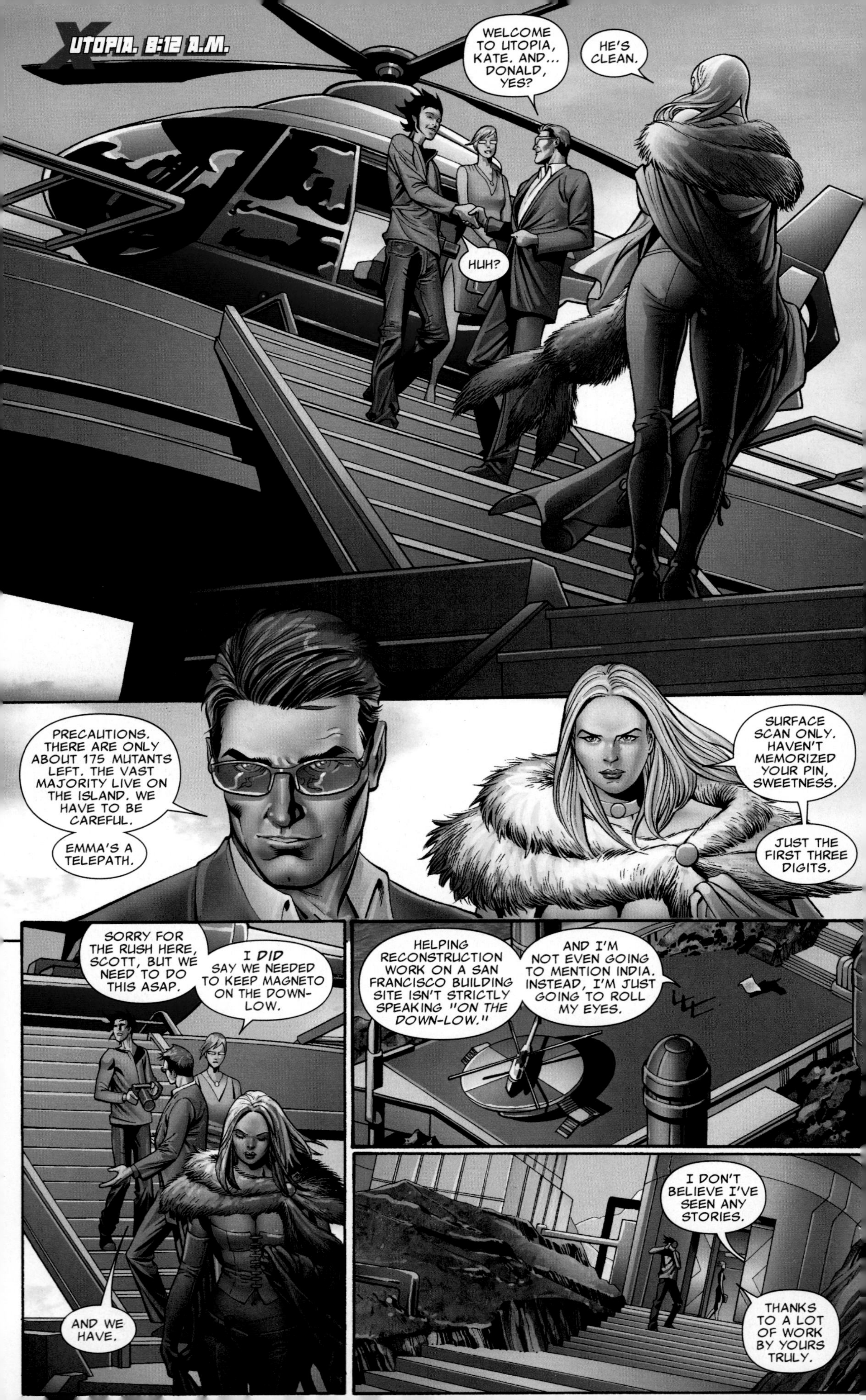
UTOPIA. 8:12 A.M.
WELCOME TO UTOPIA, KATE. AND... DONALD, YES?
HE'S CLEAN.
HUH?
PRECAUTIONS. THERE ARE ONLY ABOUT 175 MUTANTS LEFT. THE VAST MAJORITY LIVE ON THE ISLAND. WE HAVE TO BE CAREFUL.
EMMA'S A TELEPATH.
SURFACE SCAN ONLY. HAVEN'T MEMORIZED YOUR PIN, SWEETNESS.
JUST THE FIRST THREE DIGITS.
SORRY FOR THE RUSH HERE, SCOTT, BUT WE NEED TO DO THIS ASAP.
I *DID* SAY WE NEEDED TO KEEP MAGNETO ON THE DOWN-LOW.
AND WE HAVE.
HELPING RECONSTRUCTION WORK ON A SAN FRANCISCO BUILDING SITE ISN'T STRICTLY SPEAKING "ON THE DOWN-LOW."
AND I'M NOT EVEN GOING TO MENTION INDIA. INSTEAD, I'M JUST GOING TO ROLL MY EYES.
I DON'T BELIEVE I'VE SEEN ANY STORIES.
THANKS TO A LOT OF WORK BY YOURS TRULY.

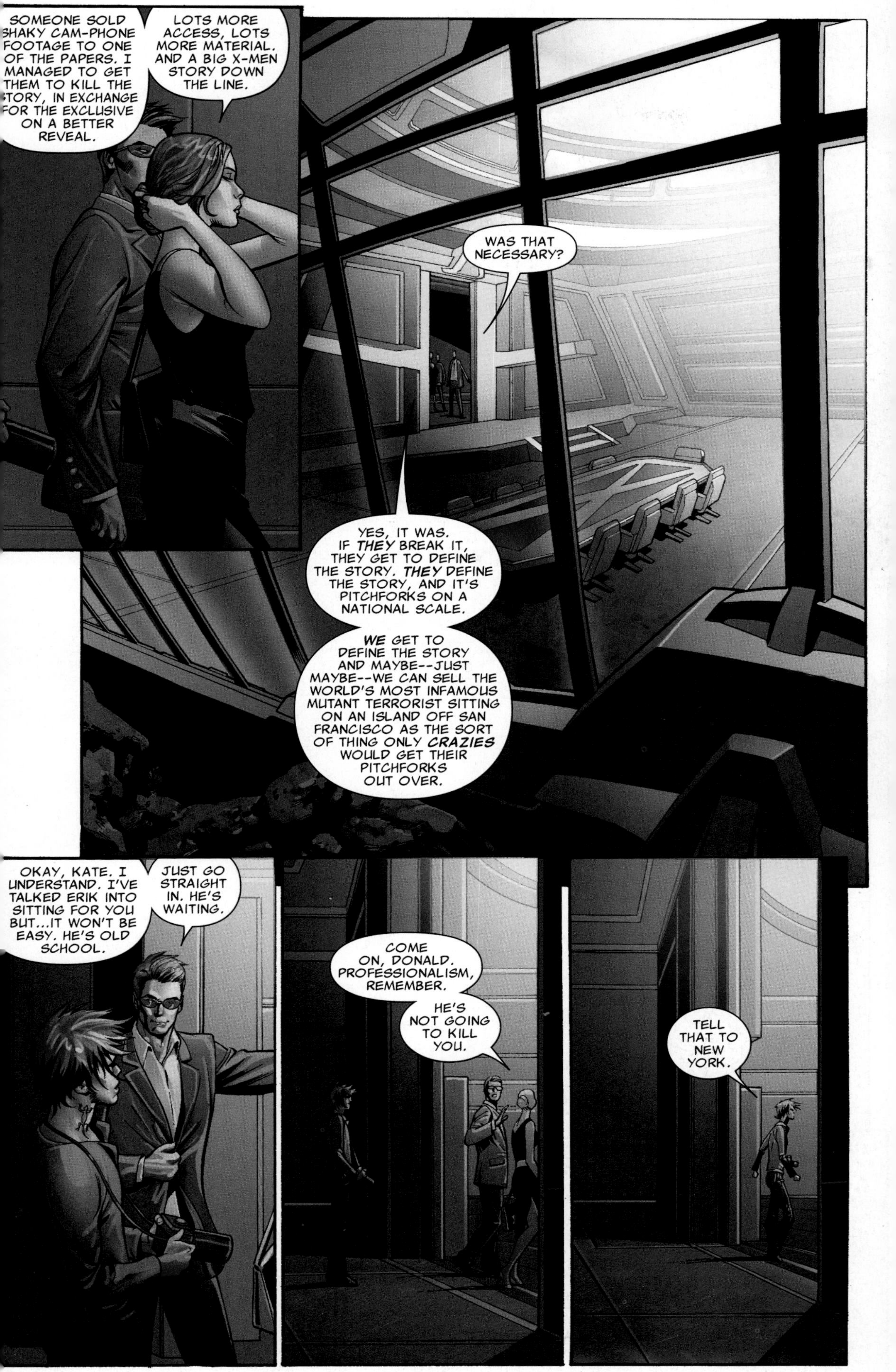
SOMEONE SOLD SHAKY CAM-PHONE FOOTAGE TO ONE OF THE PAPERS. I MANAGED TO GET THEM TO KILL THE STORY, IN EXCHANGE FOR THE EXCLUSIVE ON A BETTER REVEAL.
LOTS MORE ACCESS, LOTS MORE MATERIAL. AND A BIG X-MEN STORY DOWN THE LINE.
WAS THAT NECESSARY?
YES, IT WAS. IF *THEY* BREAK IT, THEY GET TO DEFINE THE STORY. *THEY* DEFINE THE STORY, AND IT'S PITCHFORKS ON A NATIONAL SCALE.
WE GET TO DEFINE THE STORY AND MAYBE--JUST MAYBE--WE CAN SELL THE WORLD'S MOST INFAMOUS MUTANT TERRORIST SITTING ON AN ISLAND OFF SAN FRANCISCO AS THE SORT OF THING ONLY *CRAZIES* WOULD GET THEIR PITCHFORKS OUT OVER.
OKAY, KATE. I UNDERSTAND. I'VE TALKED ERIK INTO SITTING FOR YOU BUT...IT WON'T BE EASY. HE'S OLD SCHOOL.
JUST GO STRAIGHT IN. HE'S WAITING.
COME ON, DONALD. PROFESSIONALISM, REMEMBER.
HE'S NOT GOING TO KILL YOU.
TELL THAT TO NEW YORK.

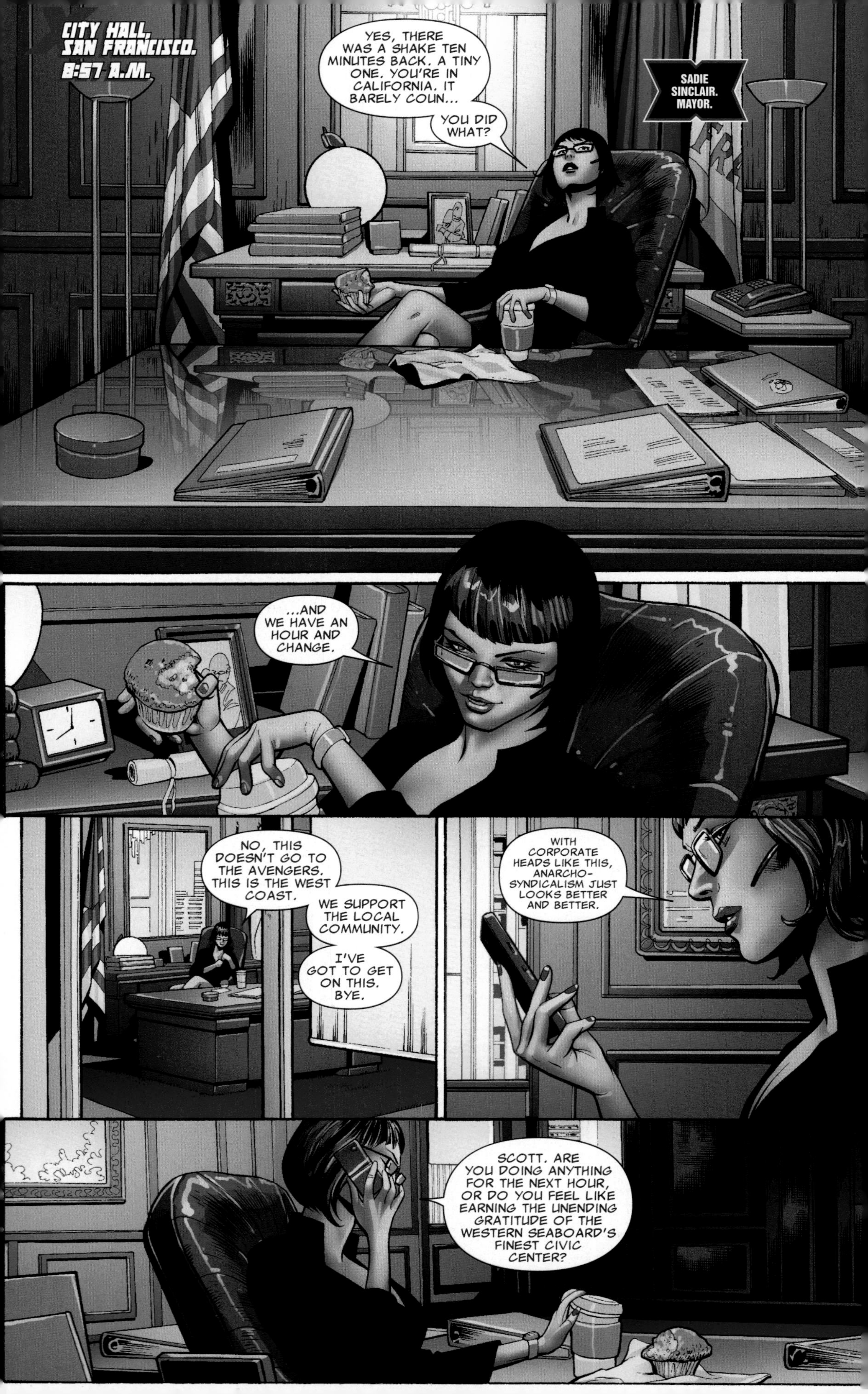
CITY HALL, SAN FRANCISCO. 8:57 A.M.
YES, THERE WAS A SHAKE TEN MINUTES BACK. A TINY ONE. YOU'RE IN CALIFORNIA. IT BARELY COUN...
YOU DID WHAT?
SADIE SINCLAIR. MAYOR.
...AND WE HAVE AN HOUR AND CHANGE.
NO, THIS DOESN'T GO TO THE AVENGERS. THIS IS THE WEST COAST.
WE SUPPORT THE LOCAL COMMUNITY.
I'VE GOT TO GET ON THIS. BYE.
WITH CORPORATE HEADS LIKE THIS, ANARCHO-SYNDICALISM JUST LOOKS BETTER AND BETTER.
SCOTT. ARE YOU DOING ANYTHING FOR THE NEXT HOUR, OR DO YOU FEEL LIKE EARNING THE UNENDING GRATITUDE OF THE WESTERN SEABOARD'S FINEST CIVIC CENTER?

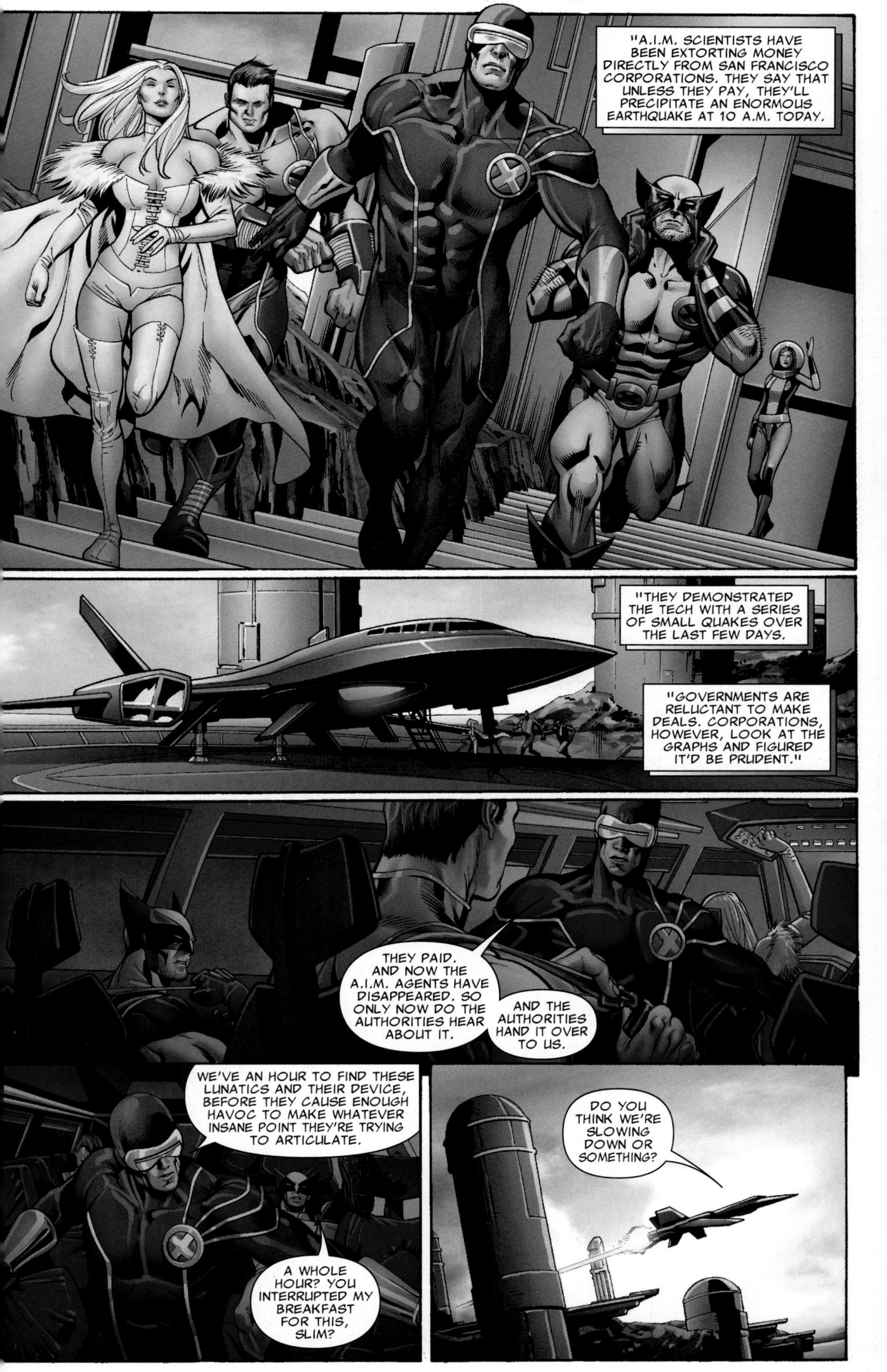
"A.I.M. SCIENTISTS HAVE BEEN EXTORTING MONEY DIRECTLY FROM SAN FRANCISCO CORPORATIONS. THEY SAY THAT UNLESS THEY PAY, THEY'LL PRECIPITATE AN ENORMOUS EARTHQUAKE AT 10 A.M. TODAY.
"THEY DEMONSTRATED THE TECH WITH A SERIES OF SMALL QUAKES OVER THE LAST FEW DAYS.
"GOVERNMENTS ARE RELUCTANT TO MAKE DEALS. CORPORATIONS, HOWEVER, LOOK AT THE GRAPHS AND FIGURED IT'D BE PRUDENT."
THEY PAID. AND NOW THE A.I.M. AGENTS HAVE DISAPPEARED. SO ONLY NOW DO THE AUTHORITIES HEAR ABOUT IT.
AND THE AUTHORITIES HAND IT OVER TO US.
WE'VE AN HOUR TO FIND THESE LUNATICS AND THEIR DEVICE, BEFORE THEY CAUSE ENOUGH HAVOC TO MAKE WHATEVER INSANE POINT THEY'RE TRYING TO ARTICULATE.
A WHOLE HOUR? YOU INTERRUPTED MY BREAKFAST FOR THIS, SLIM?
DO YOU THINK WE'RE SLOWING DOWN OR SOMETHING?

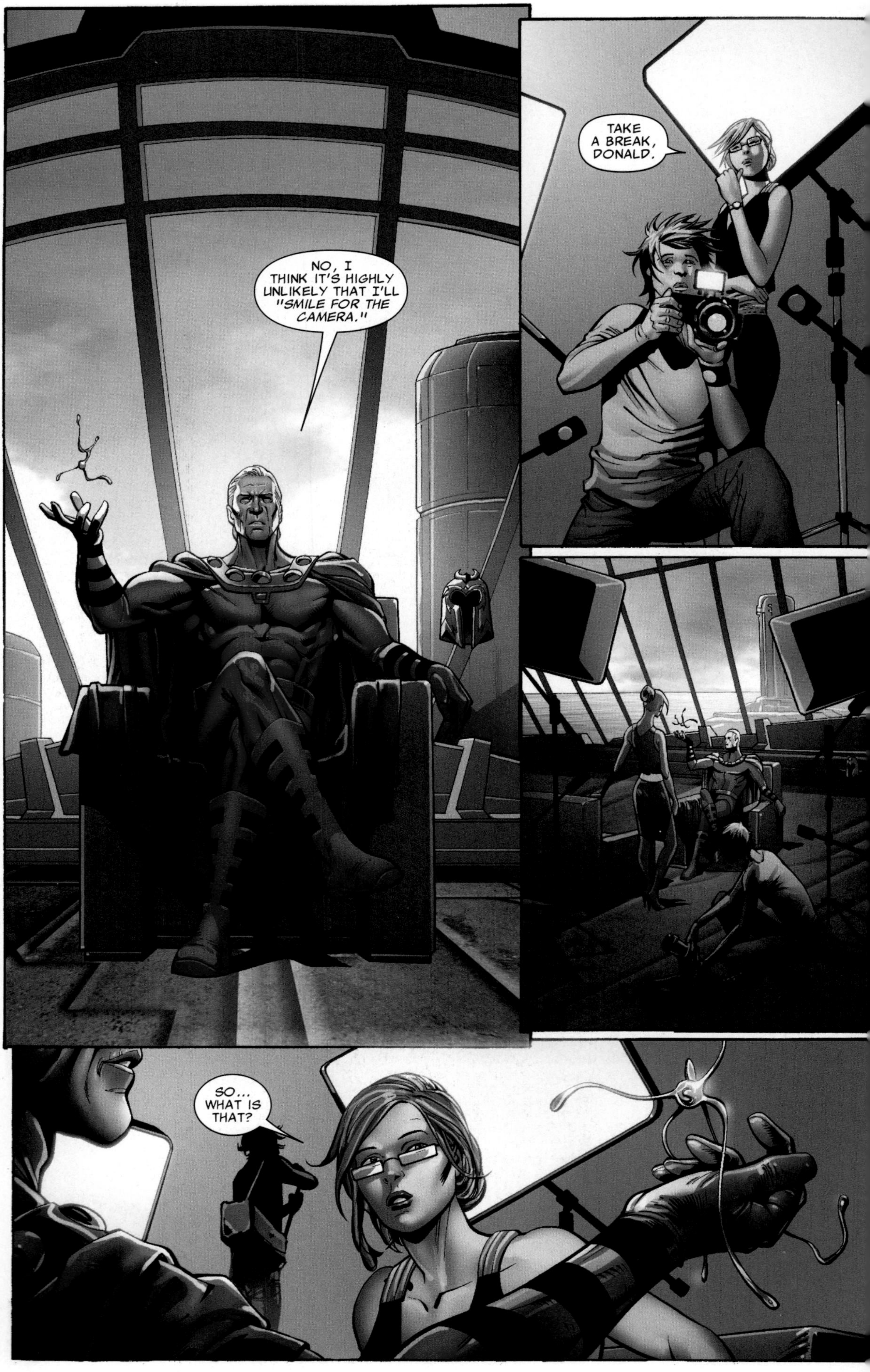
NO, I THINK IT'S HIGHLY UNLIKELY THAT I'LL "SMILE FOR THE CAMERA."
TAKE A BREAK, DONALD.
SO... WHAT IS THAT?

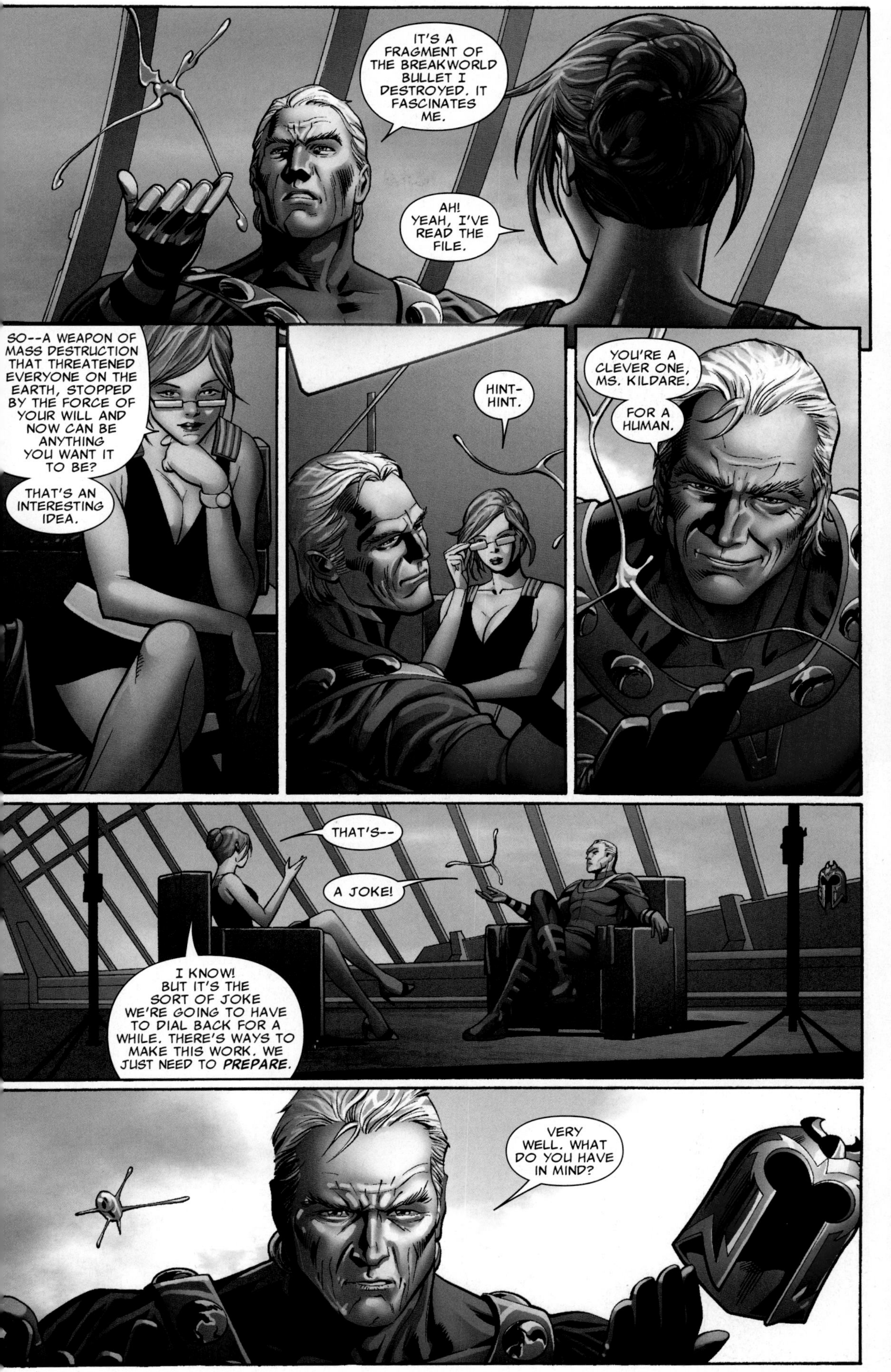

IT'S A FRAGMENT OF THE BREAKWORLD BULLET I DESTROYED. IT FASCINATES ME.
AH! YEAH, I'VE READ THE FILE.
SO--A WEAPON OF MASS DESTRUCTION THAT THREATENED EVERYONE ON THE EARTH, STOPPED BY THE FORCE OF YOUR WILL AND NOW CAN BE ANYTHING YOU WANT IT TO BE?
THAT'S AN INTERESTING IDEA.
HINT-HINT.
YOU'RE A CLEVER ONE, MS. KILDARE.
FOR A HUMAN.
THAT'S--
A JOKE!
I KNOW! BUT IT'S THE SORT OF JOKE WE'RE GOING TO HAVE TO DIAL BACK FOR A WHILE. THERE'S WAYS TO MAKE THIS WORK. WE JUST NEED TO *PREPARE*.
VERY WELL. WHAT DO YOU HAVE IN MIND?

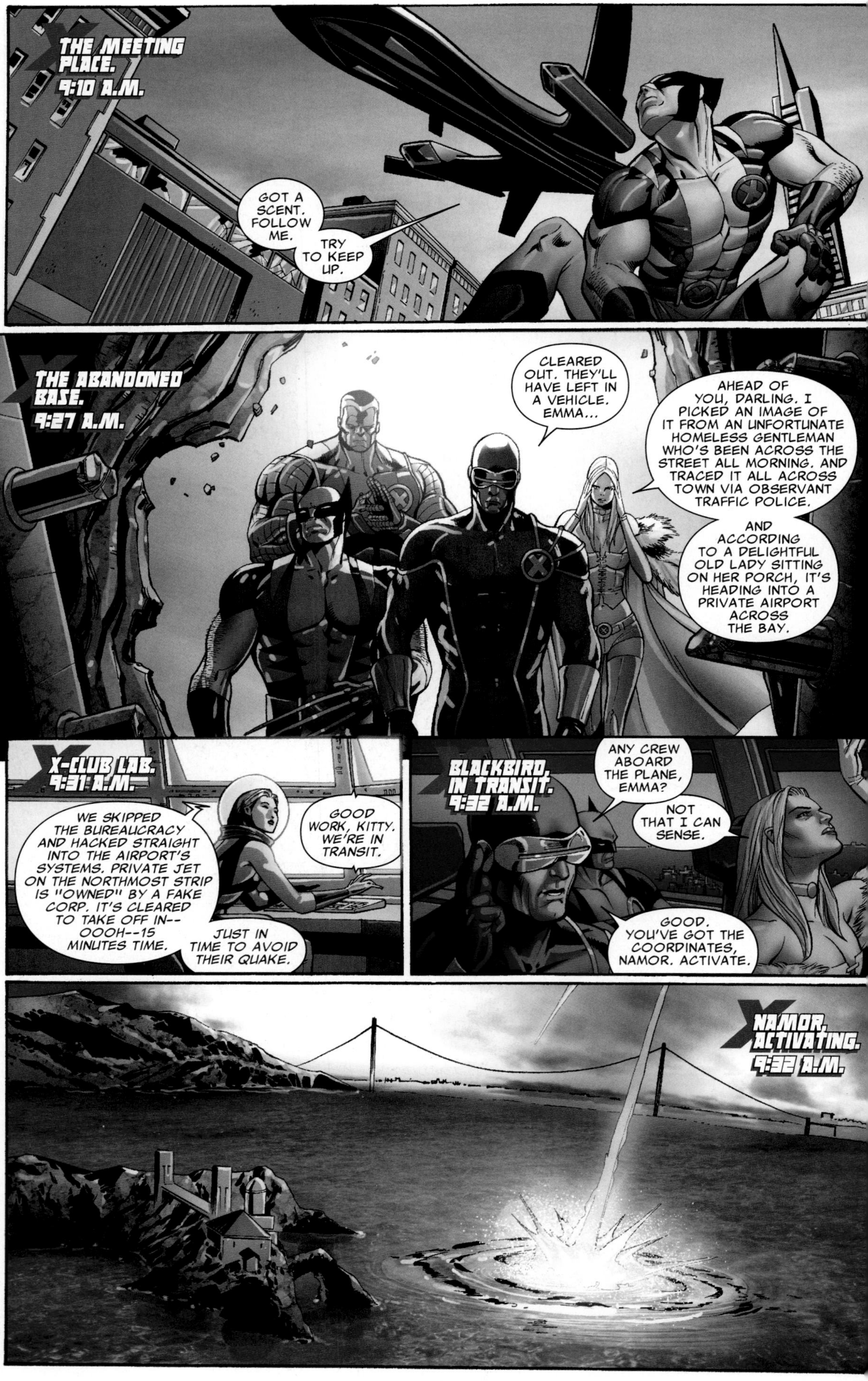
THE MEETING PLACE. 9:10 A.M.
GOT A SCENT. FOLLOW ME.
TRY TO KEEP UP.
THE ABANDONED BASE. 9:27 A.M.
CLEARED OUT. THEY'LL HAVE LEFT IN A VEHICLE. EMMA...
AHEAD OF YOU, DARLING. I PICKED AN IMAGE OF IT FROM AN UNFORTUNATE HOMELESS GENTLEMAN WHO'S BEEN ACROSS THE STREET ALL MORNING. AND TRACED IT ALL ACROSS TOWN VIA OBSERVANT TRAFFIC POLICE.
AND ACCORDING TO A DELIGHTFUL OLD LADY SITTING ON HER PORCH, IT'S HEADING INTO A PRIVATE AIRPORT ACROSS THE BAY.
X-CLUB LAB. 9:31 A.M.
WE SKIPPED THE BUREAUCRACY AND HACKED STRAIGHT INTO THE AIRPORT'S SYSTEMS. PRIVATE JET ON THE NORTHMOST STRIP IS "OWNED" BY A FAKE CORP. IT'S CLEARED TO TAKE OFF IN--OOOH--15 MINUTES TIME.
GOOD WORK, KITTY. WE'RE IN TRANSIT.
JUST IN TIME TO AVOID THEIR QUAKE.
BLACKBIRD, IN TRANSIT. 9:32 A.M.
ANY CREW ABOARD THE PLANE, EMMA?
NOT THAT I CAN SENSE.
GOOD. YOU'VE GOT THE COORDINATES, NAMOR. ACTIVATE.
NAMOR. ACTIVATING. 9:32 A.M.

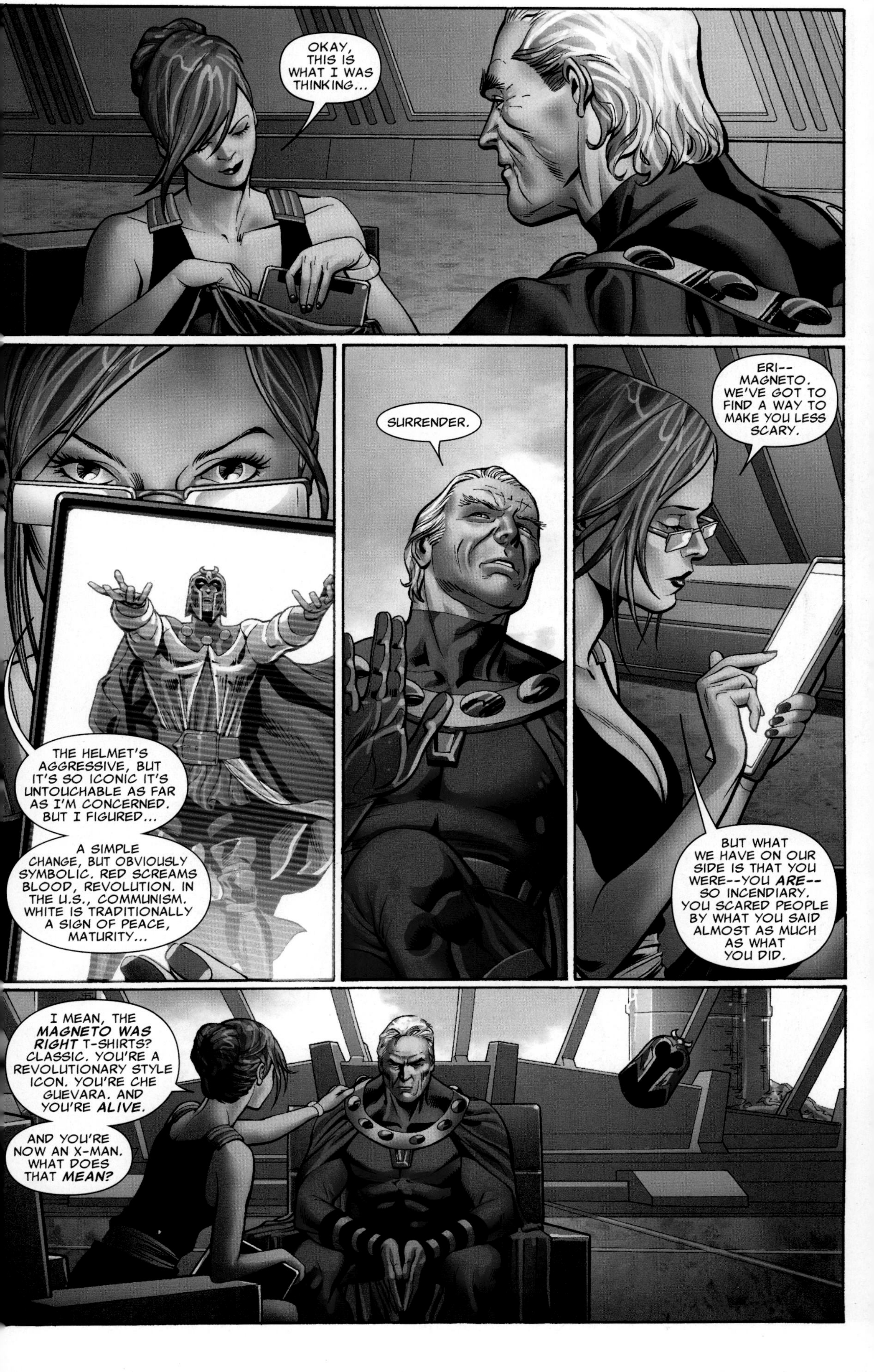
OKAY, THIS IS WHAT I WAS THINKING...
THE HELMET'S AGGRESSIVE, BUT IT'S SO ICONIC IT'S UNTOUCHABLE AS FAR AS I'M CONCERNED. BUT I FIGURED...
A SIMPLE CHANGE, BUT OBVIOUSLY SYMBOLIC. RED SCREAMS BLOOD, REVOLUTION. IN THE U.S., COMMUNISM. WHITE IS TRADITIONALLY A SIGN OF PEACE, MATURITY...
SURRENDER.
ERI-- MAGNETO. WE'VE GOT TO FIND A WAY TO MAKE YOU LESS SCARY.
BUT WHAT WE HAVE ON OUR SIDE IS THAT YOU WERE--YOU *ARE*-- SO INCENDIARY. YOU SCARED PEOPLE BY WHAT YOU SAID ALMOST AS MUCH AS WHAT YOU DID.
I MEAN, THE *MAGNETO WAS RIGHT* T-SHIRTS? CLASSIC. YOU'RE A REVOLUTIONARY STYLE ICON. YOU'RE CHE GUEVARA. AND YOU'RE *ALIVE*.
AND YOU'RE NOW AN X-MAN. WHAT DOES THAT *MEAN?*

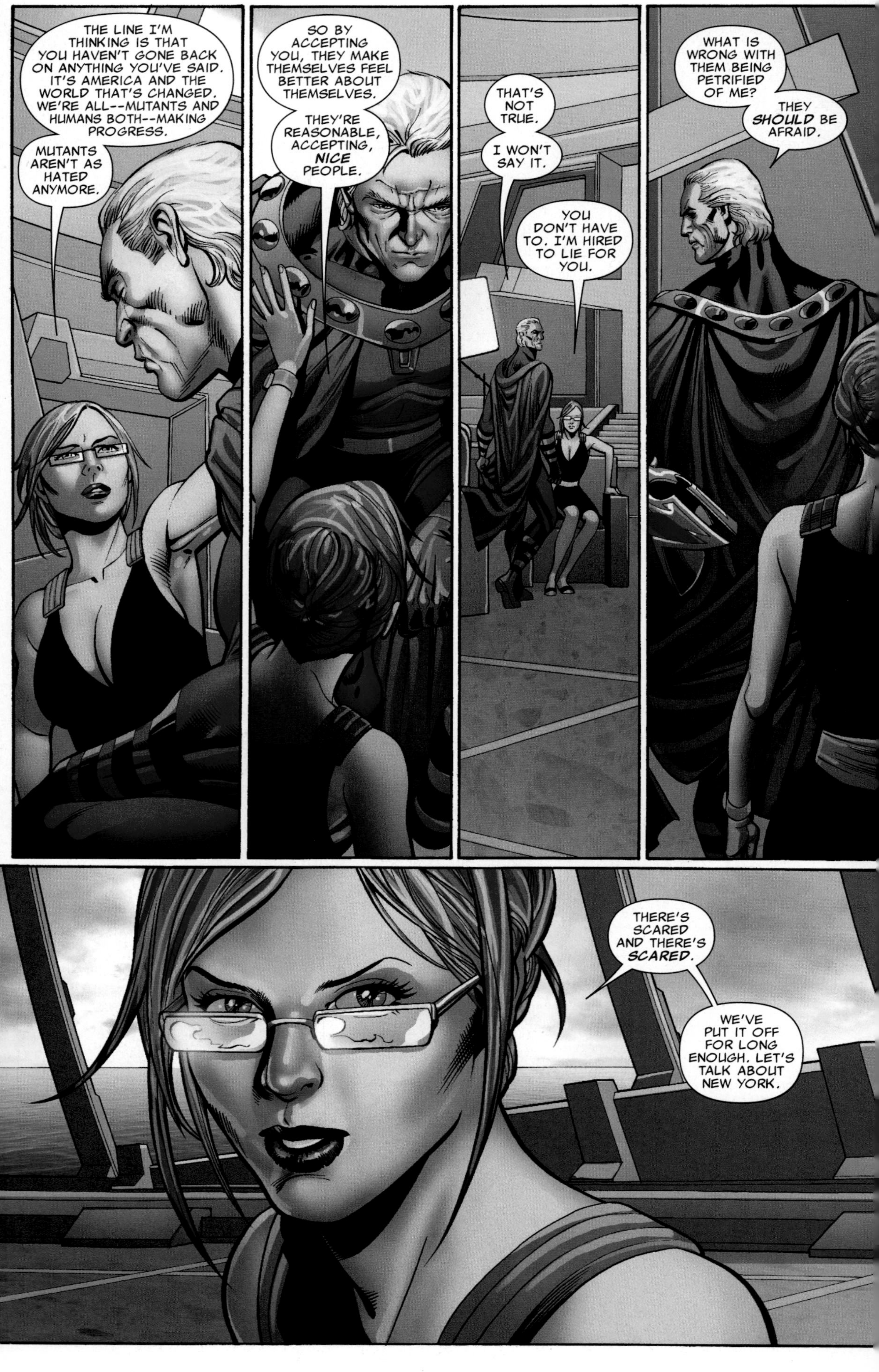
THE LINE I'M THINKING IS THAT YOU HAVEN'T GONE BACK ON ANYTHING YOU'VE SAID. IT'S AMERICA AND THE WORLD THAT'S CHANGED. WE'RE ALL--MUTANTS AND HUMANS BOTH--MAKING PROGRESS.
MUTANTS AREN'T AS HATED ANYMORE.
SO BY ACCEPTING YOU, THEY MAKE THEMSELVES FEEL BETTER ABOUT THEMSELVES.
THEY'RE REASONABLE, ACCEPTING, NICE PEOPLE.
THAT'S NOT TRUE.
I WON'T SAY IT.
YOU DON'T HAVE TO. I'M HIRED TO LIE FOR YOU.
WHAT IS WRONG WITH THEM BEING PETRIFIED OF ME?
THEY SHOULD BE AFRAID.
THERE'S SCARED AND THERE'S SCARED.
WE'VE PUT IT OFF FOR LONG ENOUGH. LET'S TALK ABOUT NEW YORK.

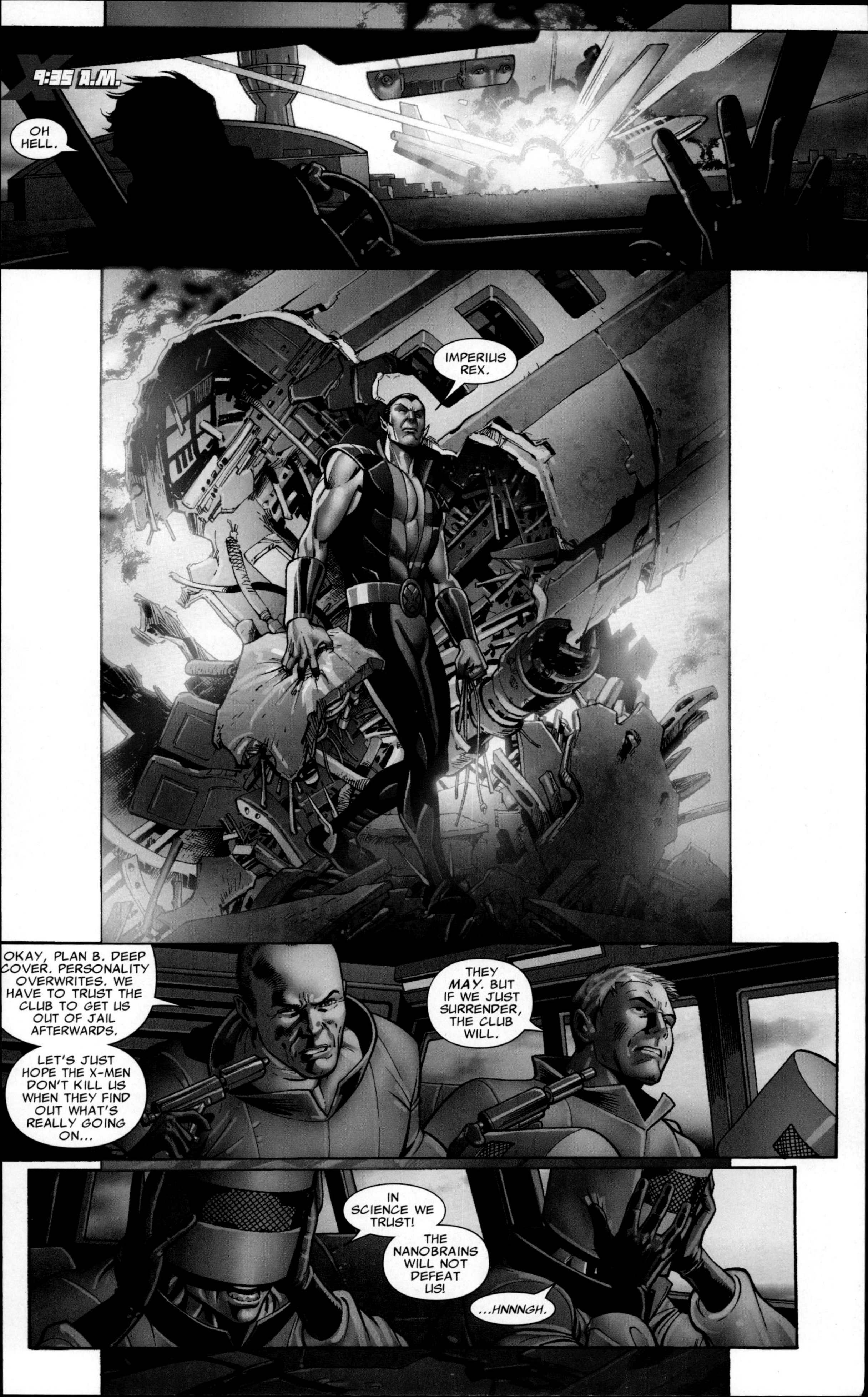
9:35 A.M.
OH HELL.
IMPERIUS REX.
OKAY, PLAN B. DEEP COVER. PERSONALITY OVERWRITES. WE HAVE TO TRUST THE CLUB TO GET US OUT OF JAIL AFTERWARDS.
LET'S JUST HOPE THE X-MEN DON'T KILL US WHEN THEY FIND OUT WHAT'S REALLY GOING ON...
THEY MAY. BUT IF WE JUST SURRENDER, THE CLUB WILL.
IN SCIENCE WE TRUST!
THE NANOBRAINS WILL NOT DEFEAT US!
...HNNNGH.

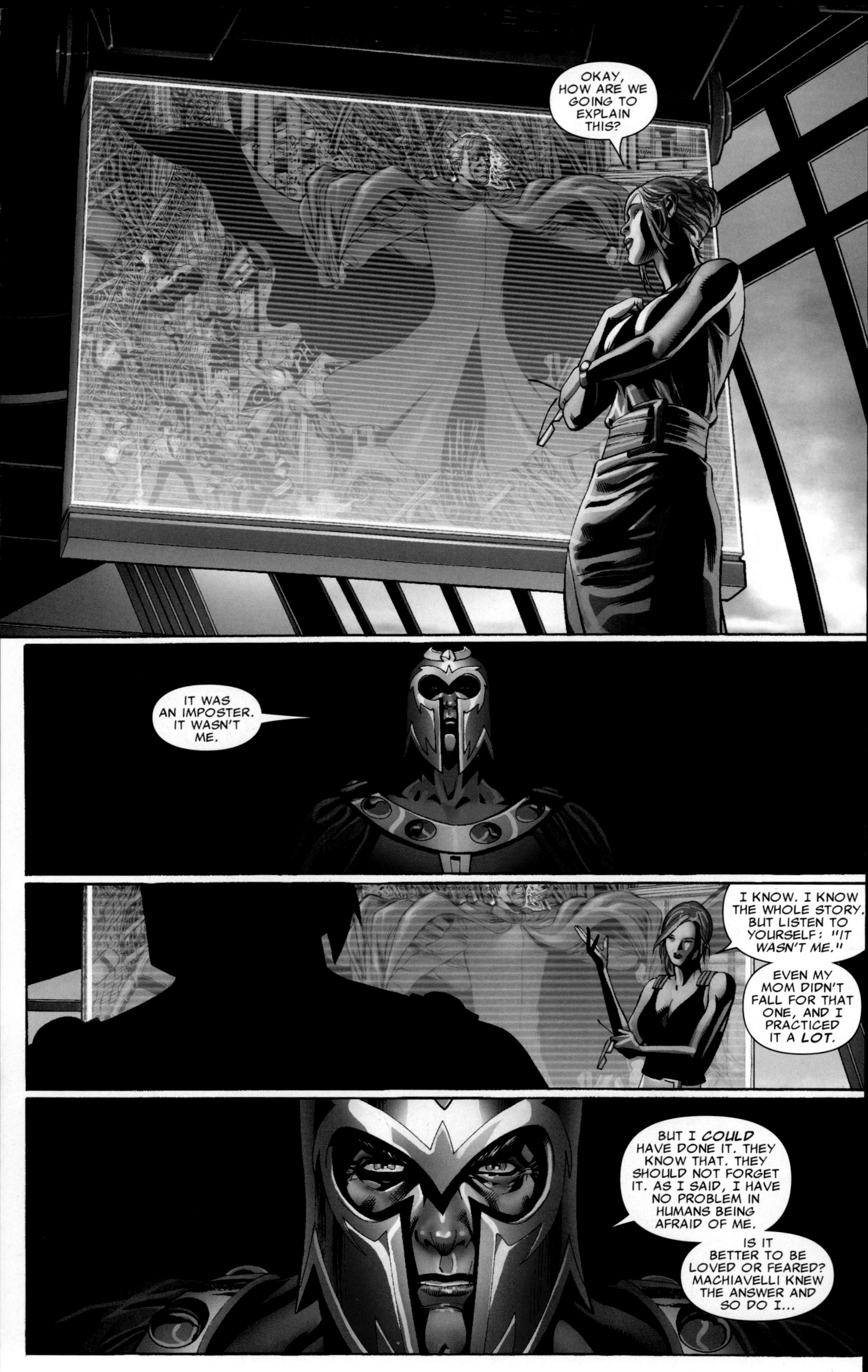
OKAY, HOW ARE WE GOING TO EXPLAIN THIS?
IT WAS AN IMPOSTER. IT WASN'T ME.
I KNOW. I KNOW THE WHOLE STORY. BUT LISTEN TO YOURSELF: "IT WASN'T ME."
EVEN MY MOM DIDN'T FALL FOR THAT ONE, AND I PRACTICED IT A *LOT*.
BUT I *COULD* HAVE DONE IT. THEY KNOW THAT. THEY SHOULD NOT FORGET IT. AS I SAID, I HAVE NO PROBLEM IN HUMANS BEING AFRAID OF ME.
IS IT BETTER TO BE LOVED OR FEARED? MACHIAVELLI KNEW THE ANSWER AND SO DO I...

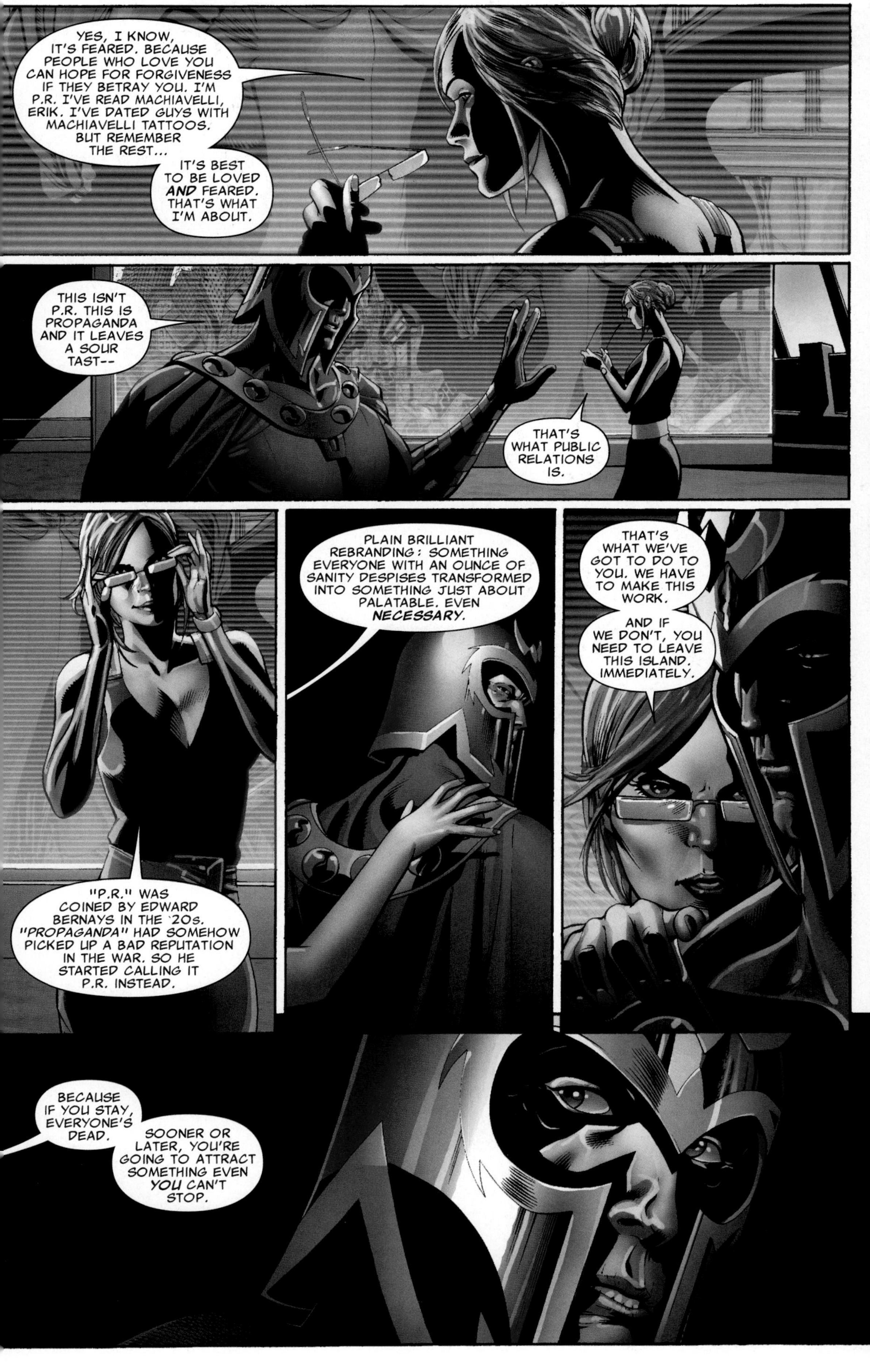
YES, I KNOW, IT'S FEARED. BECAUSE PEOPLE WHO LOVE YOU CAN HOPE FOR FORGIVENESS IF THEY BETRAY YOU. I'M P.R. I'VE READ MACHIAVELLI, ERIK. I'VE DATED GUYS WITH MACHIAVELLI TATTOOS. BUT REMEMBER THE REST...
IT'S BEST TO BE LOVED AND FEARED. THAT'S WHAT I'M ABOUT.
THIS ISN'T P.R. THIS IS PROPAGANDA AND IT LEAVES A SOUR TAST--
THAT'S WHAT PUBLIC RELATIONS IS.
"P.R." WAS COINED BY EDWARD BERNAYS IN THE '20s. "PROPAGANDA" HAD SOMEHOW PICKED UP A BAD REPUTATION IN THE WAR. SO HE STARTED CALLING IT P.R. INSTEAD.
PLAIN BRILLIANT REBRANDING: SOMETHING EVERYONE WITH AN OUNCE OF SANITY DESPISES TRANSFORMED INTO SOMETHING JUST ABOUT PALATABLE. EVEN NECESSARY.
THAT'S WHAT WE'VE GOT TO DO TO YOU. WE HAVE TO MAKE THIS WORK.
AND IF WE DON'T, YOU NEED TO LEAVE THIS ISLAND. IMMEDIATELY.
BECAUSE IF YOU STAY, EVERYONE'S DEAD.
SOONER OR LATER, YOU'RE GOING TO ATTRACT SOMETHING EVEN YOU CAN'T STOP.

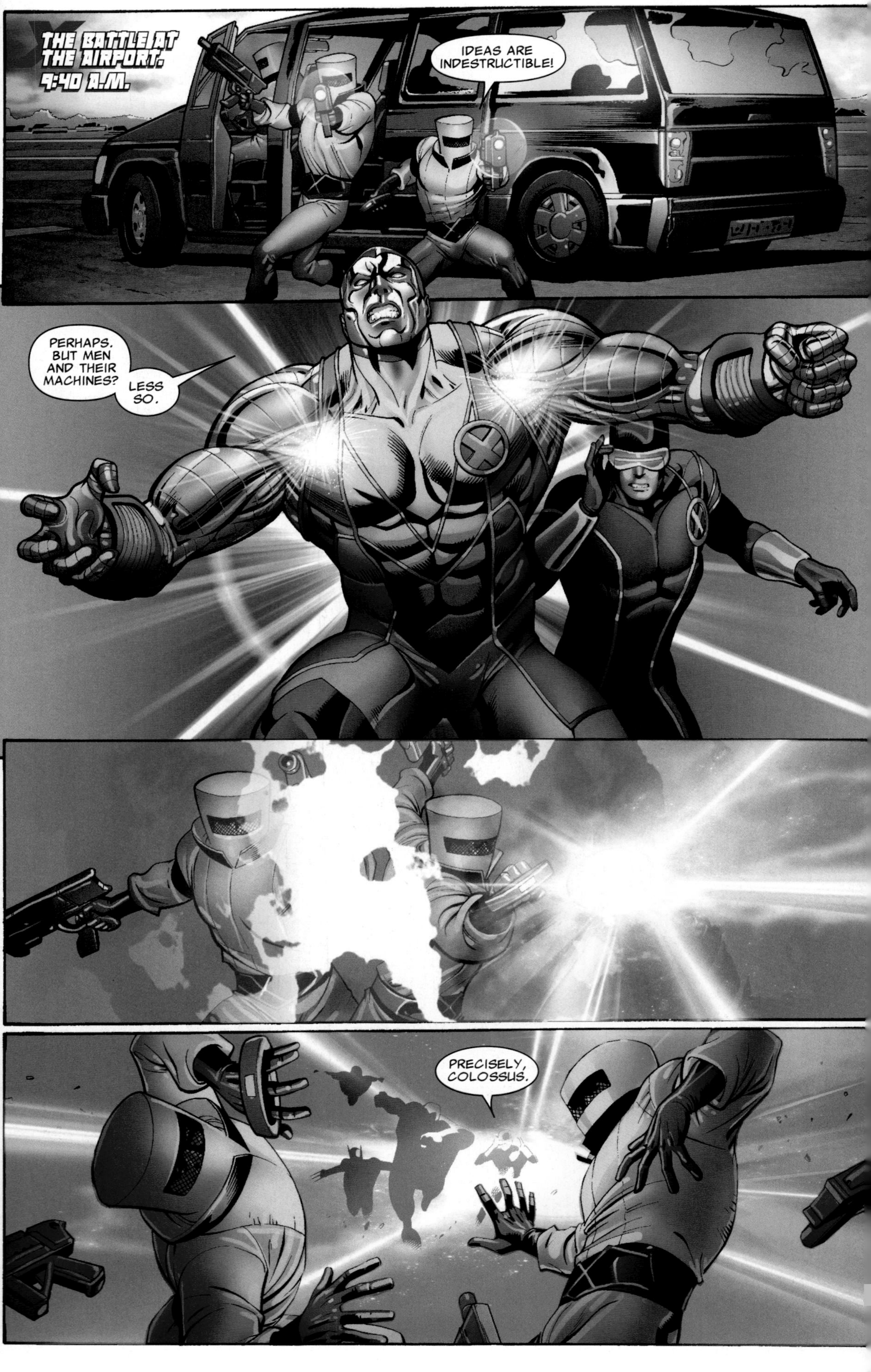
THE BATTLE AT THE AIRPORT.
9:40 A.M.
IDEAS ARE INDESTRUCTIBLE!
PERHAPS. BUT MEN AND THEIR MACHINES?
LESS SO.
PRECISELY, COLOSSUS.

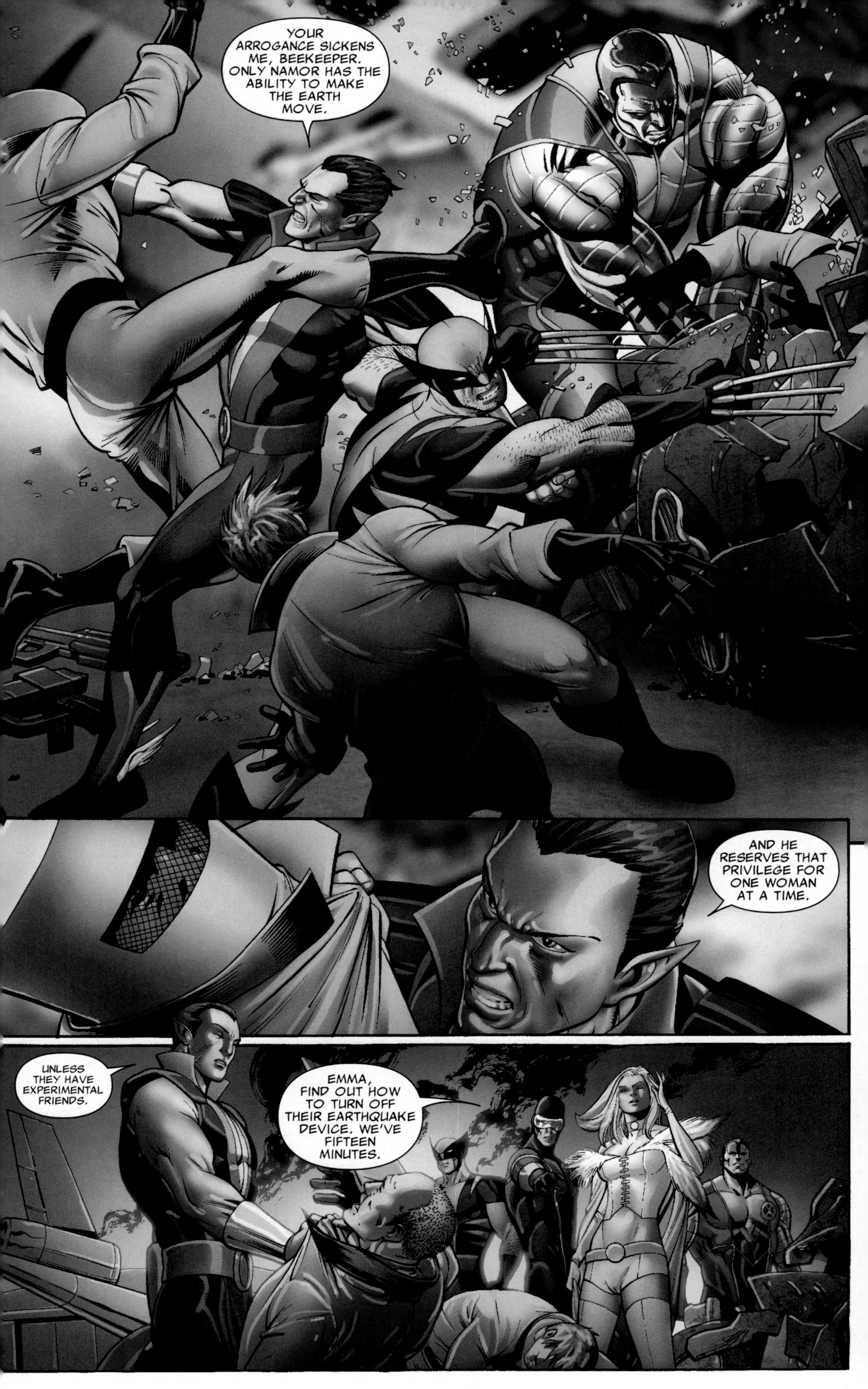
YOUR ARROGANCE SICKENS ME, BEEKEEPER. ONLY NAMOR HAS THE ABILITY TO MAKE THE EARTH MOVE.
AND HE RESERVES THAT PRIVILEGE FOR ONE WOMAN AT A TIME.
UNLESS THEY HAVE EXPERIMENTAL FRIENDS.
EMMA, FIND OUT HOW TO TURN OFF THEIR EARTHQUAKE DEVICE. WE'VE FIFTEEN MINUTES.

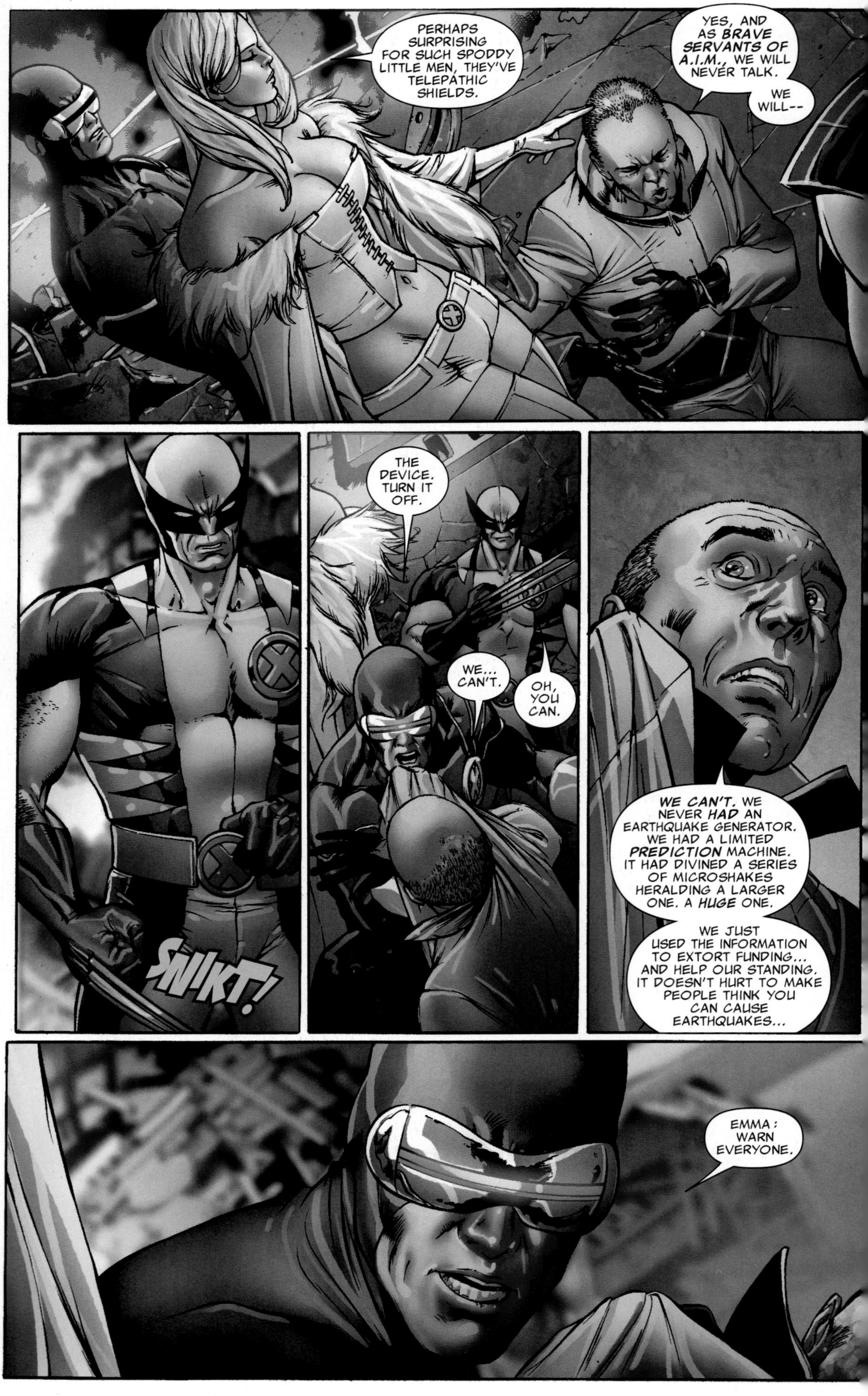
PERHAPS SURPRISING FOR SUCH SPODDY LITTLE MEN, THEY'VE TELEPATHIC SHIELDS.
YES, AND AS BRAVE SERVANTS OF A.I.M., WE WILL NEVER TALK.
WE WILL--
SNIKT!
THE DEVICE. TURN IT OFF.
WE... CAN'T.
OH, YOU CAN.
WE CAN'T. WE NEVER HAD AN EARTHQUAKE GENERATOR. WE HAD A LIMITED PREDICTION MACHINE. IT HAD DIVINED A SERIES OF MICROSHAKES HERALDING A LARGER ONE. A HUGE ONE.
WE JUST USED THE INFORMATION TO EXTORT FUNDING... AND HELP OUR STANDING. IT DOESN'T HURT TO MAKE PEOPLE THINK YOU CAN CAUSE EARTHQUAKES...
EMMA: WARN EVERYONE.

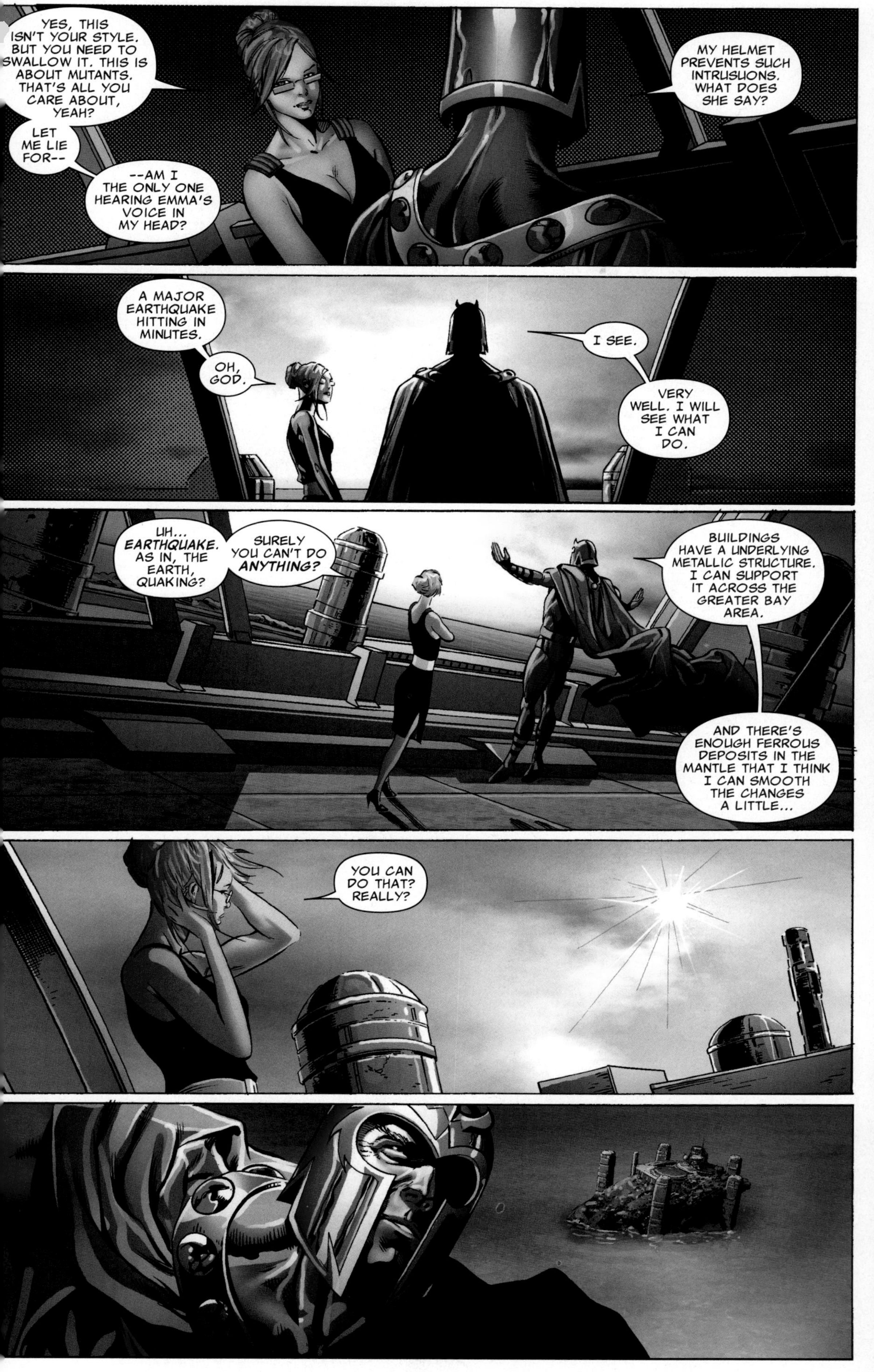
YES, THIS ISN'T YOUR STYLE. BUT YOU NEED TO SWALLOW IT. THIS IS ABOUT MUTANTS. THAT'S ALL YOU CARE ABOUT, YEAH?
LET ME LIE FOR--
--AM I THE ONLY ONE HEARING EMMA'S VOICE IN MY HEAD?
MY HELMET PREVENTS SUCH INTRUSIONS. WHAT DOES SHE SAY?
A MAJOR EARTHQUAKE HITTING IN MINUTES.
OH, GOD.
I SEE.
VERY WELL. I WILL SEE WHAT I CAN DO.
UH... EARTHQUAKE. AS IN, THE EARTH, QUAKING?
SURELY YOU CAN'T DO ANYTHING?
BUILDINGS HAVE A UNDERLYING METALLIC STRUCTURE. I CAN SUPPORT IT ACROSS THE GREATER BAY AREA.
AND THERE'S ENOUGH FERROUS DEPOSITS IN THE MANTLE THAT I THINK I CAN SMOOTH THE CHANGES A LITTLE...
YOU CAN DO THAT? REALLY?

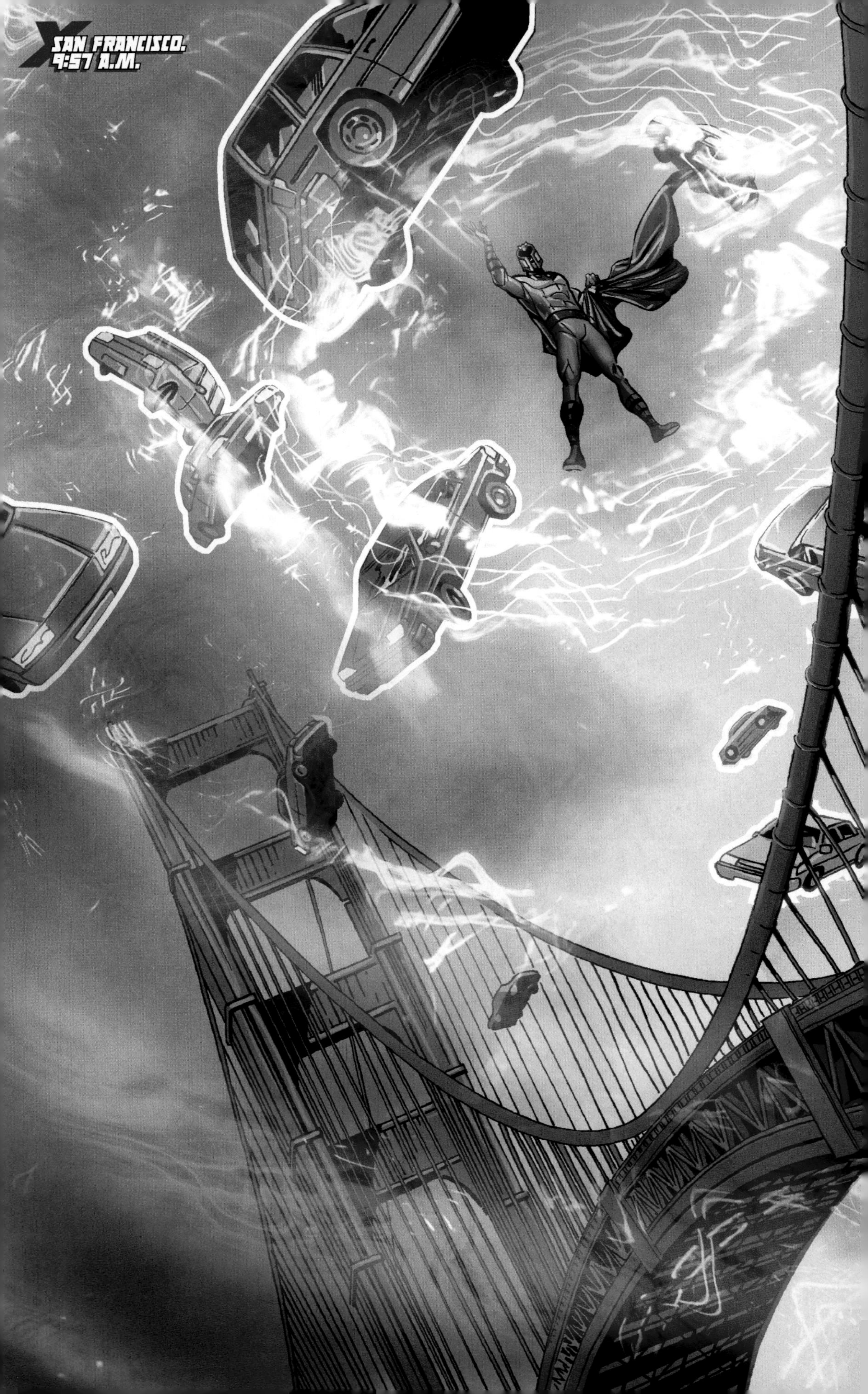
SAN FRANCISCO.
9:57 A.M.

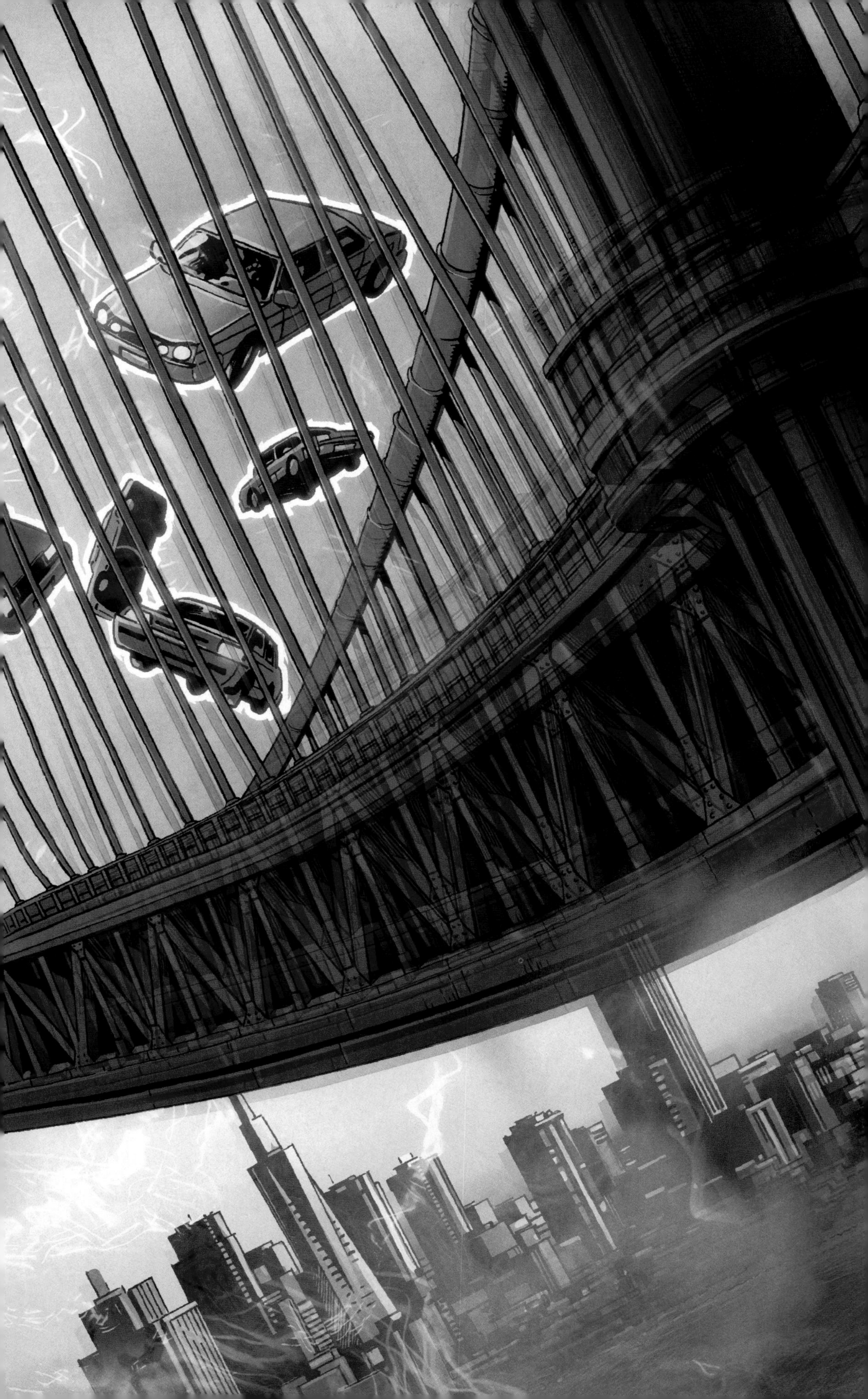

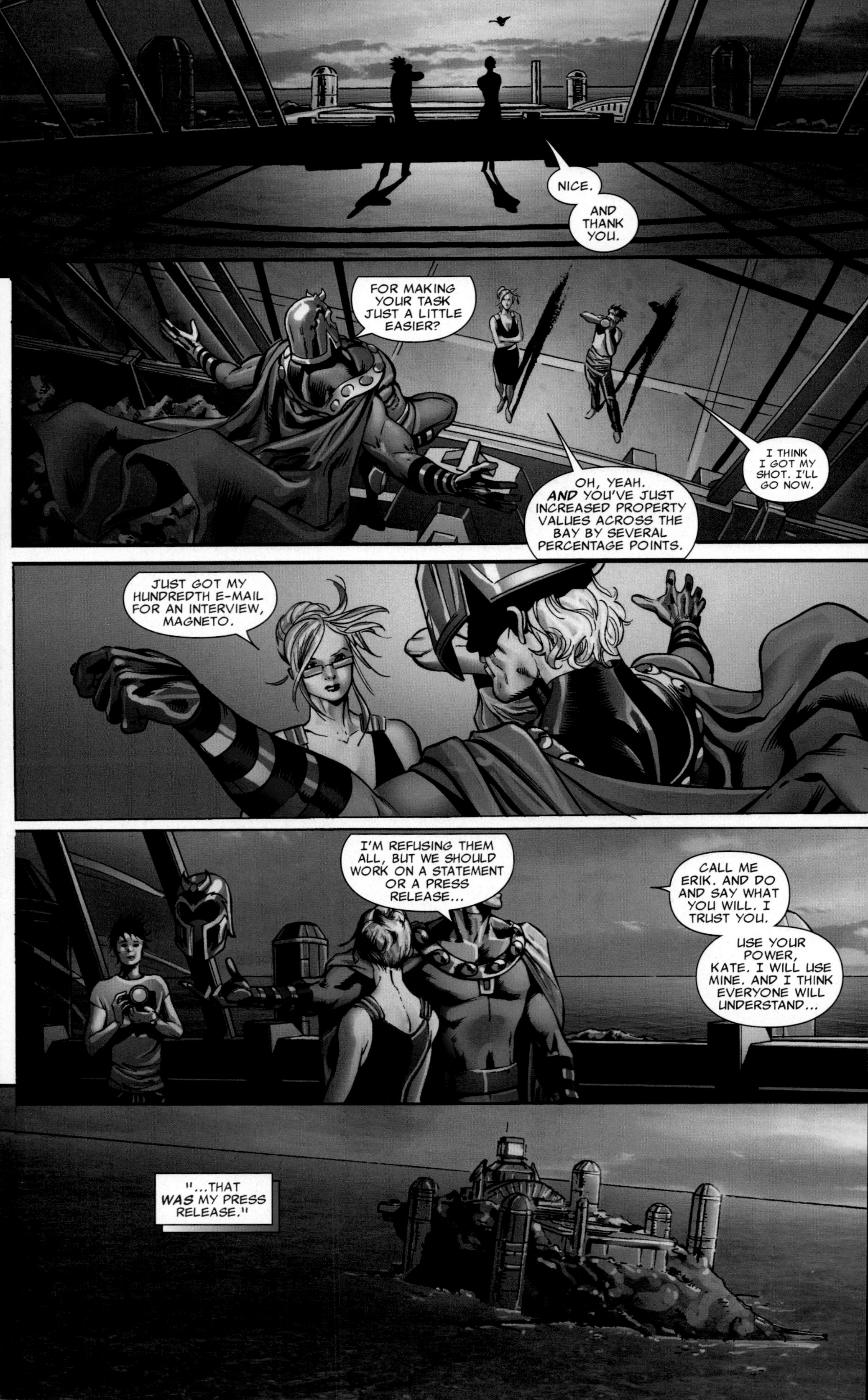
NICE.
AND THANK YOU.
FOR MAKING YOUR TASK JUST A LITTLE EASIER?
OH, YEAH. AND YOU'VE JUST INCREASED PROPERTY VALUES ACROSS THE BAY BY SEVERAL PERCENTAGE POINTS.
I THINK I GOT MY SHOT. I'LL GO NOW.
JUST GOT MY HUNDREDTH E-MAIL FOR AN INTERVIEW, MAGNETO.
I'M REFUSING THEM ALL, BUT WE SHOULD WORK ON A STATEMENT OR A PRESS RELEASE...
CALL ME ERIK. AND DO AND SAY WHAT YOU WILL. I TRUST YOU.
USE YOUR POWER, KATE. I WILL USE MINE. AND I THINK EVERYONE WILL UNDERSTAND...
"...THAT WAS MY PRESS RELEASE."

#535

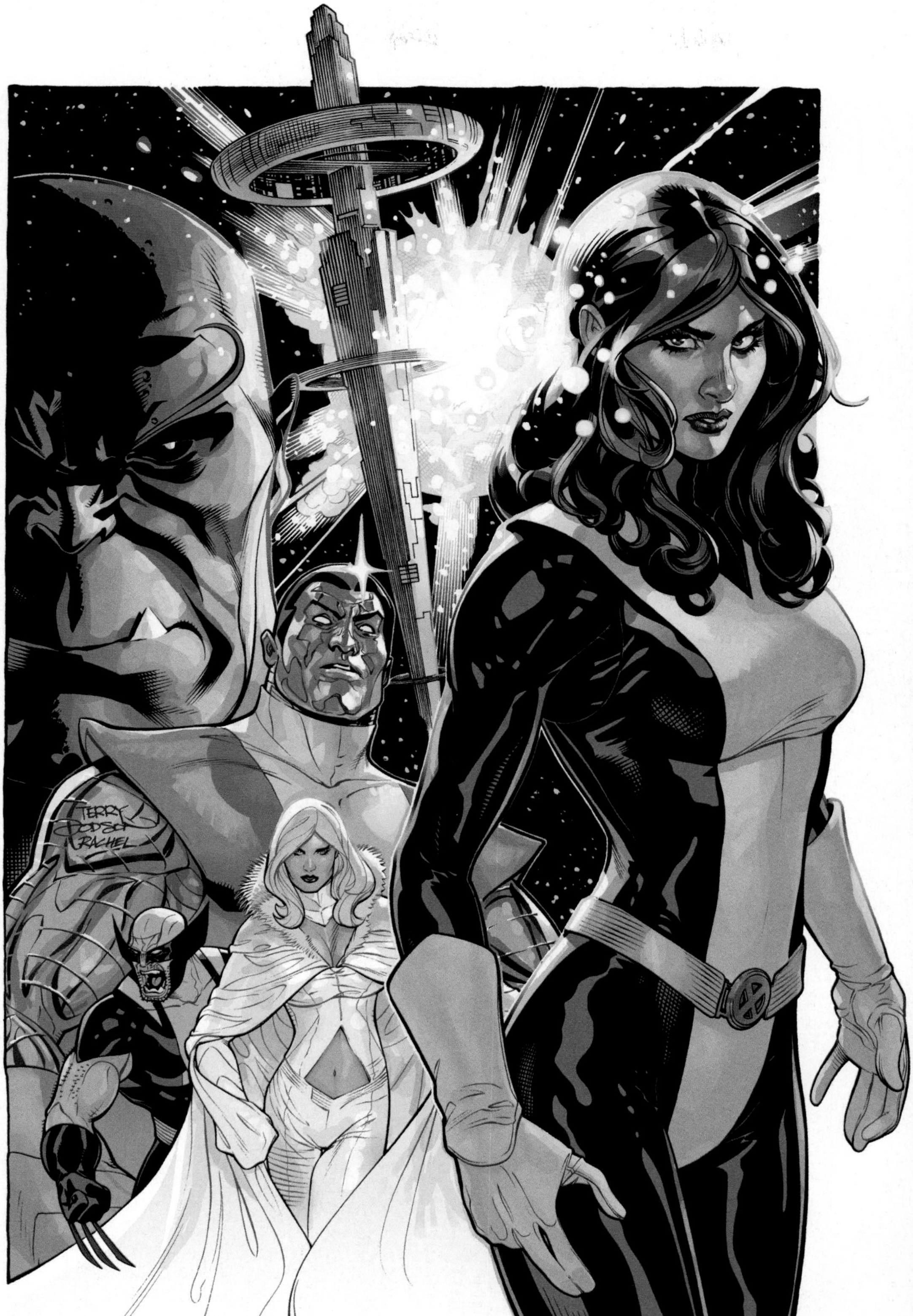
TERRY
DODSON
RACHEL

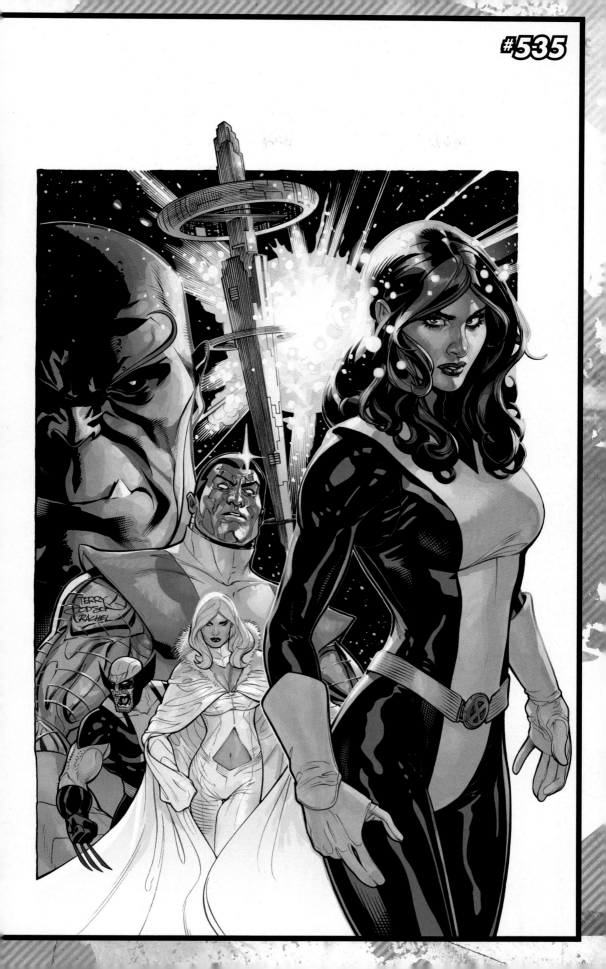

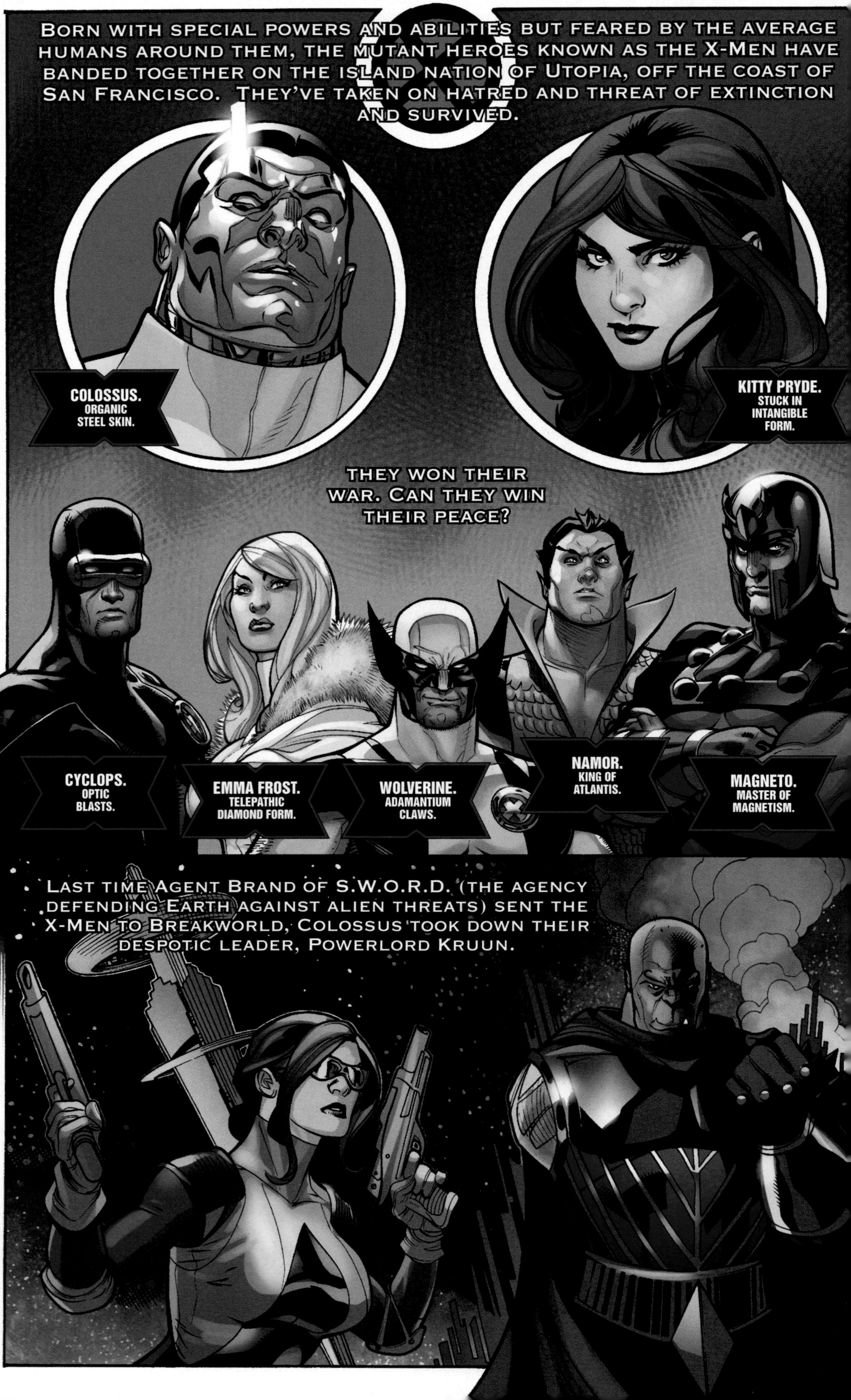
Born with special powers and abilities but feared by the average humans around them, the mutant heroes known as the X-Men have banded together on the island nation of Utopia, off the coast of San Francisco. They've taken on hatred and threat of extinction and survived.
COLOSSUS. ORGANIC STEEL SKIN.
KITTY PRYDE. STUCK IN INTANGIBLE FORM.
THEY WON THEIR WAR. CAN THEY WIN THEIR PEACE?
CYCLOPS. OPTIC BLASTS.
EMMA FROST. TELEPATHIC DIAMOND FORM.
WOLVERINE. ADAMANTIUM CLAWS.
NAMOR. KING OF ATLANTIS.
MAGNETO. MASTER OF MAGNETISM.
Last time Agent Brand of S.W.O.R.D. (the agency defending Earth against alien threats) sent the X-Men to Breakworld, Colossus took down their despotic leader, Powerlord Kruun.

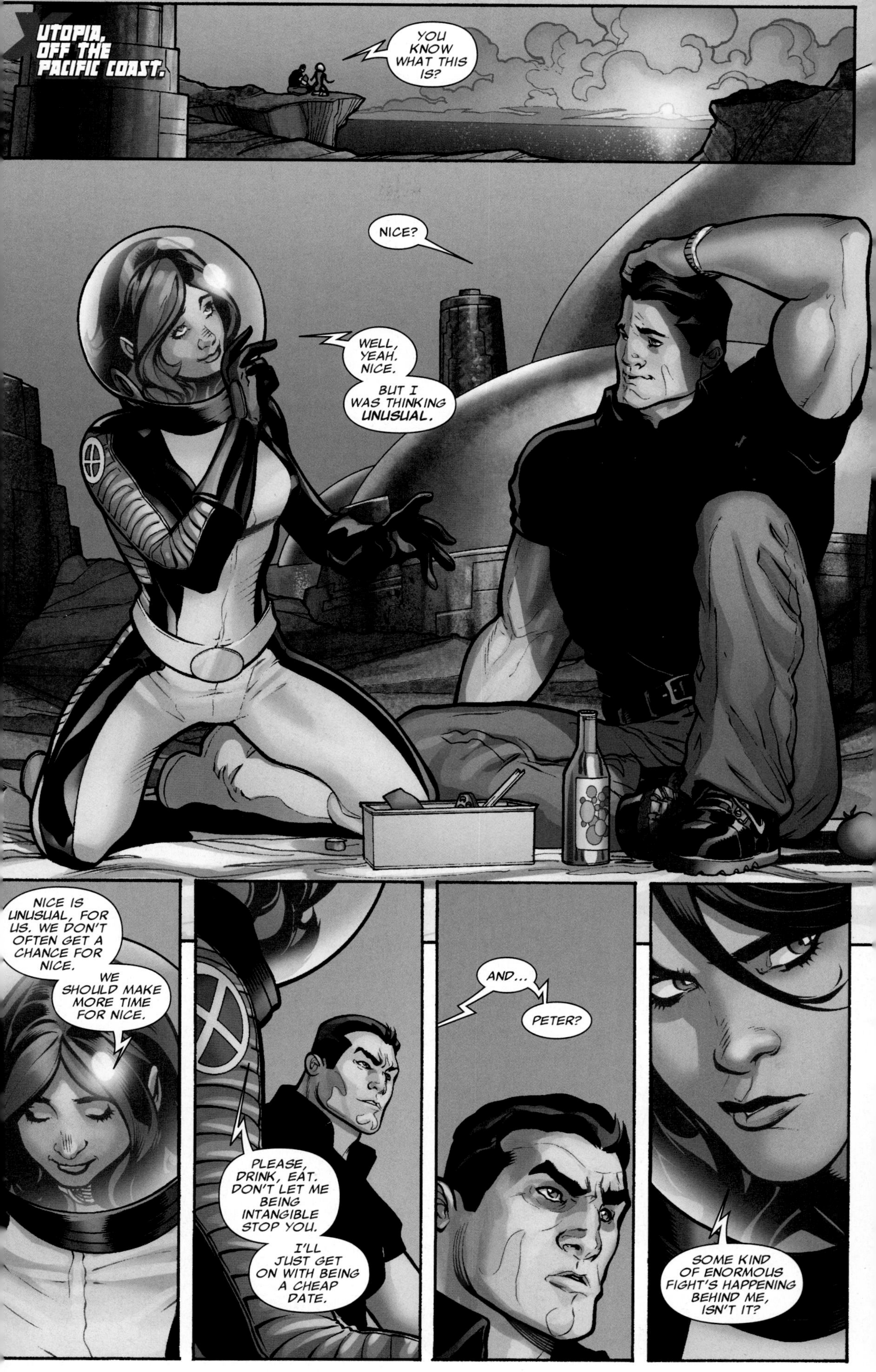
UTOPIA, OFF THE PACIFIC COAST.
YOU KNOW WHAT THIS IS?
NICE?
WELL, YEAH. NICE.
BUT I WAS THINKING UNUSUAL.
NICE IS UNUSUAL, FOR US. WE DON'T OFTEN GET A CHANCE FOR NICE.
WE SHOULD MAKE MORE TIME FOR NICE.
PLEASE, DRINK, EAT. DON'T LET ME BEING INTANGIBLE STOP YOU.
I'LL JUST GET ON WITH BEING A CHEAP DATE.
AND...
PETER?
SOME KIND OF ENORMOUS FIGHT'S HAPPENING BEHIND ME, ISN'T IT?

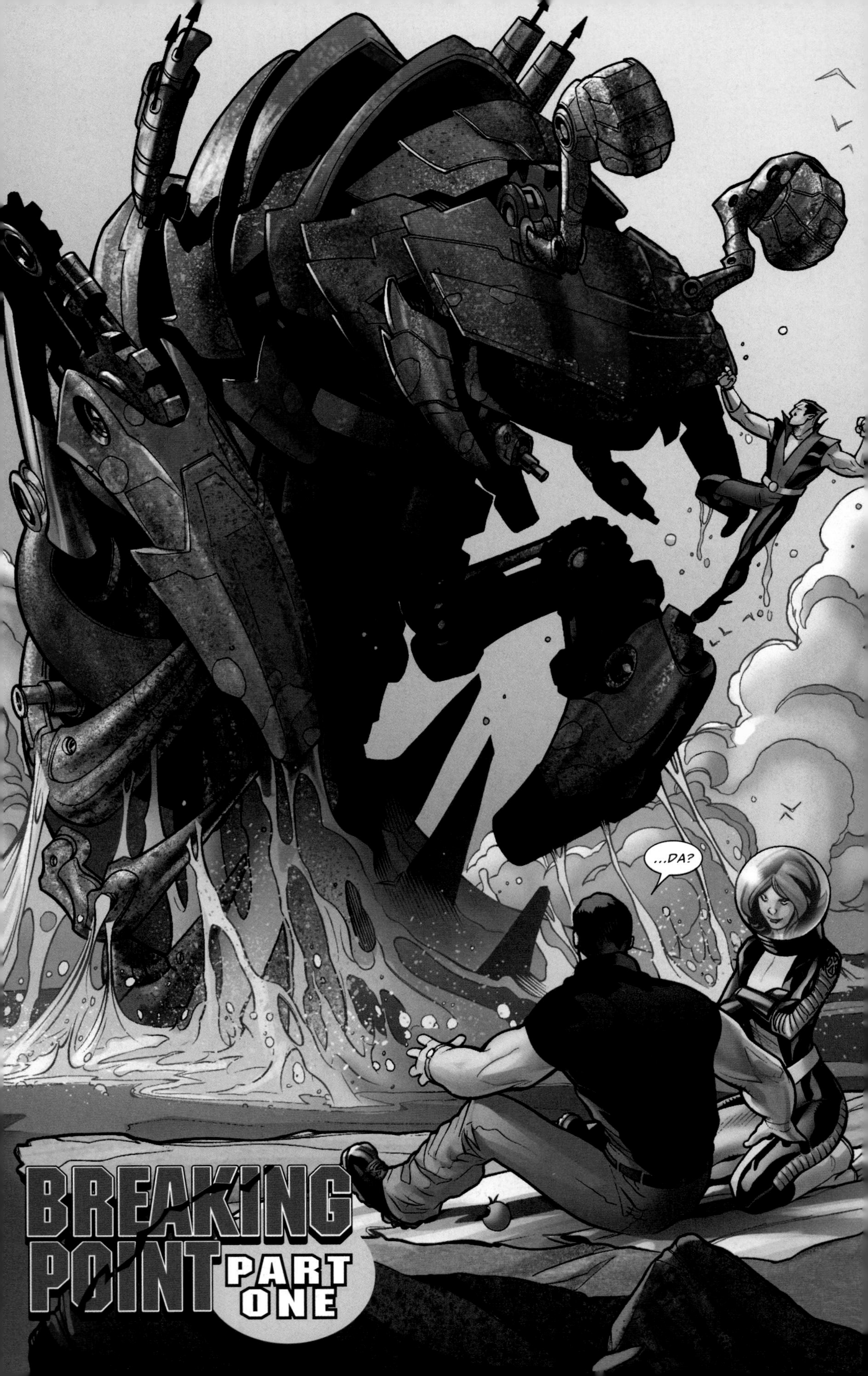
...DA?
BREAKING POINT PART ONE

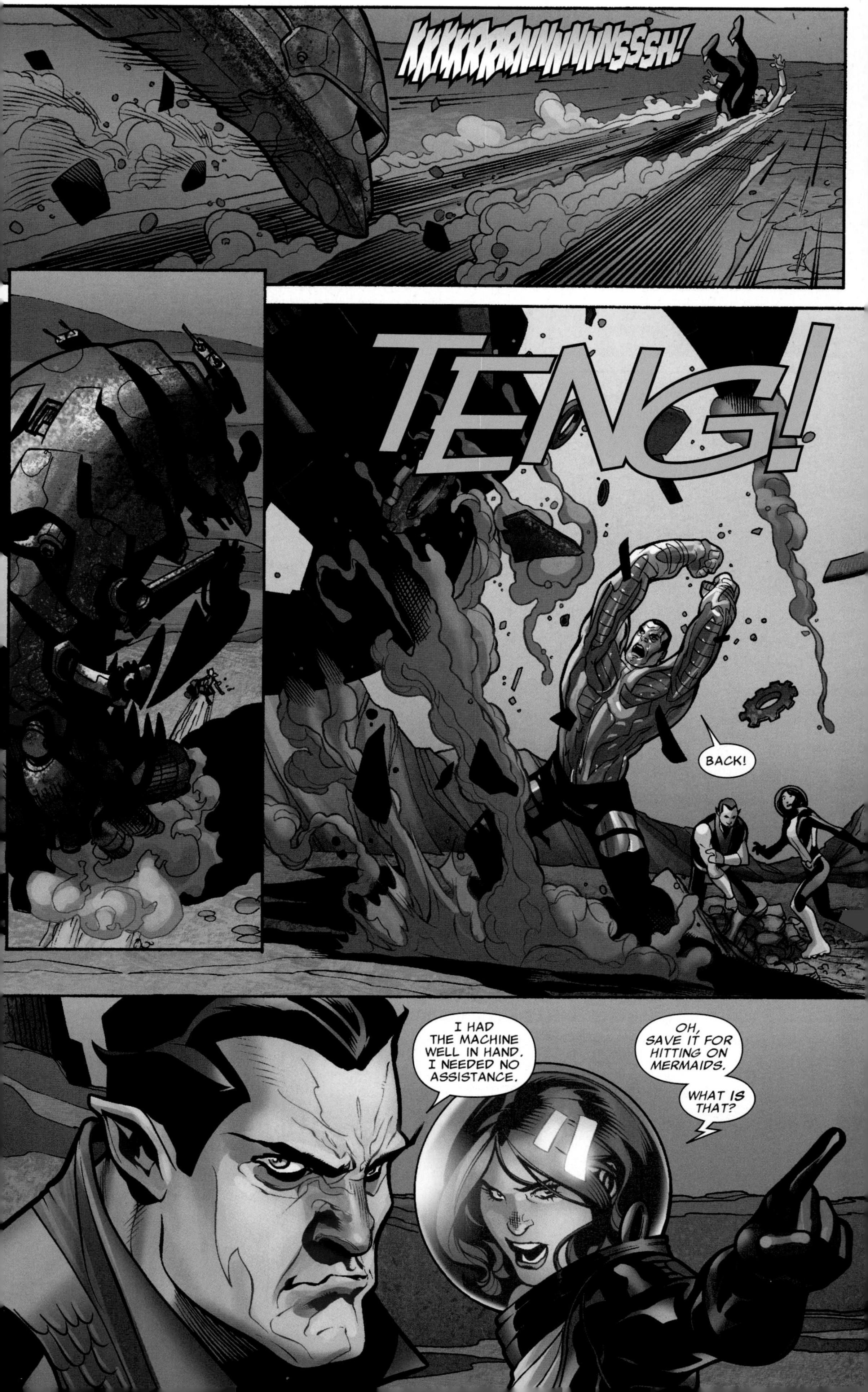
KKKKRRRRNNNNNNNSSSH!
TENG!
BACK!
I HAD THE MACHINE WELL IN HAND. I NEEDED NO ASSISTANCE.
OH, SAVE IT FOR HITTING ON MERMAIDS.
WHAT IS THAT?

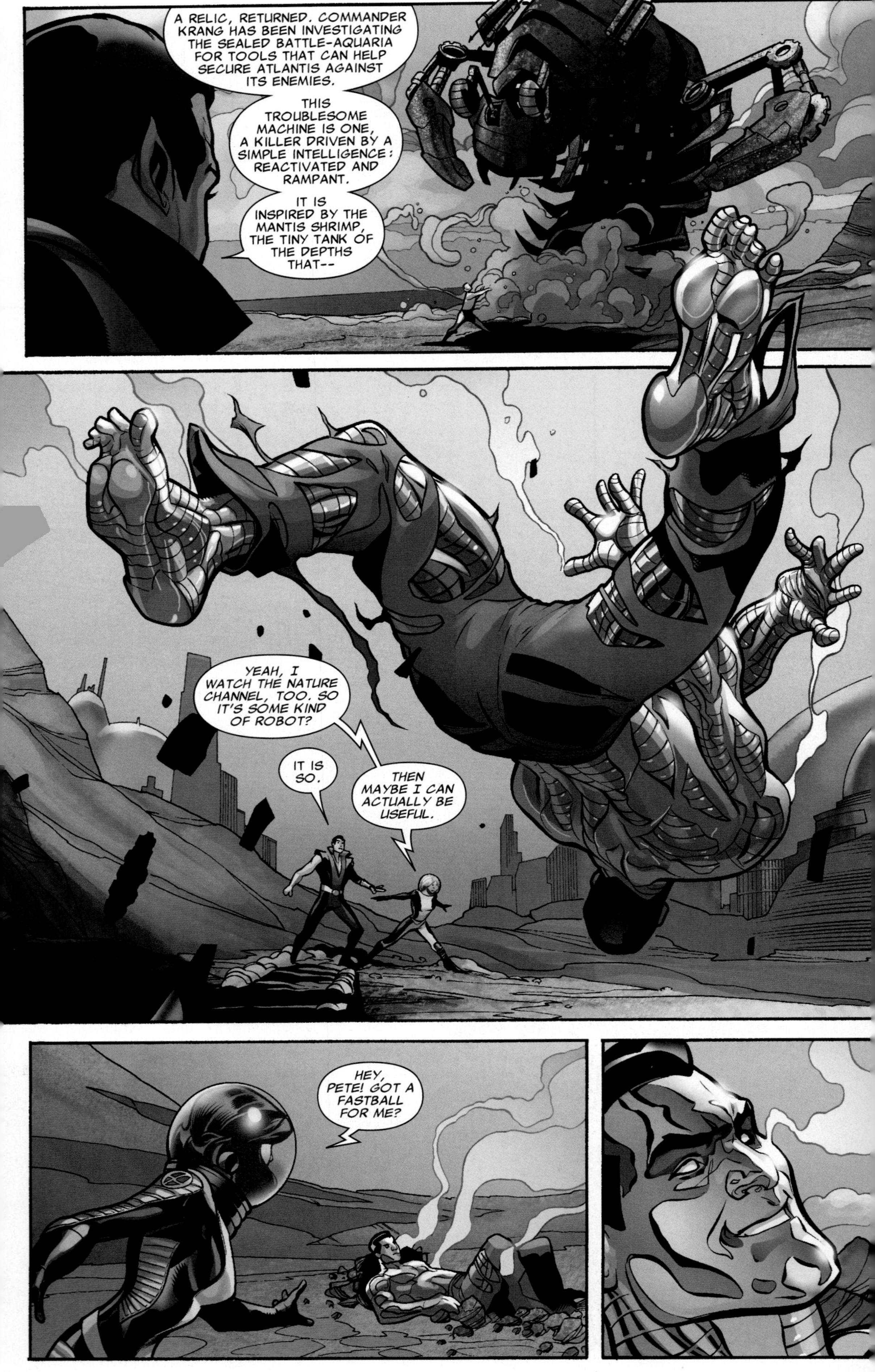
A RELIC, RETURNED. COMMANDER KRANG HAS BEEN INVESTIGATING THE SEALED BATTLE-AQUARIA FOR TOOLS THAT CAN HELP SECURE ATLANTIS AGAINST ITS ENEMIES.
THIS TROUBLESOME MACHINE IS ONE, A KILLER DRIVEN BY A SIMPLE INTELLIGENCE: REACTIVATED AND RAMPANT.
IT IS INSPIRED BY THE MANTIS SHRIMP, THE TINY TANK OF THE DEPTHS THAT--
YEAH, I WATCH THE NATURE CHANNEL, TOO. SO IT'S SOME KIND OF ROBOT?
IT IS SO.
THEN MAYBE I CAN ACTUALLY BE USEFUL.
HEY, PETE! GOT A FASTBALL FOR ME?

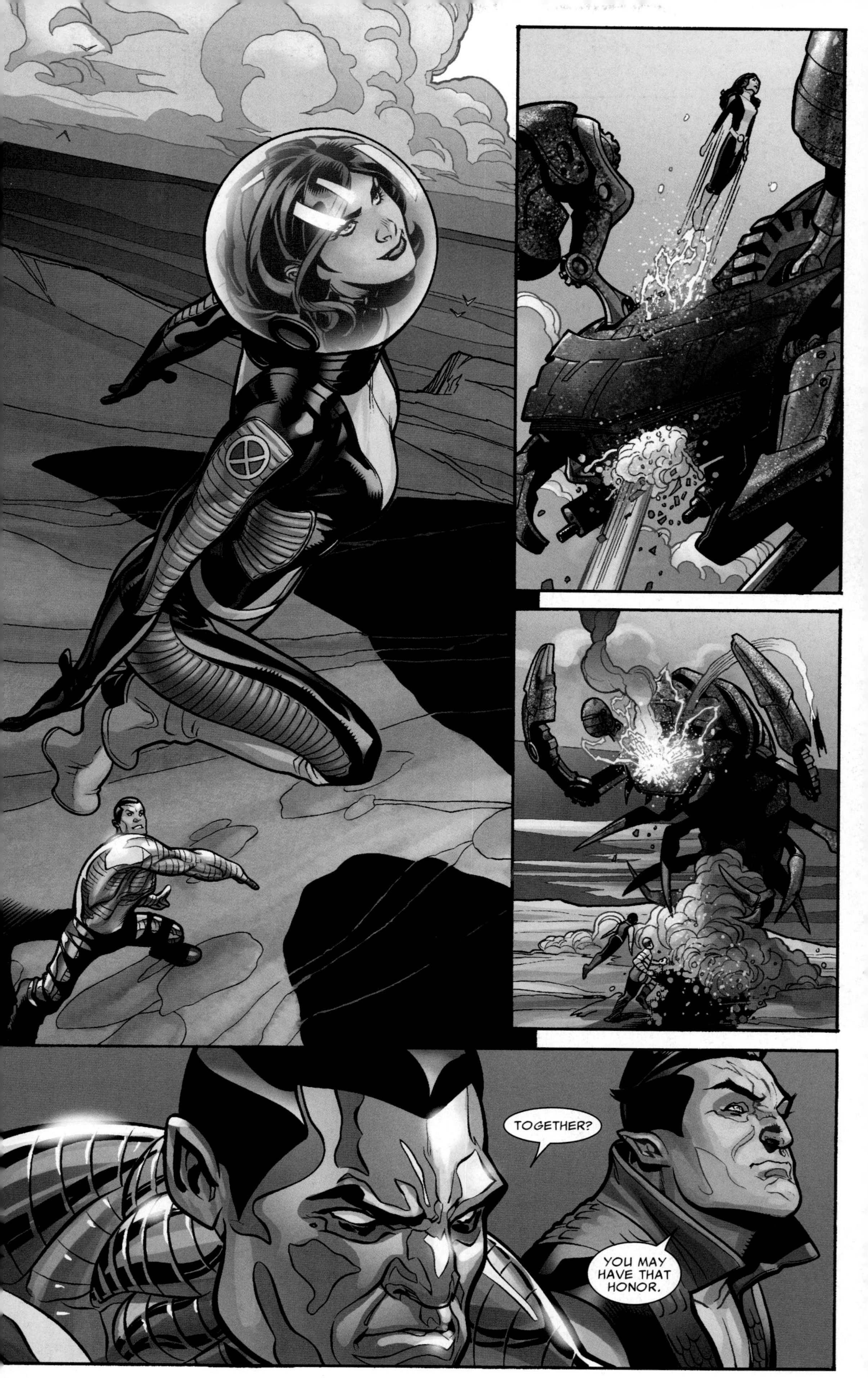
TOGETHER?
YOU MAY HAVE THAT HONOR.

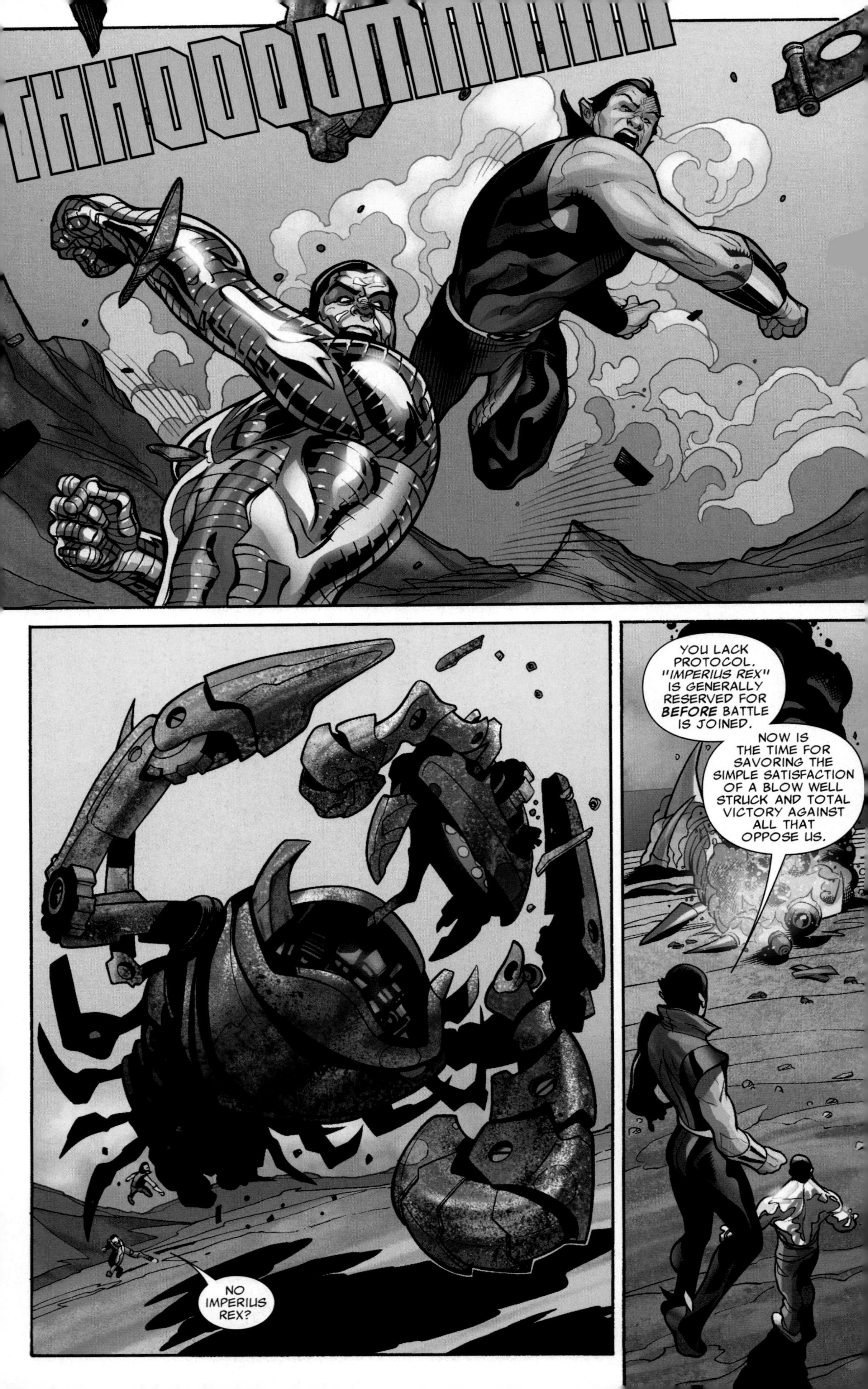
THHOOOOMMMMMM
NO IMPERIUS REX?
YOU LACK PROTOCOL. "IMPERIUS REX" IS GENERALLY RESERVED FOR **BEFORE** BATTLE IS JOINED.
NOW IS THE TIME FOR SAVORING THE SIMPLE SATISFACTION OF A BLOW WELL STRUCK AND TOTAL VICTORY AGAINST ALL THAT OPPOSE US.

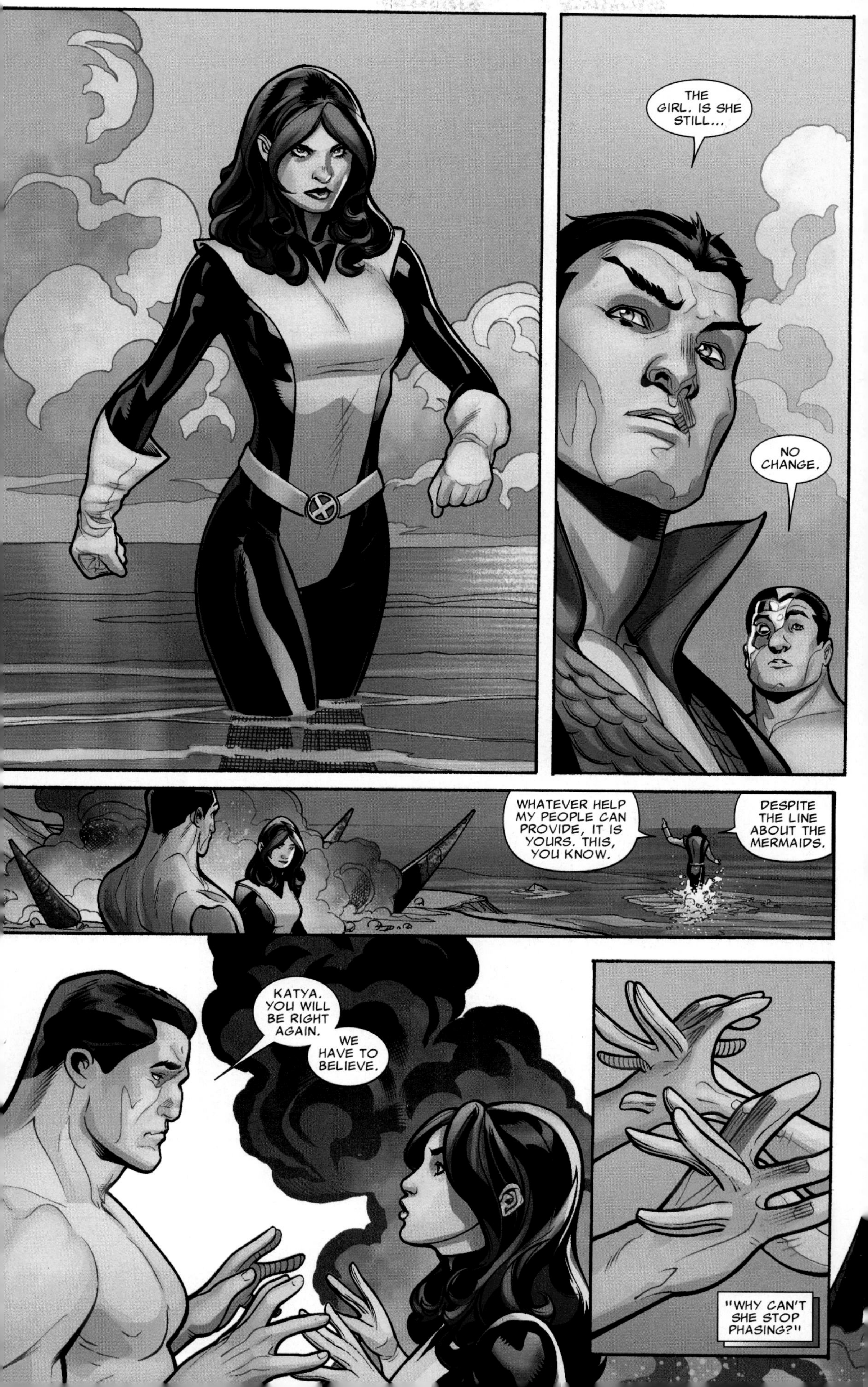
THE GIRL. IS SHE STILL...
NO CHANGE.
WHATEVER HELP MY PEOPLE CAN PROVIDE, IT IS YOURS. THIS, YOU KNOW.
DESPITE THE LINE ABOUT THE MERMAIDS.
KATYA. YOU WILL BE RIGHT AGAIN.
WE HAVE TO BELIEVE.
"WHY CAN'T SHE STOP PHASING?"

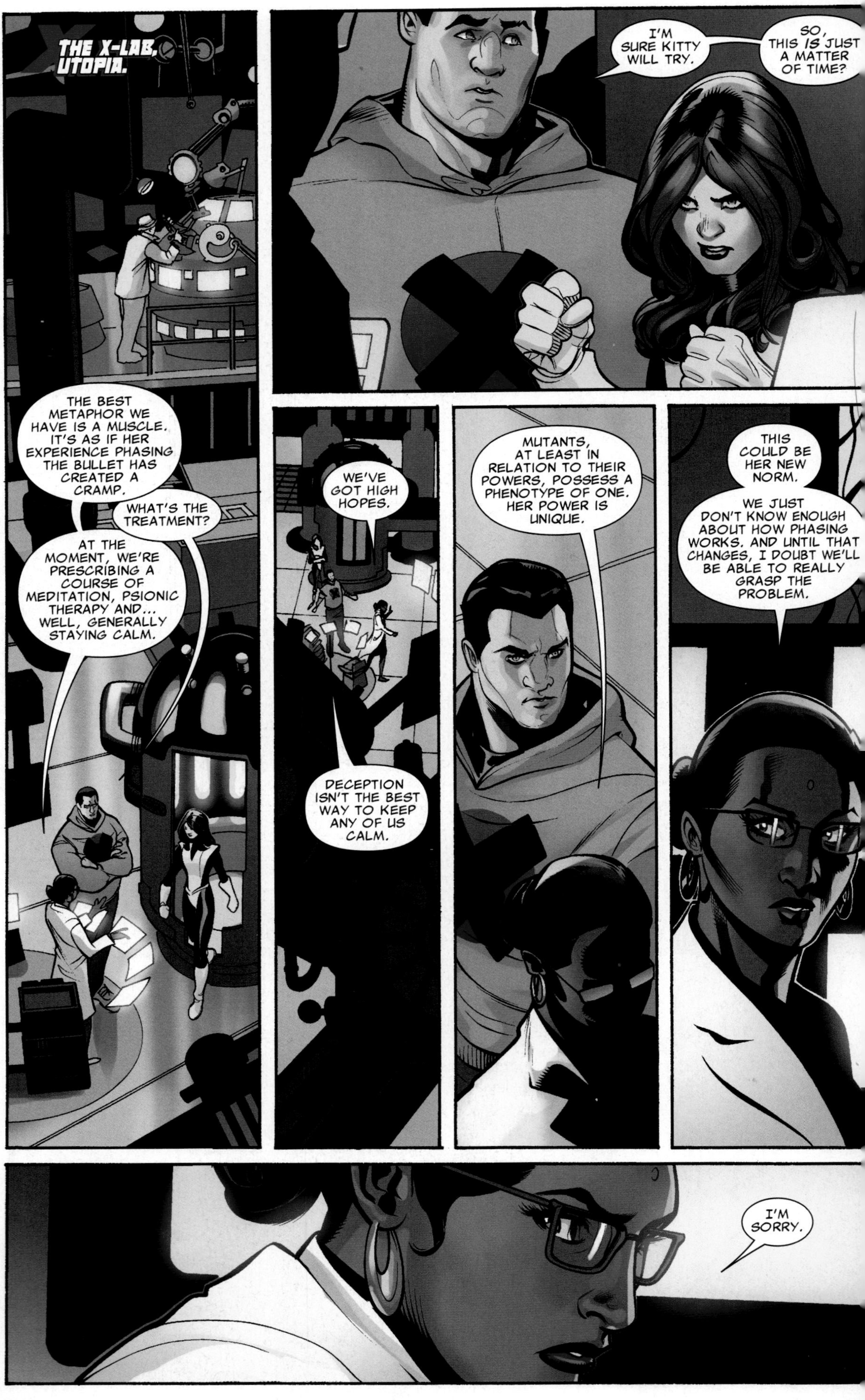
THE X-LAB, UTOPIA.
I'M SURE KITTY WILL TRY.
SO, THIS IS JUST A MATTER OF TIME?
THE BEST METAPHOR WE HAVE IS A MUSCLE. IT'S AS IF HER EXPERIENCE PHASING THE BULLET HAS CREATED A CRAMP.
WHAT'S THE TREATMENT?
AT THE MOMENT, WE'RE PRESCRIBING A COURSE OF MEDITATION, PSIONIC THERAPY AND... WELL, GENERALLY STAYING CALM.
WE'VE GOT HIGH HOPES.
DECEPTION ISN'T THE BEST WAY TO KEEP ANY OF US CALM.
MUTANTS, AT LEAST IN RELATION TO THEIR POWERS, POSSESS A PHENOTYPE OF ONE. HER POWER IS UNIQUE.
THIS COULD BE HER NEW NORM.
WE JUST DON'T KNOW ENOUGH ABOUT HOW PHASING WORKS, AND UNTIL THAT CHANGES, I DOUBT WE'LL BE ABLE TO REALLY GRASP THE PROBLEM.
I'M SORRY.

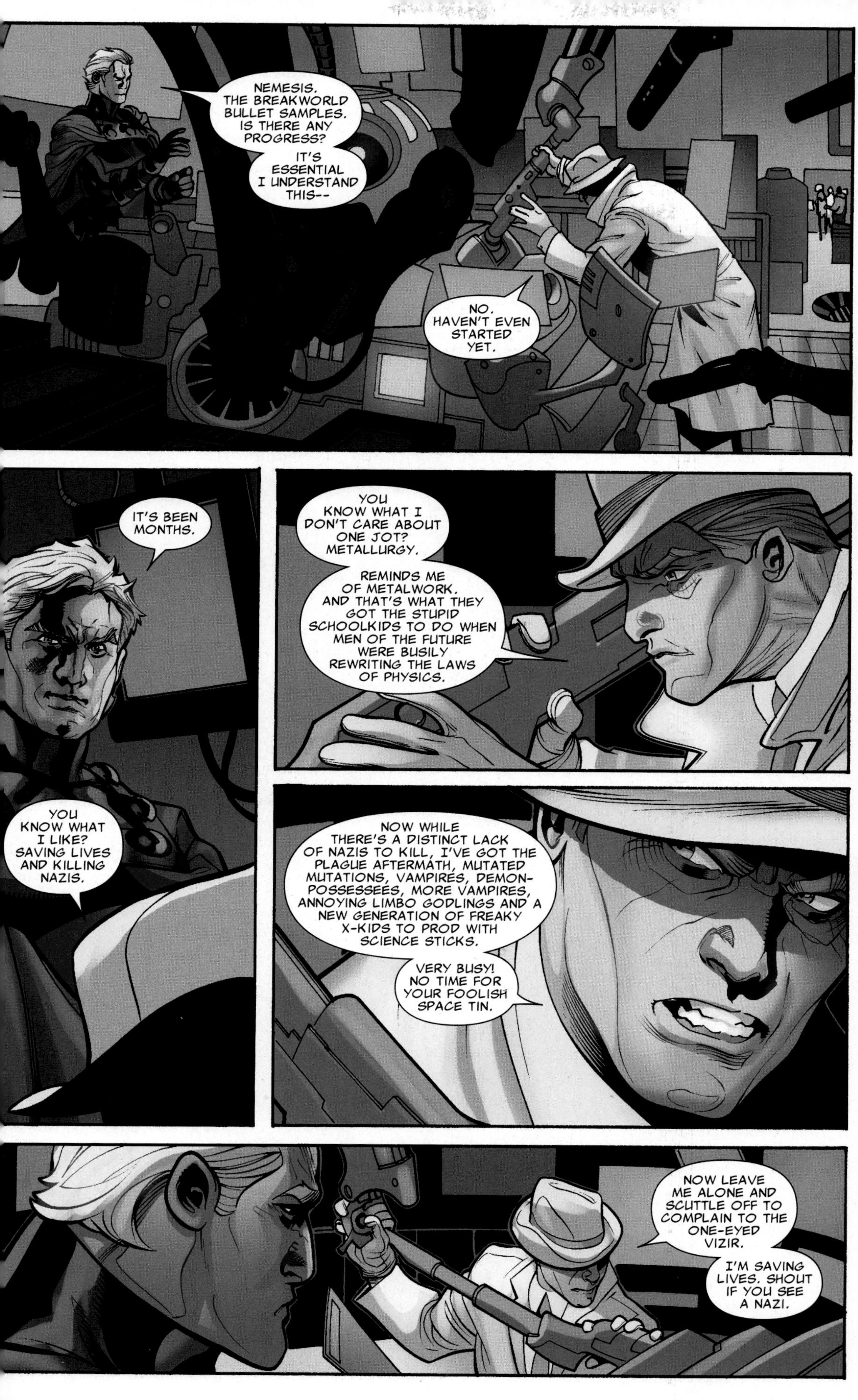
NEMESIS. THE BREAKWORLD BULLET SAMPLES. IS THERE ANY PROGRESS?
IT'S ESSENTIAL I UNDERSTAND THIS--
NO. HAVEN'T EVEN STARTED YET.
IT'S BEEN MONTHS.
YOU KNOW WHAT I DON'T CARE ABOUT ONE JOT? METALLURGY.
REMINDS ME OF METALWORK. AND THAT'S WHAT THEY GOT THE STUPID SCHOOLKIDS TO DO WHEN MEN OF THE FUTURE WERE BUSILY REWRITING THE LAWS OF PHYSICS.
YOU KNOW WHAT I LIKE? SAVING LIVES AND KILLING NAZIS.
NOW WHILE THERE'S A DISTINCT LACK OF NAZIS TO KILL, I'VE GOT THE PLAGUE AFTERMATH, MUTATED MUTATIONS, VAMPIRES, DEMON-POSSESSEES, MORE VAMPIRES, ANNOYING LIMBO GODLINGS AND A NEW GENERATION OF FREAKY X-KIDS TO PROD WITH SCIENCE STICKS.
VERY BUSY! NO TIME FOR YOUR FOOLISH SPACE TIN.
NOW LEAVE ME ALONE AND SCUTTLE OFF TO COMPLAIN TO THE ONE-EYED VIZIR.
I'M SAVING LIVES. SHOUT IF YOU SEE A NAZI.

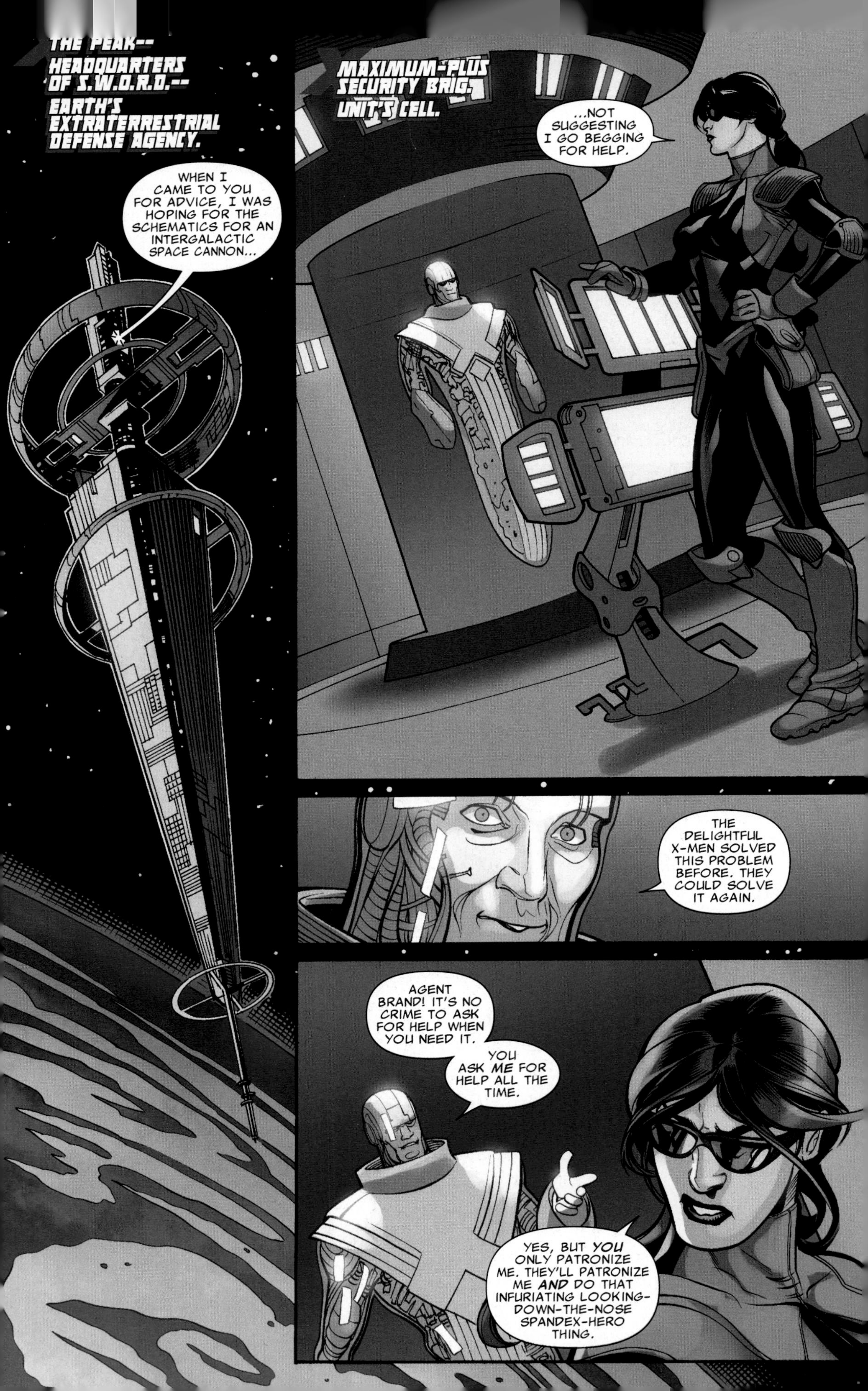
THE PEAK--
HEADQUARTERS OF S.W.O.R.D.--
EARTH'S EXTRATERRESTRIAL DEFENSE AGENCY.
WHEN I CAME TO YOU FOR ADVICE, I WAS HOPING FOR THE SCHEMATICS FOR AN INTERGALACTIC SPACE CANNON...
MAXIMUM-PLUS SECURITY BRIG. UNIT'S CELL.
...NOT SUGGESTING I GO BEGGING FOR HELP.
THE DELIGHTFUL X-MEN SOLVED THIS PROBLEM BEFORE. THEY COULD SOLVE IT AGAIN.
AGENT BRAND! IT'S NO CRIME TO ASK FOR HELP WHEN YOU NEED IT.
YOU ASK ME FOR HELP ALL THE TIME.
YES, BUT YOU ONLY PATRONIZE ME. THEY'LL PATRONIZE ME AND DO THAT INFURIATING LOOKING-DOWN-THE-NOSE SPANDEX-HERO THING.

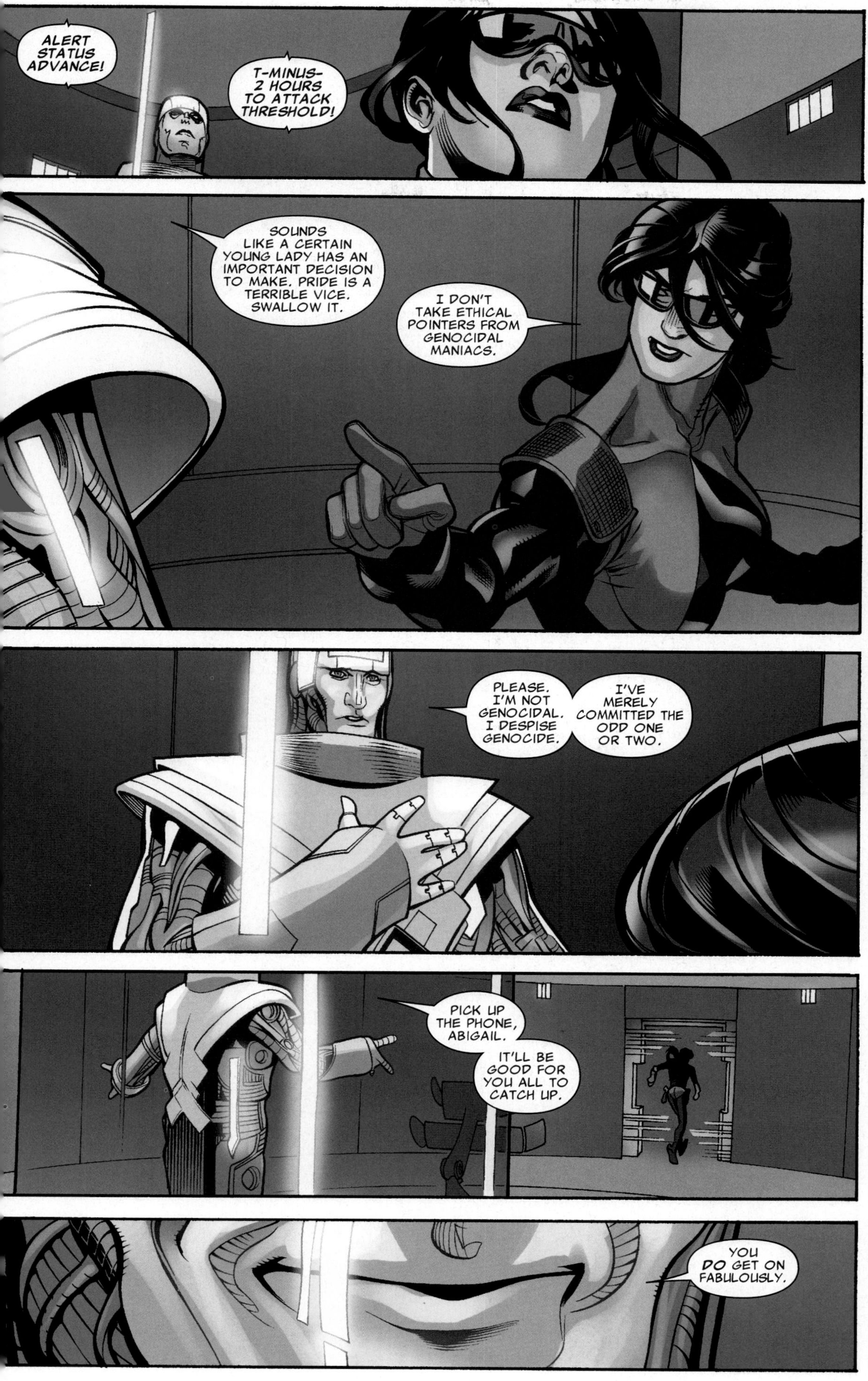
ALERT STATUS ADVANCE!
T-MINUS-2 HOURS TO ATTACK THRESHOLD!
SOUNDS LIKE A CERTAIN YOUNG LADY HAS AN IMPORTANT DECISION TO MAKE. PRIDE IS A TERRIBLE VICE. SWALLOW IT.
I DON'T TAKE ETHICAL POINTERS FROM GENOCIDAL MANIACS.
PLEASE. I'M NOT GENOCIDAL. I DESPISE GENOCIDE.
I'VE MERELY COMMITTED THE ODD ONE OR TWO.
PICK UP THE PHONE, ABIGAIL.
IT'LL BE GOOD FOR YOU ALL TO CATCH UP.
YOU **DO** GET ON FABULOUSLY.

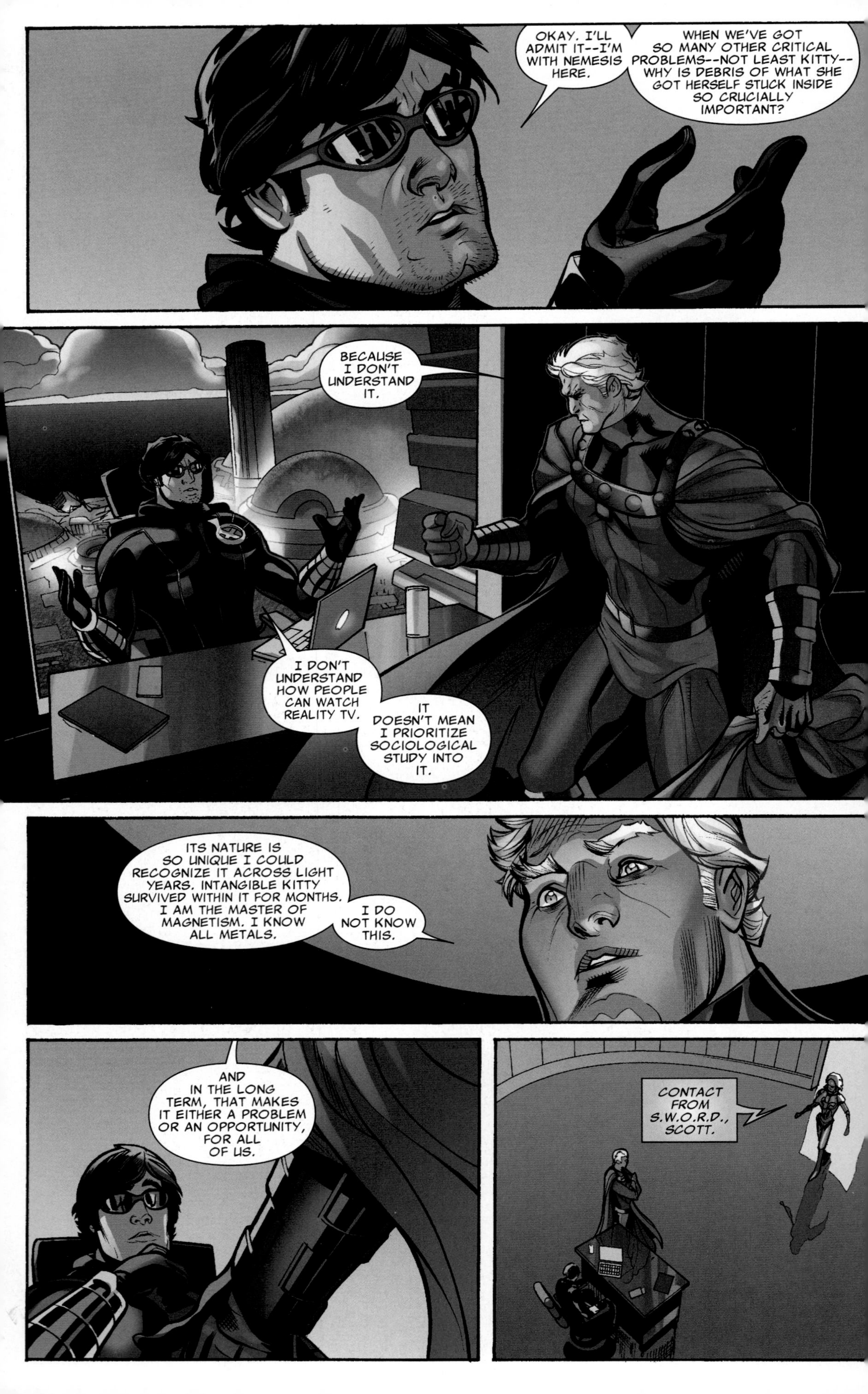
OKAY. I'LL ADMIT IT--I'M WITH NEMESIS HERE.
WHEN WE'VE GOT SO MANY OTHER CRITICAL PROBLEMS--NOT LEAST KITTY--WHY IS DEBRIS OF WHAT SHE GOT HERSELF STUCK INSIDE SO CRUCIALLY IMPORTANT?
BECAUSE I DON'T UNDERSTAND IT.
I DON'T UNDERSTAND HOW PEOPLE CAN WATCH REALITY TV.
IT DOESN'T MEAN I PRIORITIZE SOCIOLOGICAL STUDY INTO IT.
ITS NATURE IS SO UNIQUE I COULD RECOGNIZE IT ACROSS LIGHT YEARS. INTANGIBLE KITTY SURVIVED WITHIN IT FOR MONTHS. I AM THE MASTER OF MAGNETISM. I KNOW ALL METALS.
I DO NOT KNOW THIS.
AND IN THE LONG TERM, THAT MAKES IT EITHER A PROBLEM OR AN OPPORTUNITY, FOR ALL OF US.
CONTACT FROM S.W.O.R.D., SCOTT.

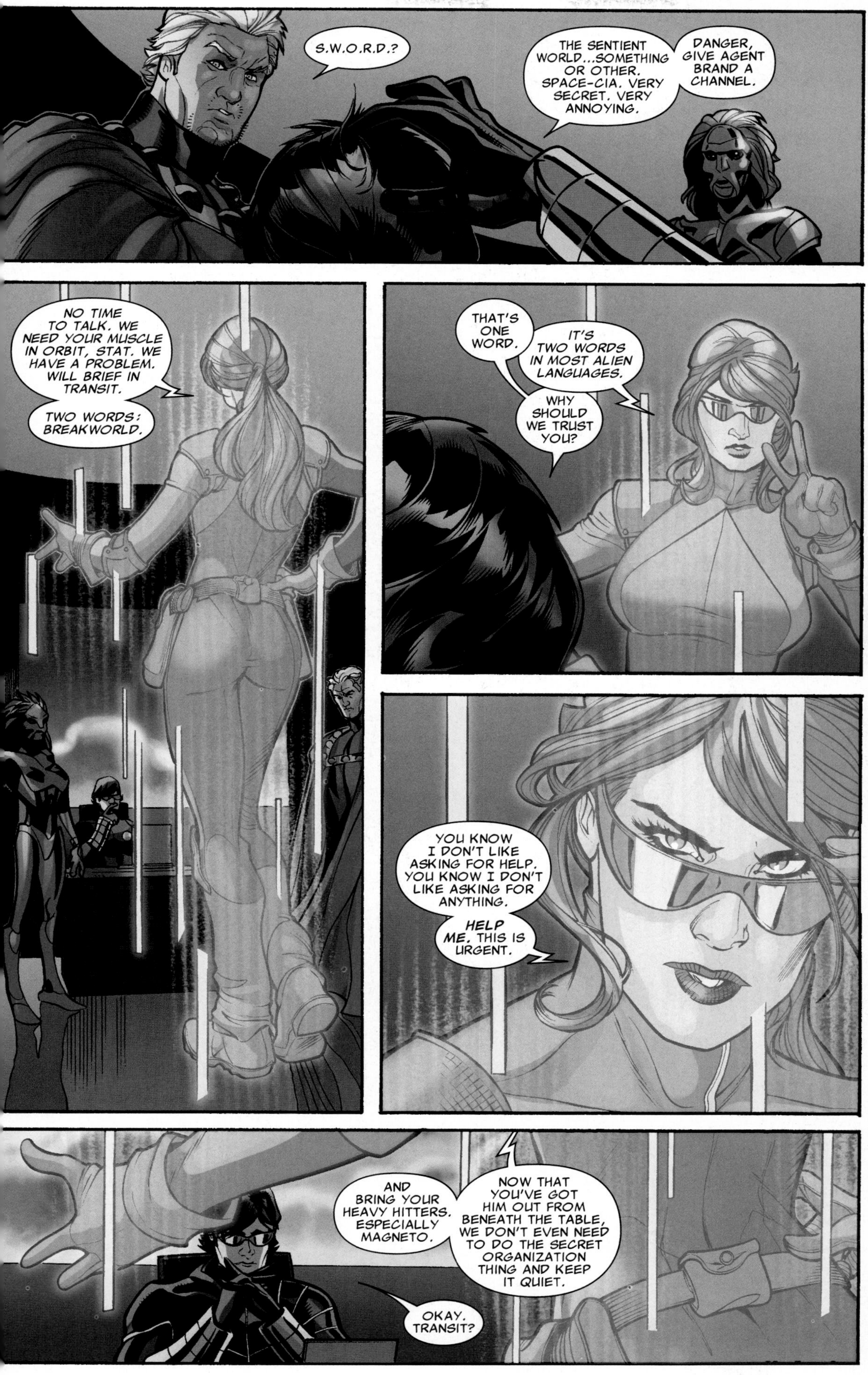
S.W.O.R.D.?
THE SENTIENT WORLD...SOMETHING OR OTHER. SPACE-CIA. VERY SECRET. VERY ANNOYING.
DANGER, GIVE AGENT BRAND A CHANNEL.
NO TIME TO TALK. WE NEED YOUR MUSCLE IN ORBIT, STAT. WE HAVE A PROBLEM. WILL BRIEF IN TRANSIT.
TWO WORDS: BREAKWORLD.
THAT'S ONE WORD.
IT'S TWO WORDS IN MOST ALIEN LANGUAGES.
WHY SHOULD WE TRUST YOU?
YOU KNOW I DON'T LIKE ASKING FOR HELP. YOU KNOW I DON'T LIKE ASKING FOR ANYTHING.
HELP ME. THIS IS URGENT.
AND BRING YOUR HEAVY HITTERS. ESPECIALLY MAGNETO.
NOW THAT YOU'VE GOT HIM OUT FROM BENEATH THE TABLE, WE DON'T EVEN NEED TO DO THE SECRET ORGANIZATION THING AND KEEP IT QUIET.
OKAY. TRANSIT?

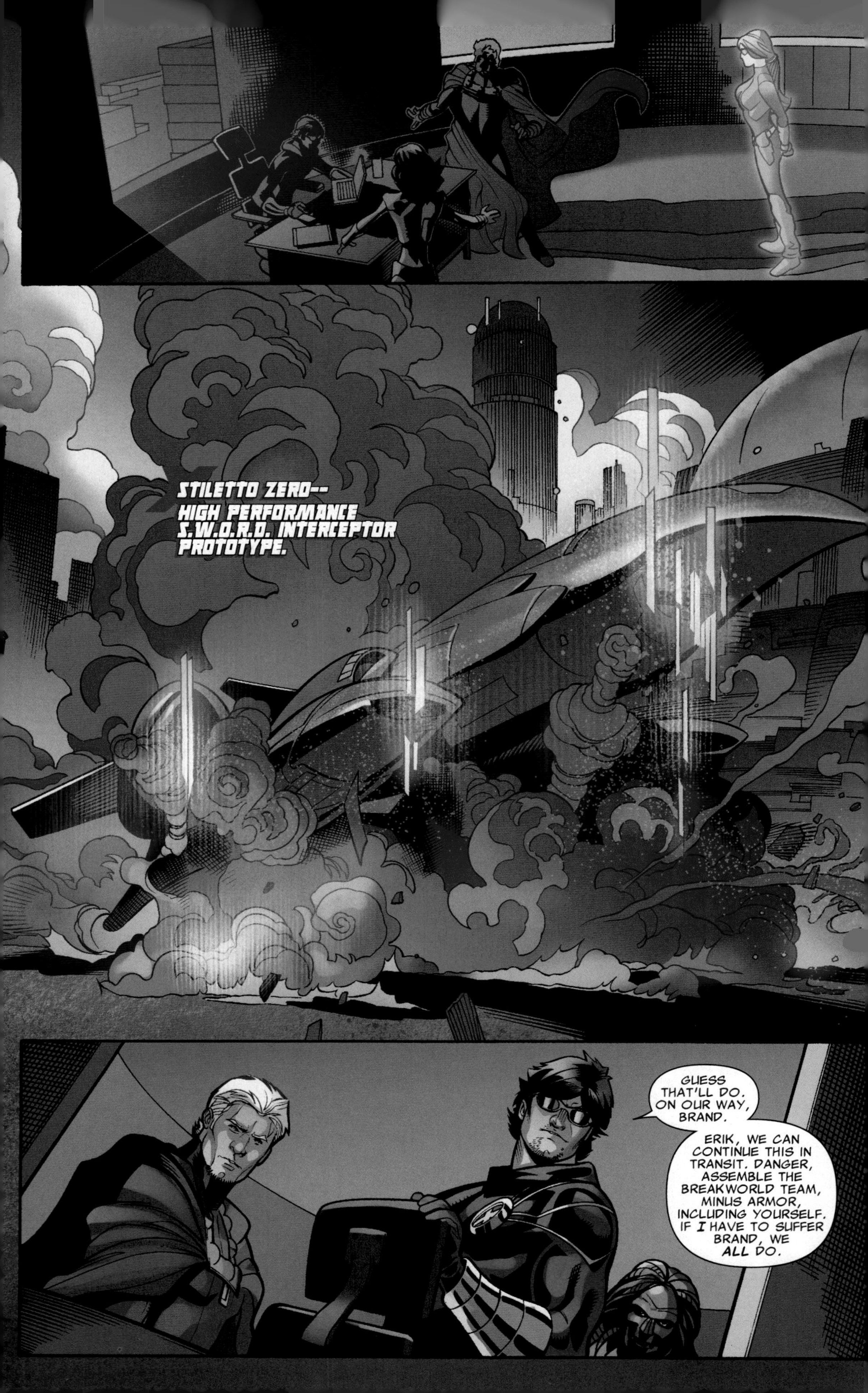
STILETTO ZERO--
HIGH PERFORMANCE S.W.O.R.D. INTERCEPTOR PROTOTYPE.
GUESS THAT'LL DO. ON OUR WAY, BRAND.
ERIK, WE CAN CONTINUE THIS IN TRANSIT. DANGER, ASSEMBLE THE BREAKWORLD TEAM, MINUS ARMOR, INCLUDING YOURSELF. IF I HAVE TO SUFFER BRAND, WE ALL DO.

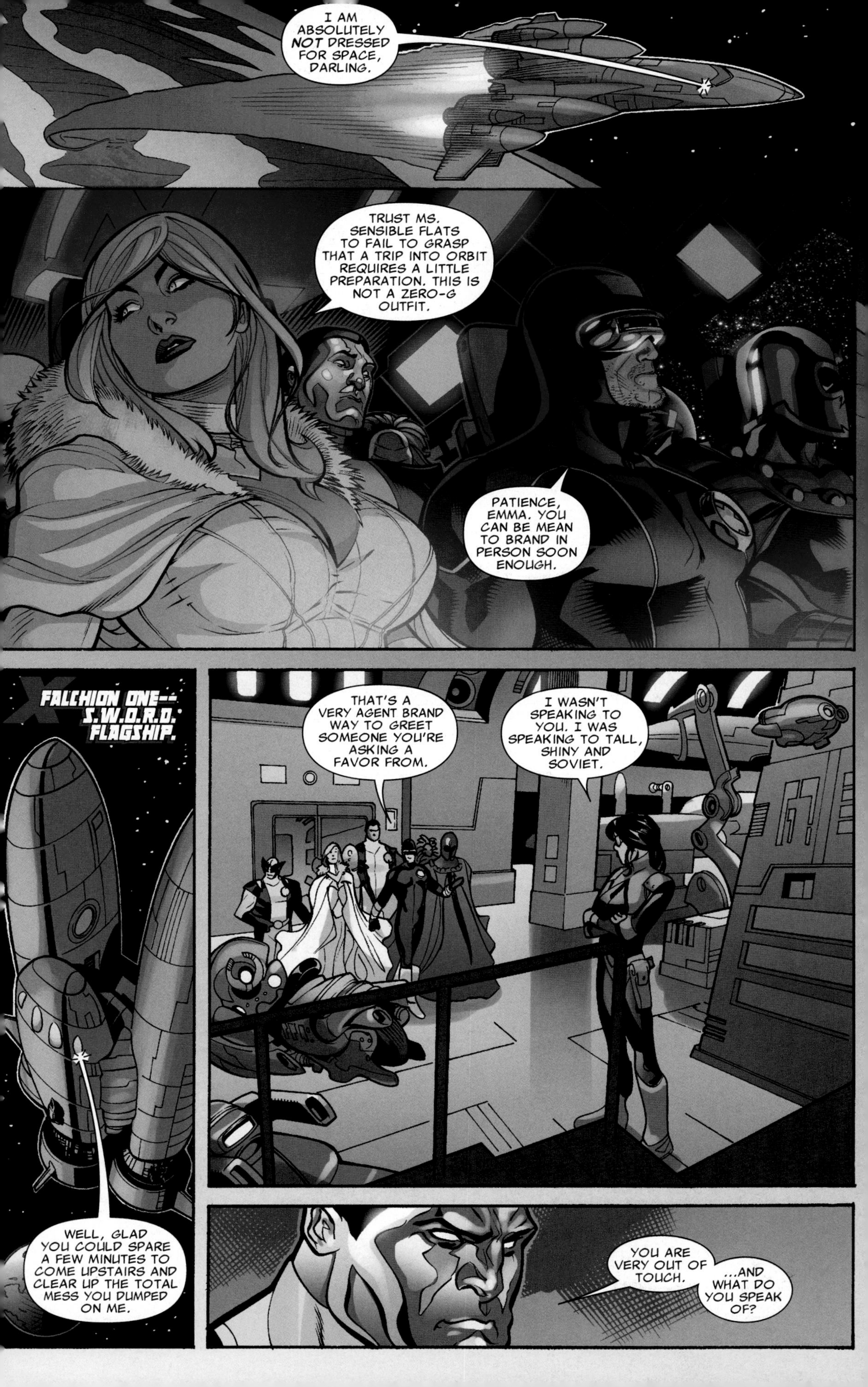
I AM ABSOLUTELY NOT DRESSED FOR SPACE, DARLING.
TRUST MS. SENSIBLE FLATS TO FAIL TO GRASP THAT A TRIP INTO ORBIT REQUIRES A LITTLE PREPARATION. THIS IS NOT A ZERO-G OUTFIT.
PATIENCE, EMMA. YOU CAN BE MEAN TO BRAND IN PERSON SOON ENOUGH.
FALCHION ONE-- S.W.O.R.D. FLAGSHIP.
WELL, GLAD YOU COULD SPARE A FEW MINUTES TO COME UPSTAIRS AND CLEAR UP THE TOTAL MESS YOU DUMPED ON ME.
THAT'S A VERY AGENT BRAND WAY TO GREET SOMEONE YOU'RE ASKING A FAVOR FROM.
I WASN'T SPEAKING TO YOU. I WAS SPEAKING TO TALL, SHINY AND SOVIET.
YOU ARE VERY OUT OF TOUCH.
...AND WHAT DO YOU SPEAK OF?

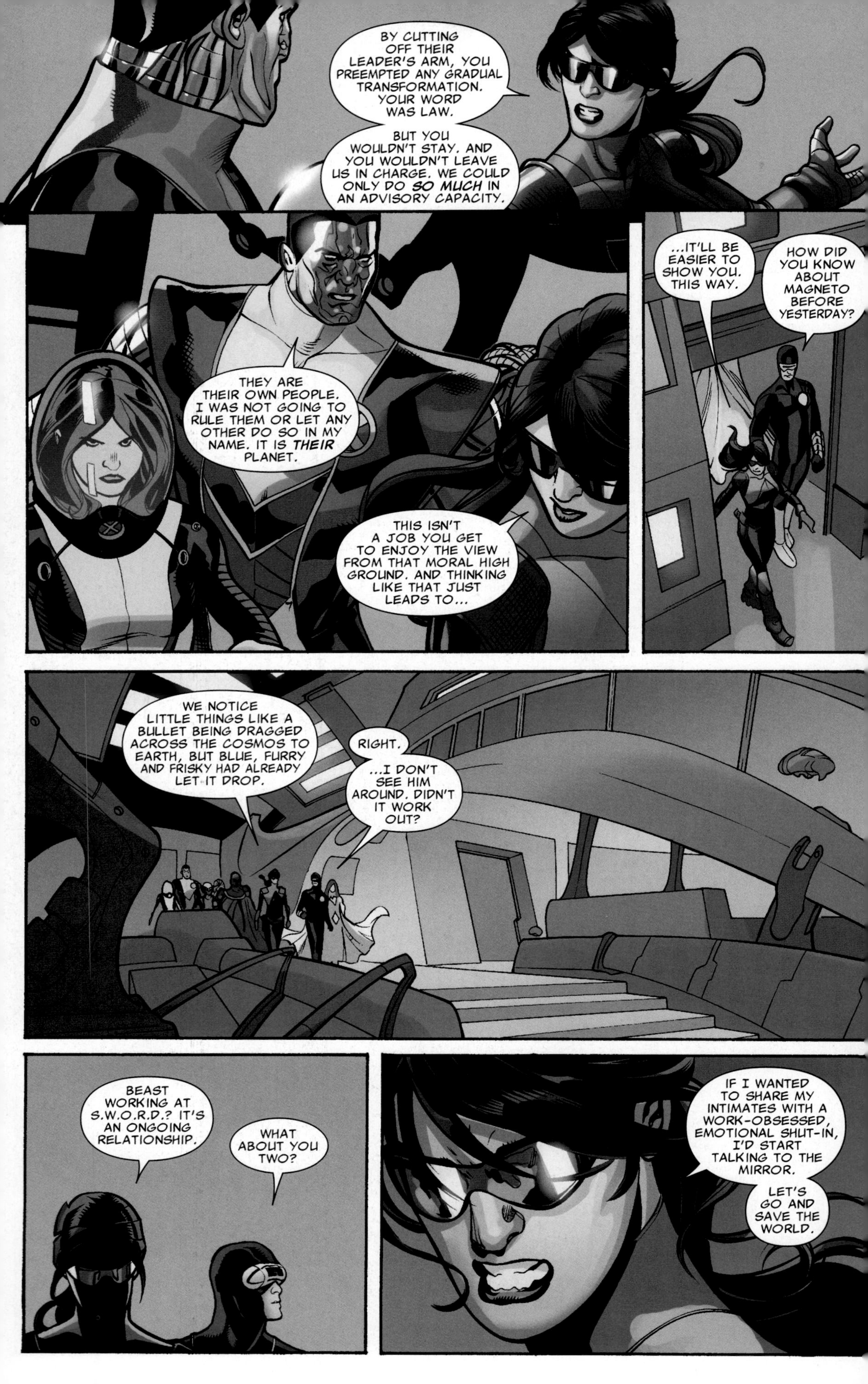
BY CUTTING OFF THEIR LEADER'S ARM, YOU PREEMPTED ANY GRADUAL TRANSFORMATION. YOUR WORD WAS LAW.
BUT YOU WOULDN'T STAY. AND YOU WOULDN'T LEAVE US IN CHARGE. WE COULD ONLY DO SO MUCH IN AN ADVISORY CAPACITY.
THEY ARE THEIR OWN PEOPLE. I WAS NOT GOING TO RULE THEM OR LET ANY OTHER DO SO IN MY NAME. IT IS THEIR PLANET.
THIS ISN'T A JOB YOU GET TO ENJOY THE VIEW FROM THAT MORAL HIGH GROUND. AND THINKING LIKE THAT JUST LEADS TO...
...IT'LL BE EASIER TO SHOW YOU. THIS WAY.
HOW DID YOU KNOW ABOUT MAGNETO BEFORE YESTERDAY?
WE NOTICE LITTLE THINGS LIKE A BULLET BEING DRAGGED ACROSS THE COSMOS TO EARTH, BUT BLUE, FURRY AND FRISKY HAD ALREADY LET IT DROP.
RIGHT.
...I DON'T SEE HIM AROUND. DIDN'T IT WORK OUT?
BEAST WORKING AT S.W.O.R.D.? IT'S AN ONGOING RELATIONSHIP.
WHAT ABOUT YOU TWO?
IF I WANTED TO SHARE MY INTIMATES WITH A WORK-OBSESSED, EMOTIONAL SHUT-IN, I'D START TALKING TO THE MIRROR.
LET'S GO AND SAVE THE WORLD.

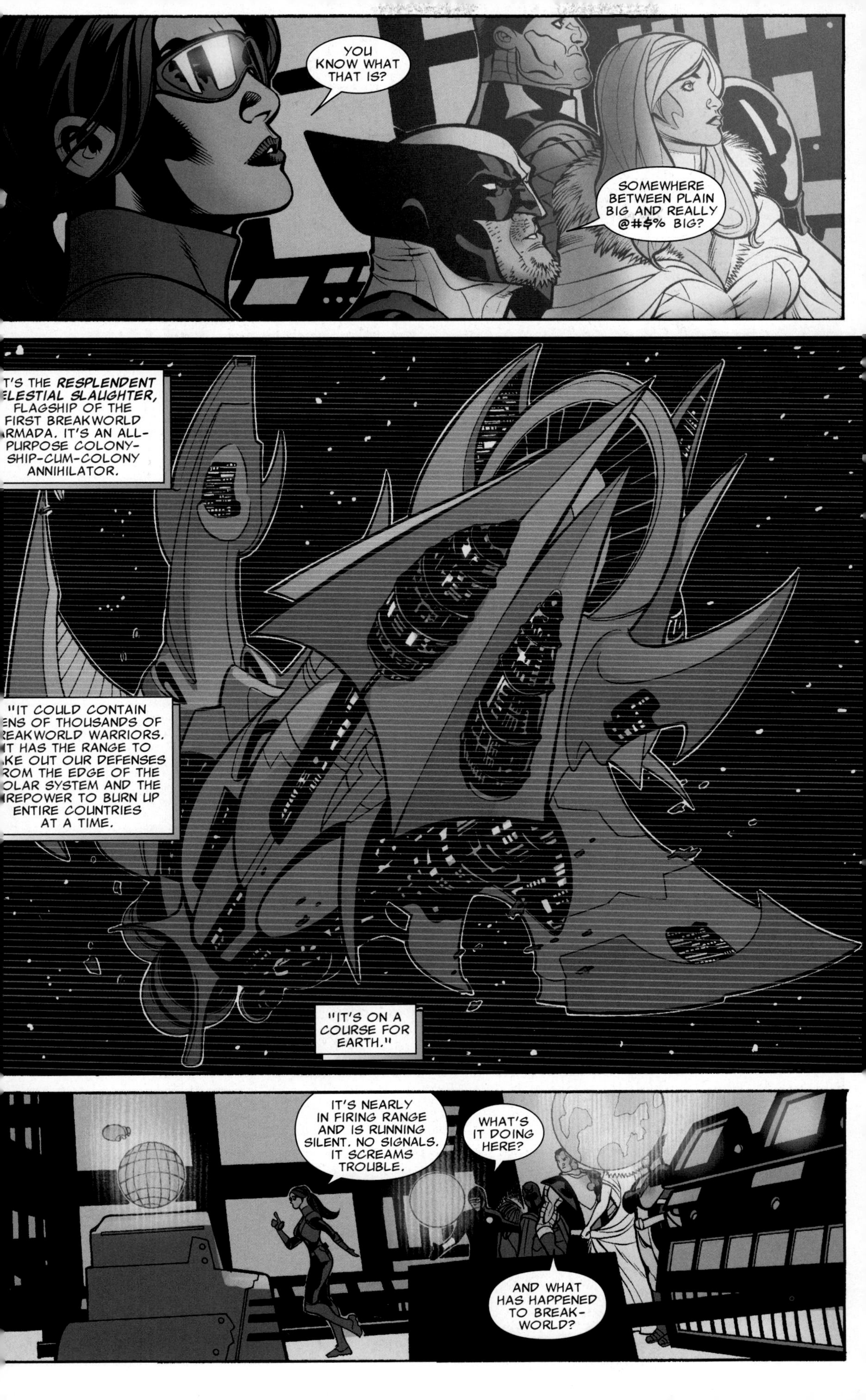

YOU KNOW WHAT THAT IS?
SOMEWHERE BETWEEN PLAIN BIG AND REALLY @#$% BIG?
T'S THE RESPLENDENT ELESTIAL SLAUGHTER, FLAGSHIP OF THE FIRST BREAKWORLD RMADA. IT'S AN ALL-PURPOSE COLONY-SHIP-CUM-COLONY ANNIHILATOR.
"IT COULD CONTAIN ENS OF THOUSANDS OF REAKWORLD WARRIORS. T HAS THE RANGE TO AKE OUT OUR DEFENSES ROM THE EDGE OF THE OLAR SYSTEM AND THE REPOWER TO BURN UP ENTIRE COUNTRIES AT A TIME.
"IT'S ON A COURSE FOR EARTH."
IT'S NEARLY IN FIRING RANGE AND IS RUNNING SILENT. NO SIGNALS. IT SCREAMS TROUBLE.
WHAT'S IT DOING HERE?
AND WHAT HAS HAPPENED TO BREAK-WORLD?

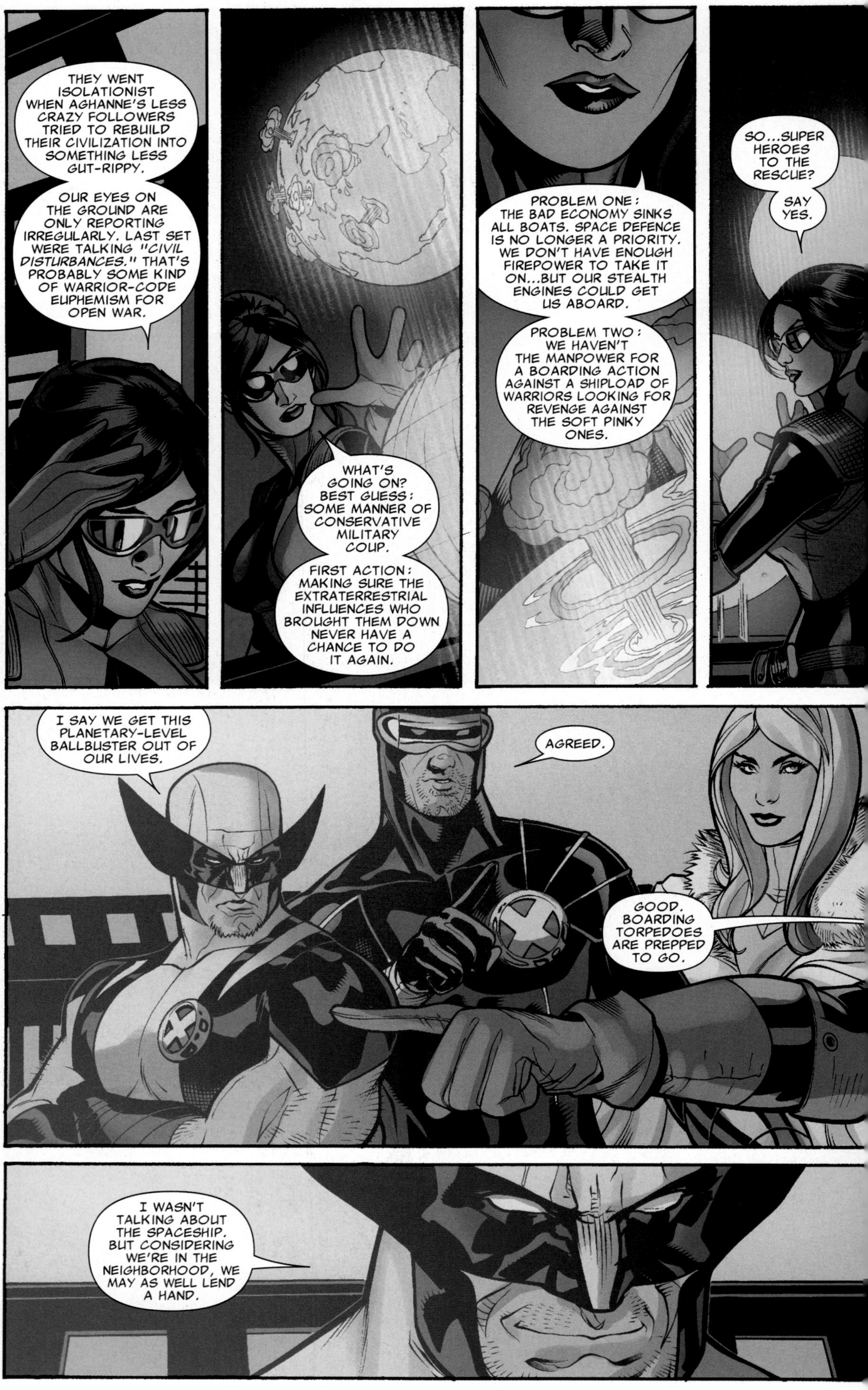
THEY WENT ISOLATIONIST WHEN AGHANNE'S LESS CRAZY FOLLOWERS TRIED TO REBUILD THEIR CIVILIZATION INTO SOMETHING LESS GUT-RIPPY.
OUR EYES ON THE GROUND ARE ONLY REPORTING IRREGULARLY. LAST SET WERE TALKING "CIVIL DISTURBANCES." THAT'S PROBABLY SOME KIND OF WARRIOR-CODE EUPHEMISM FOR OPEN WAR.
WHAT'S GOING ON? BEST GUESS: SOME MANNER OF CONSERVATIVE MILITARY COUP.
FIRST ACTION: MAKING SURE THE EXTRATERRESTRIAL INFLUENCES WHO BROUGHT THEM DOWN NEVER HAVE A CHANCE TO DO IT AGAIN.
PROBLEM ONE: THE BAD ECONOMY SINKS ALL BOATS. SPACE DEFENCE IS NO LONGER A PRIORITY. WE DON'T HAVE ENOUGH FIREPOWER TO TAKE IT ON...BUT OUR STEALTH ENGINES COULD GET US ABOARD.
PROBLEM TWO: WE HAVEN'T THE MANPOWER FOR A BOARDING ACTION AGAINST A SHIPLOAD OF WARRIORS LOOKING FOR REVENGE AGAINST THE SOFT PINKY ONES.
SO...SUPER HEROES TO THE RESCUE?
SAY YES.
I SAY WE GET THIS PLANETARY-LEVEL BALLBUSTER OUT OF OUR LIVES.
AGREED.
GOOD. BOARDING TORPEDOES ARE PREPPED TO GO.
I WASN'T TALKING ABOUT THE SPACESHIP. BUT CONSIDERING WE'RE IN THE NEIGHBORHOOD, WE MAY AS WELL LEND A HAND.

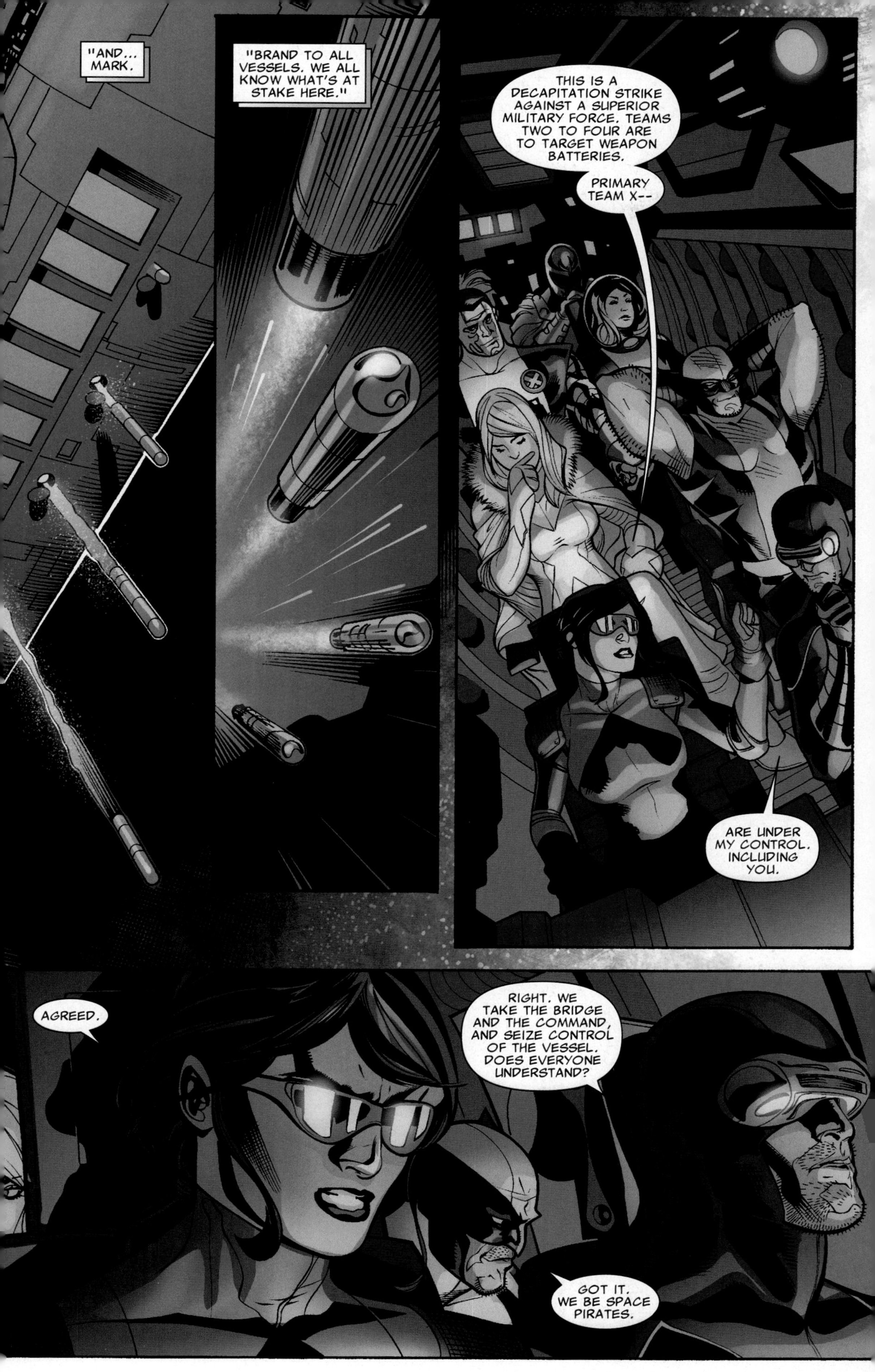
"AND... MARK.
"BRAND TO ALL VESSELS. WE ALL KNOW WHAT'S AT STAKE HERE."
THIS IS A DECAPITATION STRIKE AGAINST A SUPERIOR MILITARY FORCE. TEAMS TWO TO FOUR ARE TO TARGET WEAPON BATTERIES.
PRIMARY TEAM X--
ARE UNDER MY CONTROL. INCLUDING YOU.
AGREED.
RIGHT. WE TAKE THE BRIDGE AND THE COMMAND, AND SEIZE CONTROL OF THE VESSEL. DOES EVERYONE UNDERSTAND?
GOT IT. WE BE SPACE PIRATES.

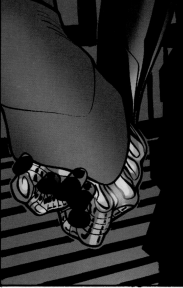

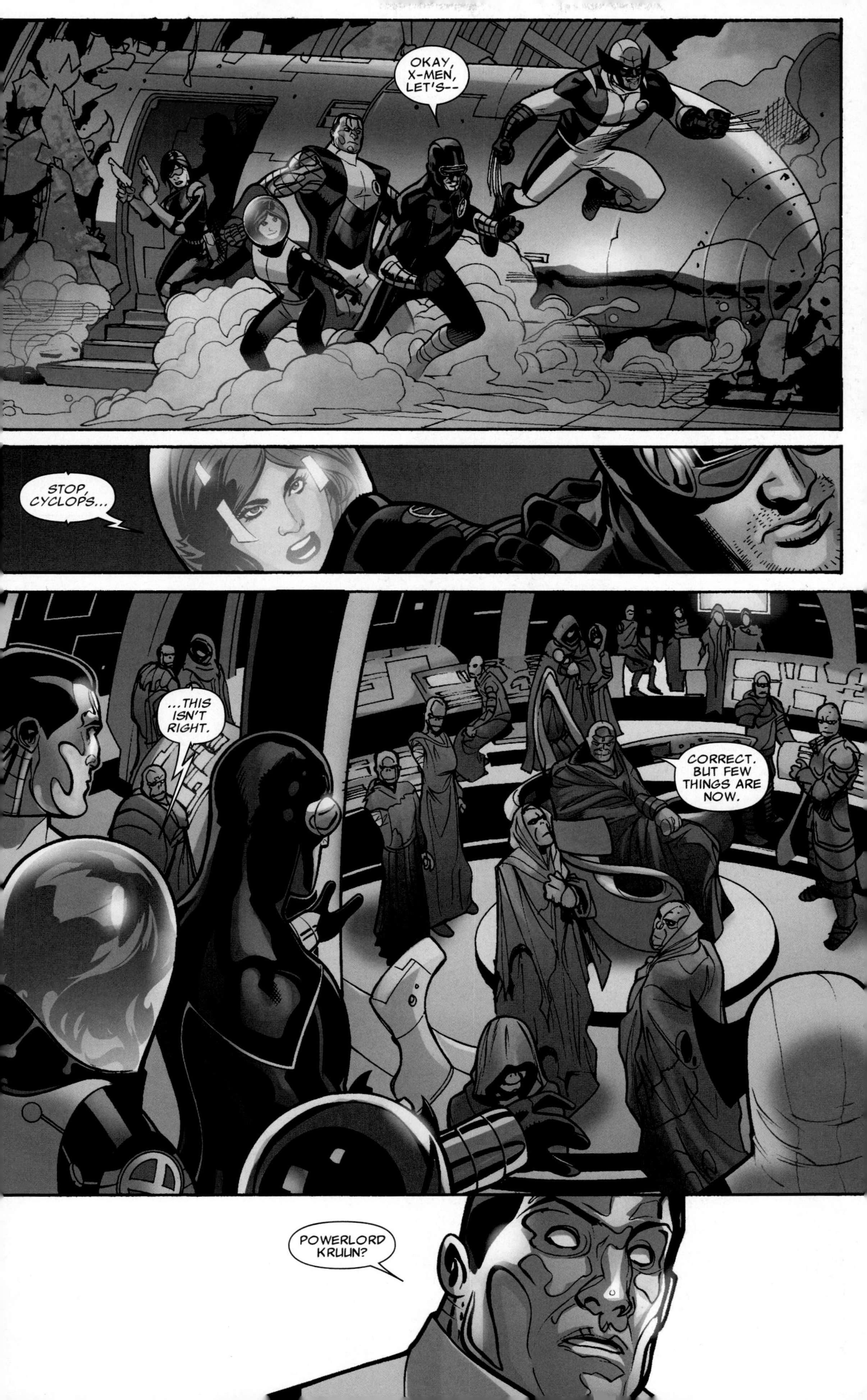
OKAY, X-MEN, LET'S--
STOP, CYCLOPS...
...THIS ISN'T RIGHT.
CORRECT. BUT FEW THINGS ARE NOW.
POWERLORD KRULN?

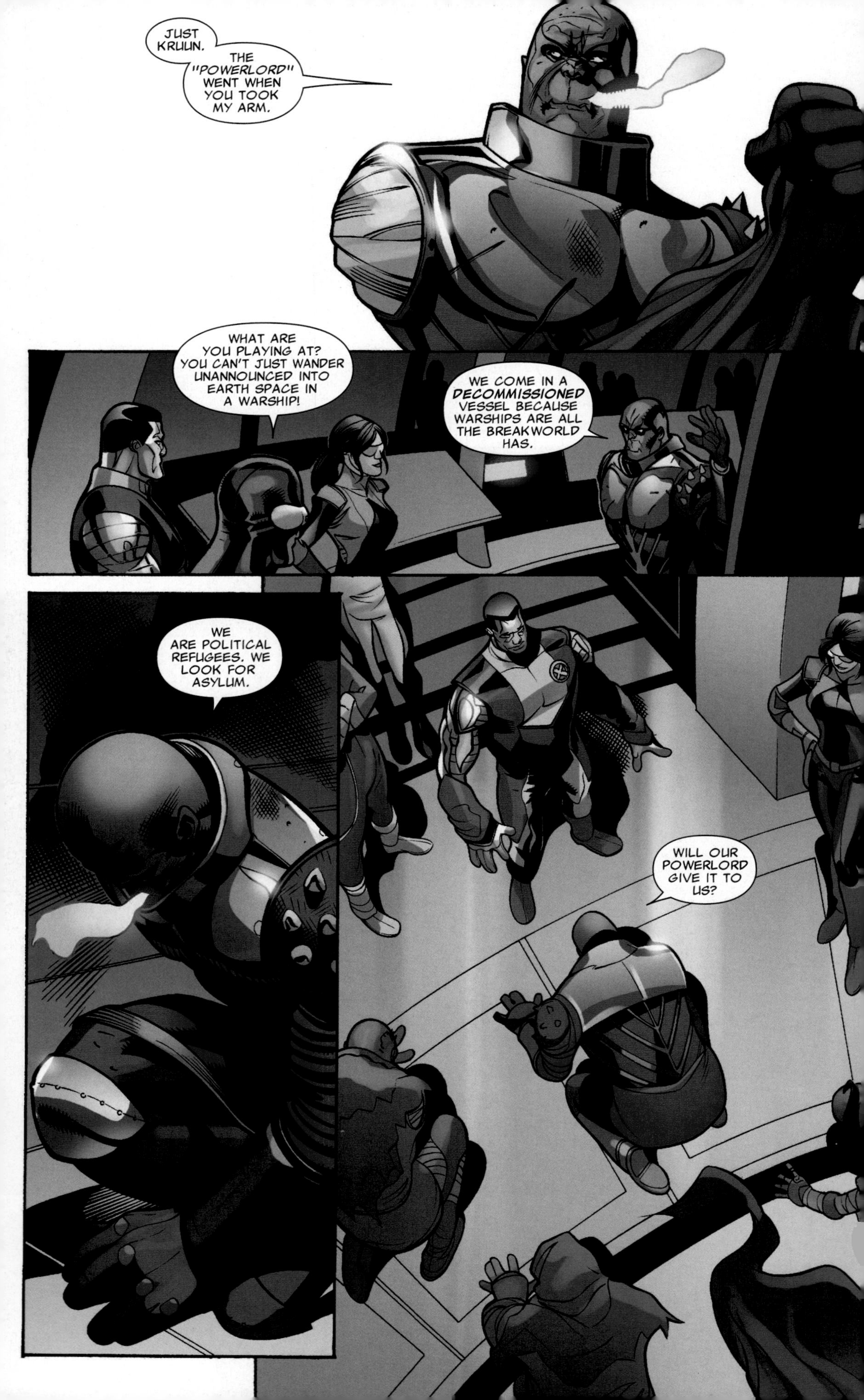
JUST KRUUN.
THE "POWERLORD" WENT WHEN YOU TOOK MY ARM.
WHAT ARE YOU PLAYING AT? YOU CAN'T JUST WANDER UNANNOUNCED INTO EARTH SPACE IN A WARSHIP!
WE COME IN A DECOMMISSIONED VESSEL BECAUSE WARSHIPS ARE ALL THE BREAKWORLD HAS.
WE ARE POLITICAL REFUGEES. WE LOOK FOR ASYLUM.
WILL OUR POWERLORD GIVE IT TO US?

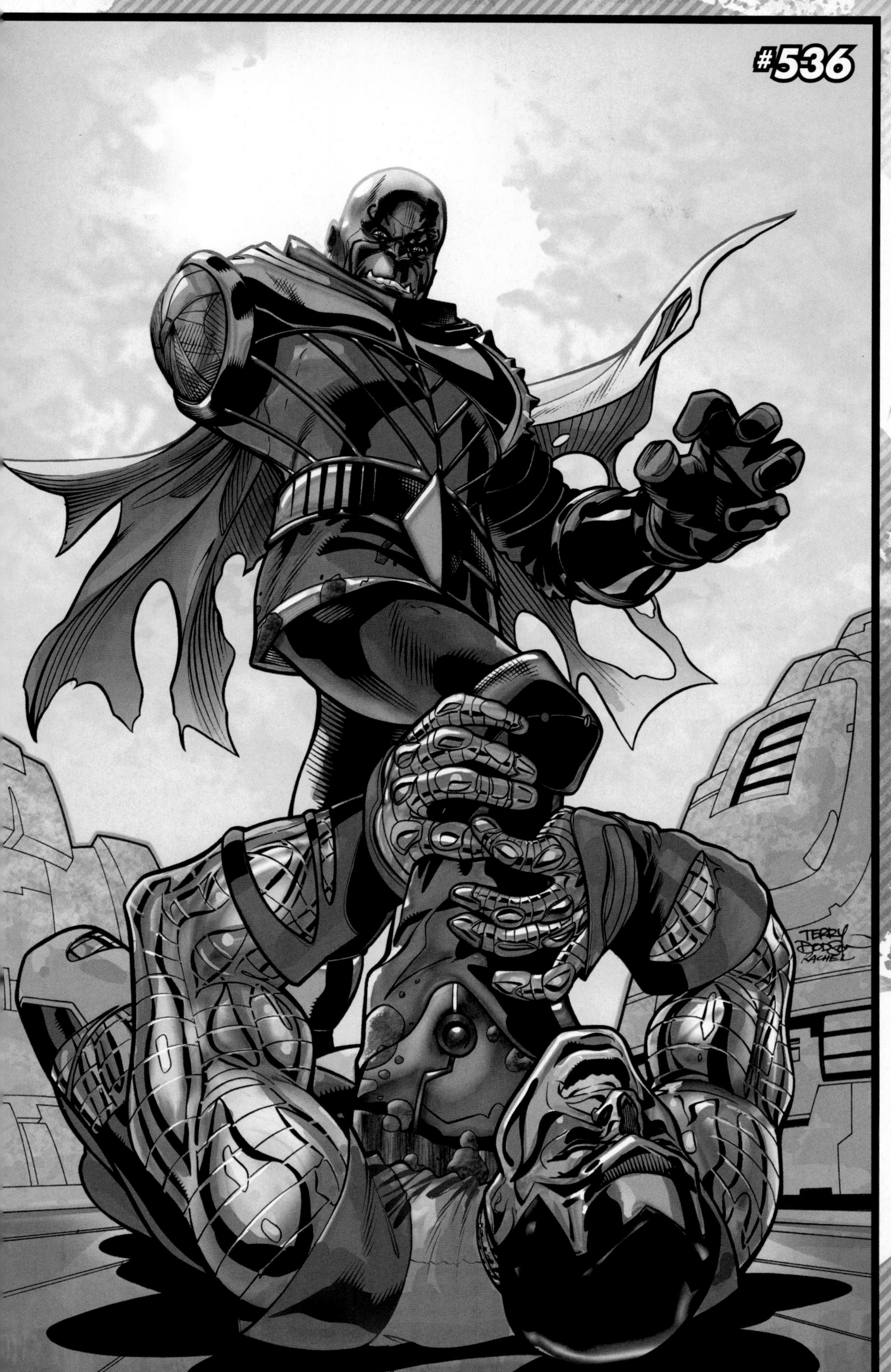
#536

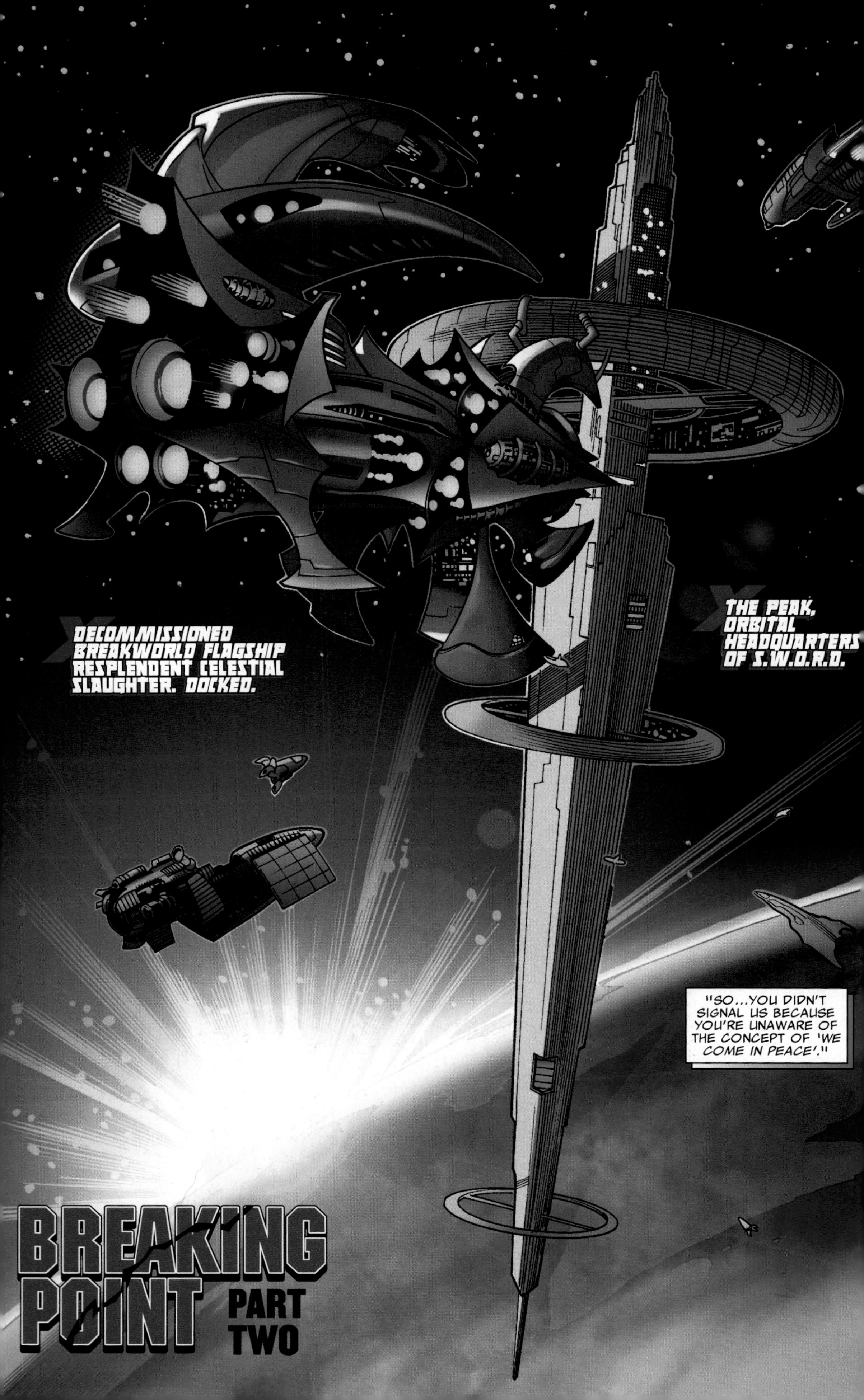

DECOMMISSIONED BREAKWORLD FLAGSHIP RESPLENDENT CELESTIAL SLAUGHTER. DOCKED.
THE PEAK, ORBITAL HEADQUARTERS OF S.W.O.R.D.
"SO...YOU DIDN'T SIGNAL US BECAUSE YOU'RE UNAWARE OF THE CONCEPT OF 'WE COME IN PEACE'."
BREAKING POINT PART TWO

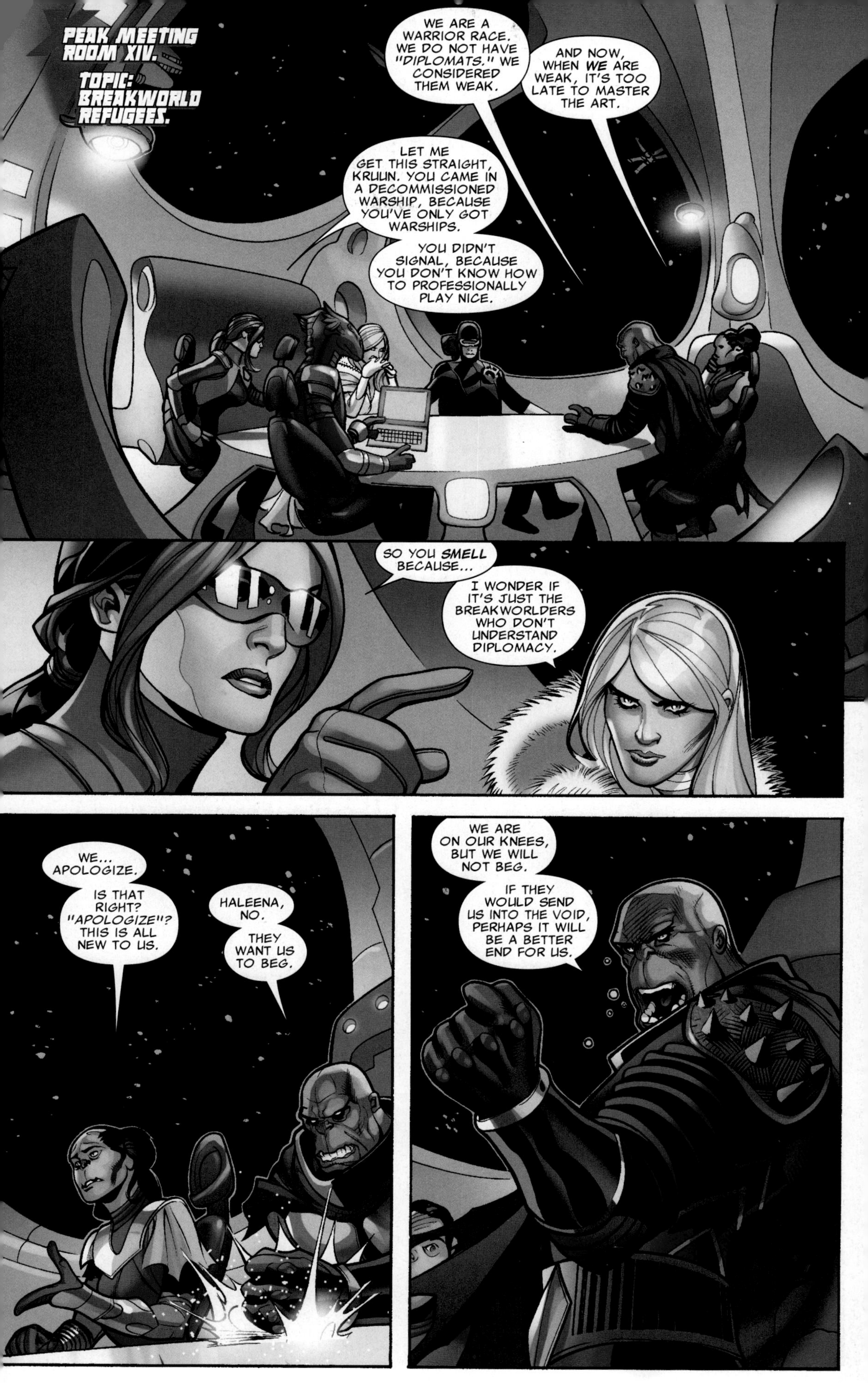
PEAK MEETING ROOM XIV.
TOPIC: BREAKWORLD REFUGEES.
WE ARE A WARRIOR RACE. WE DO NOT HAVE "DIPLOMATS." WE CONSIDERED THEM WEAK.
AND NOW, WHEN WE ARE WEAK, IT'S TOO LATE TO MASTER THE ART.
LET ME GET THIS STRAIGHT, KRUUN. YOU CAME IN A DECOMMISSIONED WARSHIP, BECAUSE YOU'VE ONLY GOT WARSHIPS.
YOU DIDN'T SIGNAL, BECAUSE YOU DON'T KNOW HOW TO PROFESSIONALLY PLAY NICE.
SO YOU SMELL BECAUSE...
I WONDER IF IT'S JUST THE BREAKWORLDERS WHO DON'T UNDERSTAND DIPLOMACY.
WE... APOLOGIZE.
IS THAT RIGHT? "APOLOGIZE"? THIS IS ALL NEW TO US.
HALEENA, NO.
THEY WANT US TO BEG.
WE ARE ON OUR KNEES, BUT WE WILL NOT BEG.
IF THEY WOULD SEND US INTO THE VOID, PERHAPS IT WILL BE A BETTER END FOR US.

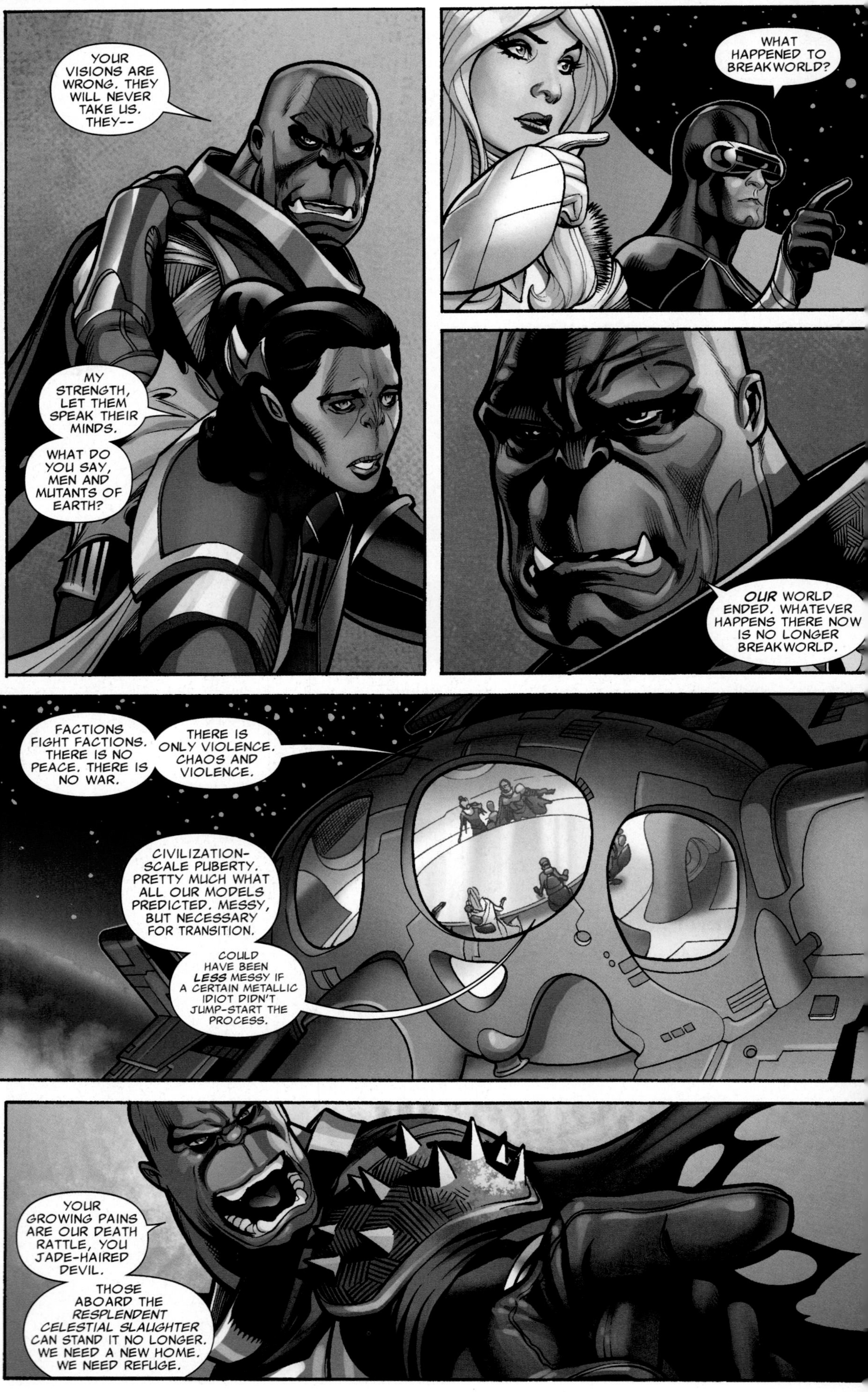
YOUR VISIONS ARE WRONG. THEY WILL NEVER TAKE US. THEY--
MY STRENGTH, LET THEM SPEAK THEIR MINDS.
WHAT DO YOU SAY, MEN AND MUTANTS OF EARTH?
WHAT HAPPENED TO BREAKWORLD?
OUR WORLD ENDED. WHATEVER HAPPENS THERE NOW IS NO LONGER BREAKWORLD.
FACTIONS FIGHT FACTIONS. THERE IS NO PEACE. THERE IS NO WAR.
THERE IS ONLY VIOLENCE. CHAOS AND VIOLENCE.
CIVILIZATION-SCALE PUBERTY. PRETTY MUCH WHAT ALL OUR MODELS PREDICTED. MESSY, BUT NECESSARY FOR TRANSITION.
COULD HAVE BEEN LESS MESSY IF A CERTAIN METALLIC IDIOT DIDN'T JUMP-START THE PROCESS.
YOUR GROWING PAINS ARE OUR DEATH RATTLE, YOU JADE-HAIRED DEVIL.
THOSE ABOARD THE RESPLENDENT CELESTIAL SLAUGHTER CAN STAND IT NO LONGER. WE NEED A NEW HOME. WE NEED REFUGE.

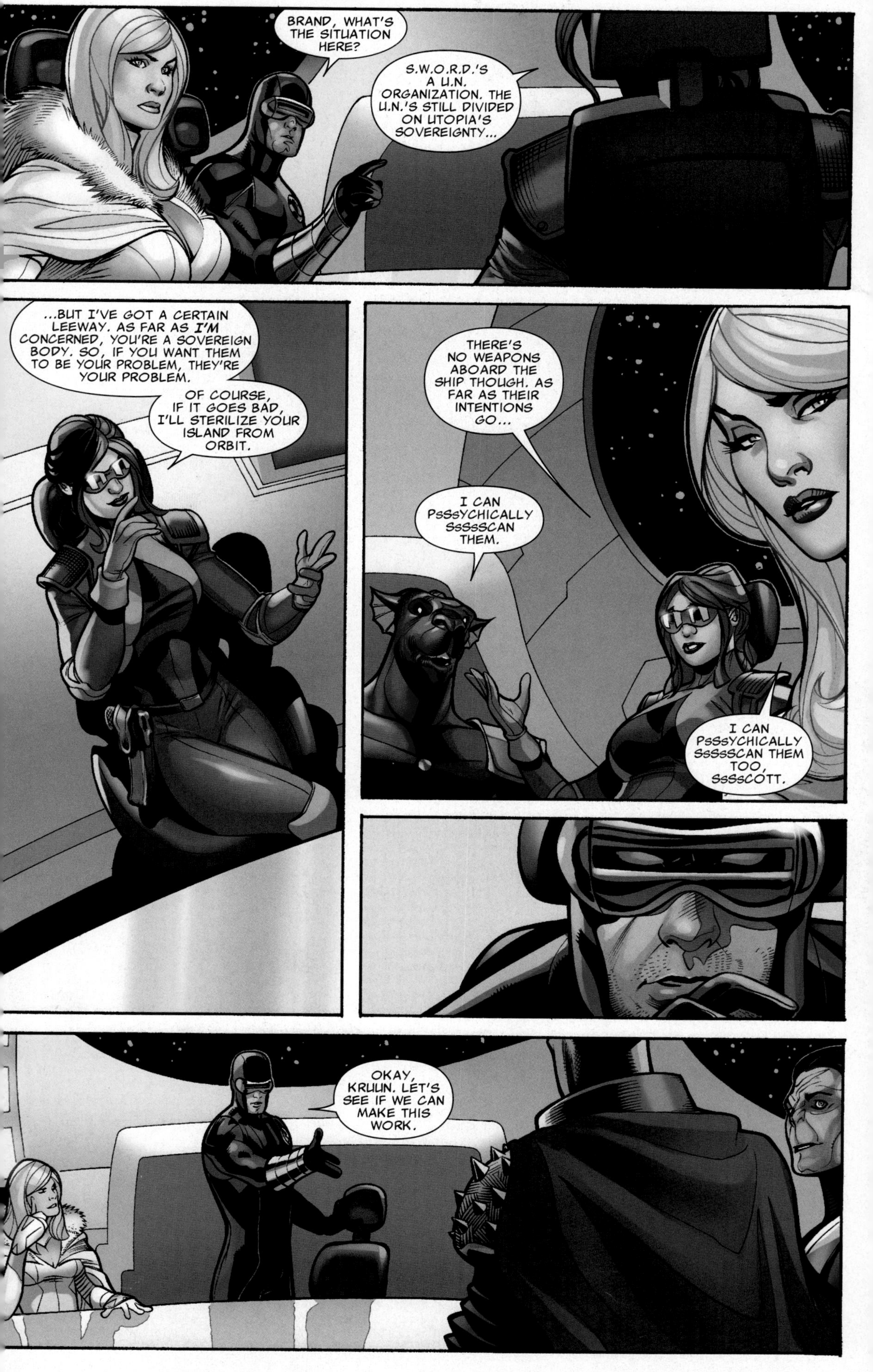
BRAND, WHAT'S THE SITUATION HERE?
S.W.O.R.D.'S A U.N. ORGANIZATION. THE U.N.'S STILL DIVIDED ON UTOPIA'S SOVEREIGNTY...
...BUT I'VE GOT A CERTAIN LEEWAY. AS FAR AS *I'M* CONCERNED, YOU'RE A SOVEREIGN BODY. SO, IF YOU WANT THEM TO BE YOUR PROBLEM, THEY'RE YOUR PROBLEM.
OF COURSE, IF IT GOES BAD, I'LL STERILIZE YOUR ISLAND FROM ORBIT.
THERE'S NO WEAPONS ABOARD THE SHIP THOUGH. AS FAR AS THEIR INTENTIONS GO...
I CAN PsSSYCHICALLY SSSSSCAN THEM.
I CAN PsSSYCHICALLY SSSSSCAN THEM TOO, SSSSCOTT.
OKAY, KRUUN. LET'S SEE IF WE CAN MAKE THIS WORK.

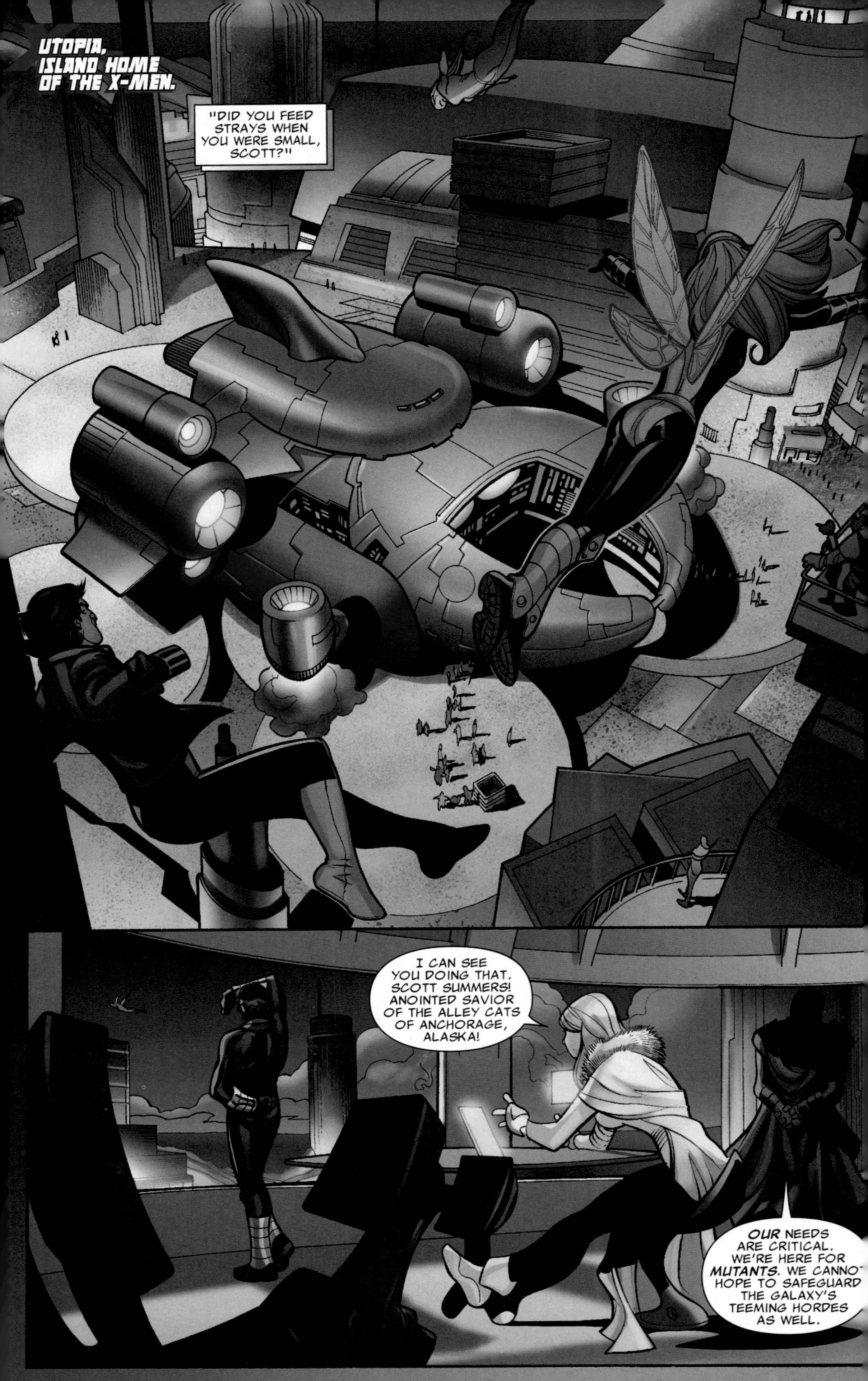
UTOPIA, ISLAND HOME OF THE X-MEN.
"DID YOU FEED STRAYS WHEN YOU WERE SMALL, SCOTT?"
I CAN SEE YOU DOING THAT. SCOTT SUMMERS! ANOINTED SAVIOR OF THE ALLEY CATS OF ANCHORAGE, ALASKA!
OUR NEEDS ARE CRITICAL. WE'RE HERE FOR MUTANTS. WE CANNOT HOPE TO SAFEGUARD THE GALAXY'S TEEMING HORDES AS WELL.

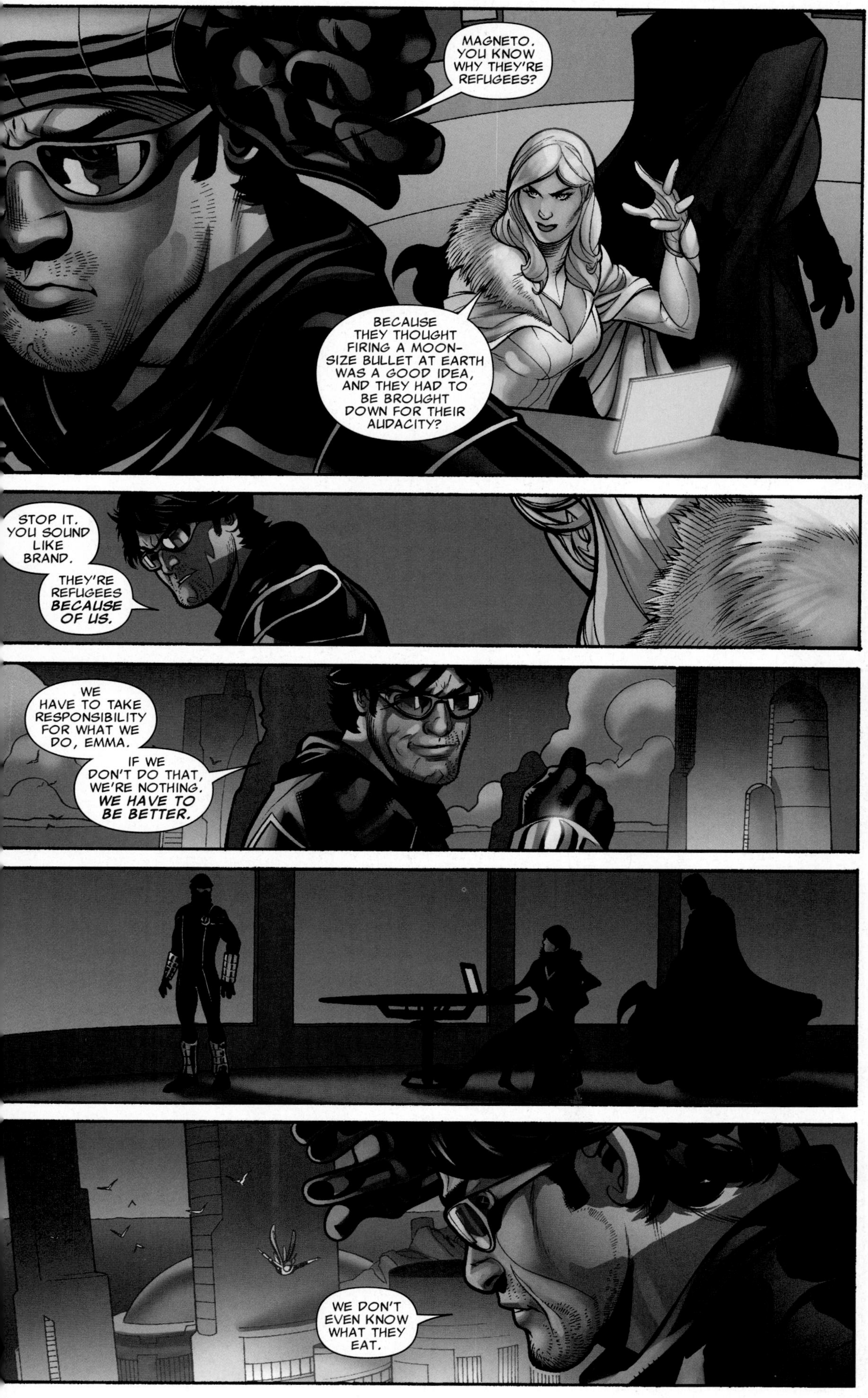
MAGNETO. YOU KNOW WHY THEY'RE REFUGEES?
BECAUSE THEY THOUGHT FIRING A MOON-SIZE BULLET AT EARTH WAS A GOOD IDEA, AND THEY HAD TO BE BROUGHT DOWN FOR THEIR AUDACITY?
STOP IT. YOU SOUND LIKE BRAND.
THEY'RE REFUGEES *BECAUSE OF US.*
WE HAVE TO TAKE RESPONSIBILITY FOR WHAT WE DO, EMMA.
IF WE DON'T DO THAT, WE'RE NOTHING. *WE HAVE TO BE BETTER.*
WE DON'T EVEN KNOW WHAT THEY EAT.

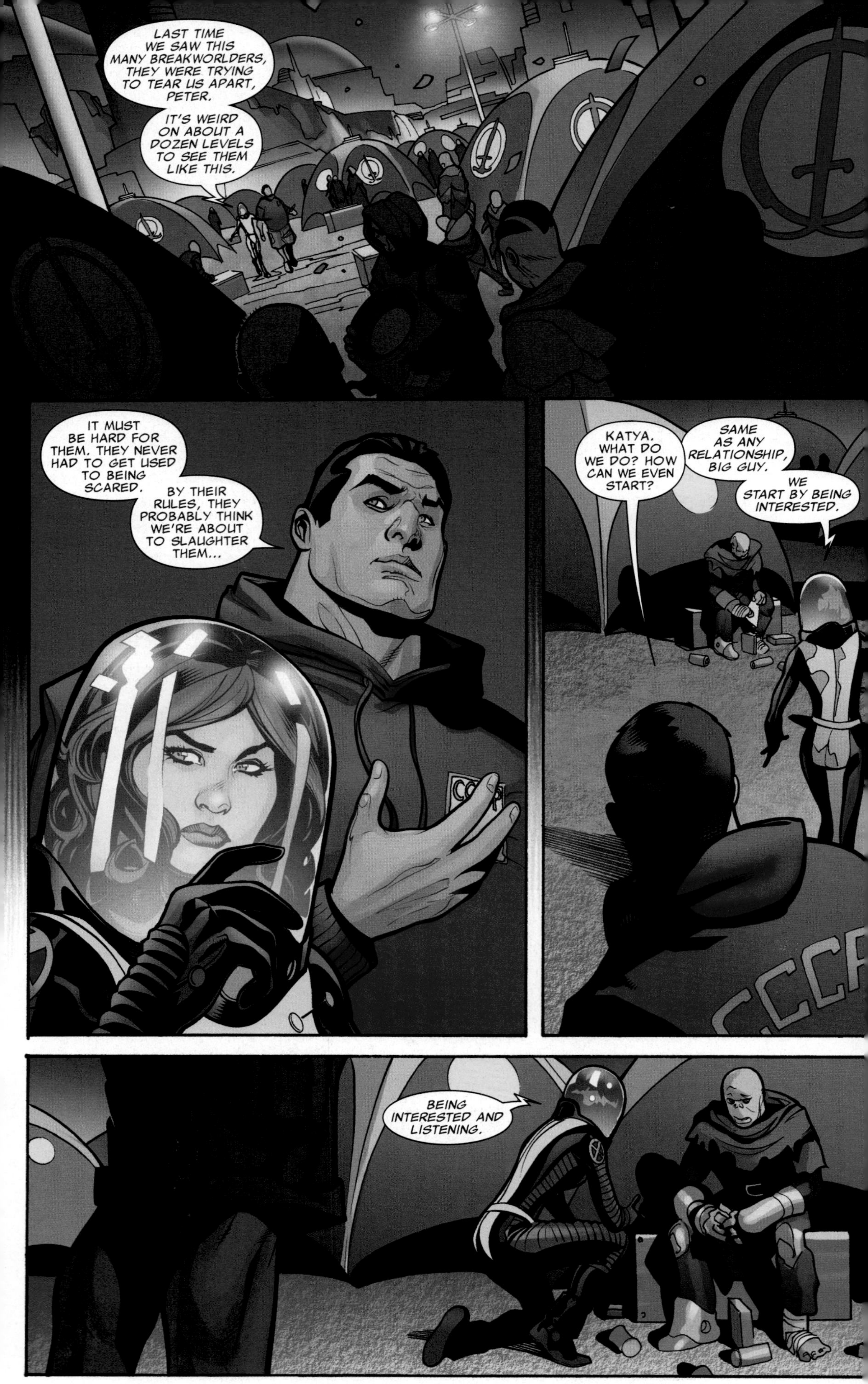
LAST TIME WE SAW THIS MANY BREAKWORLDERS, THEY WERE TRYING TO TEAR US APART, PETER.
IT'S WEIRD ON ABOUT A DOZEN LEVELS TO SEE THEM LIKE THIS.
IT MUST BE HARD FOR THEM. THEY NEVER HAD TO GET USED TO BEING SCARED.
BY THEIR RULES, THEY PROBABLY THINK WE'RE ABOUT TO SLAUGHTER THEM...
KATYA, WHAT DO WE DO? HOW CAN WE EVEN START?
SAME AS ANY RELATIONSHIP, BIG GUY.
WE START BY BEING INTERESTED.
BEING INTERESTED AND LISTENING.

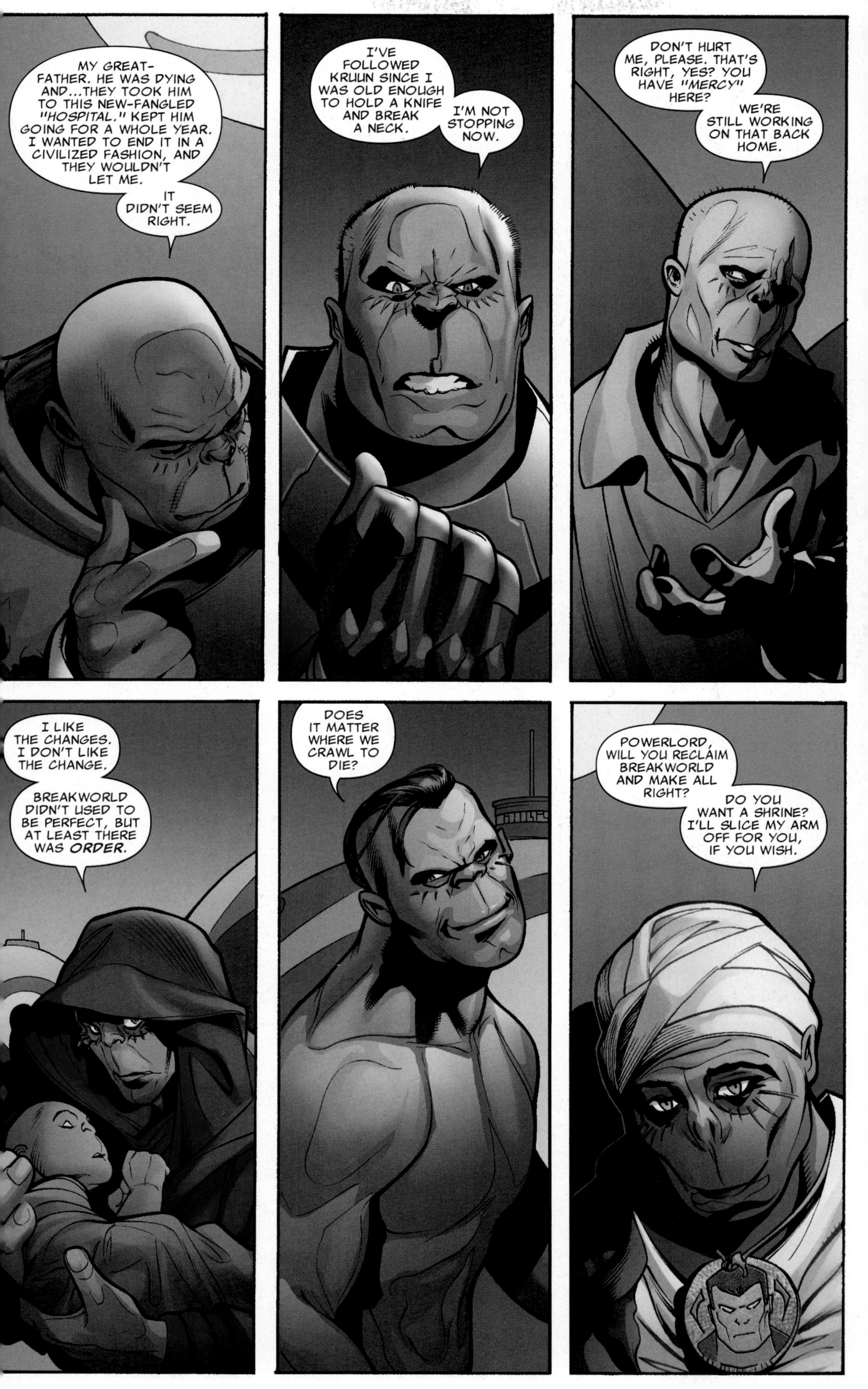

MY GREAT-FATHER. HE WAS DYING AND...THEY TOOK HIM TO THIS NEW-FANGLED "HOSPITAL." KEPT HIM GOING FOR A WHOLE YEAR. I WANTED TO END IT IN A CIVILIZED FASHION, AND THEY WOULDN'T LET ME.
IT DIDN'T SEEM RIGHT.
I'VE FOLLOWED KRUUN SINCE I WAS OLD ENOUGH TO HOLD A KNIFE AND BREAK A NECK.
I'M NOT STOPPING NOW.
DON'T HURT ME, PLEASE. THAT'S RIGHT, YES? YOU HAVE "MERCY" HERE?
WE'RE STILL WORKING ON THAT BACK HOME.
I LIKE THE CHANGES. I DON'T LIKE THE CHANGE.
BREAKWORLD DIDN'T USED TO BE PERFECT, BUT AT LEAST THERE WAS ORDER.
DOES IT MATTER WHERE WE CRAWL TO DIE?
POWERLORD, WILL YOU RECLAIM BREAKWORLD AND MAKE ALL RIGHT?
DO YOU WANT A SHRINE? I'LL SLICE MY ARM OFF FOR YOU, IF YOU WISH.

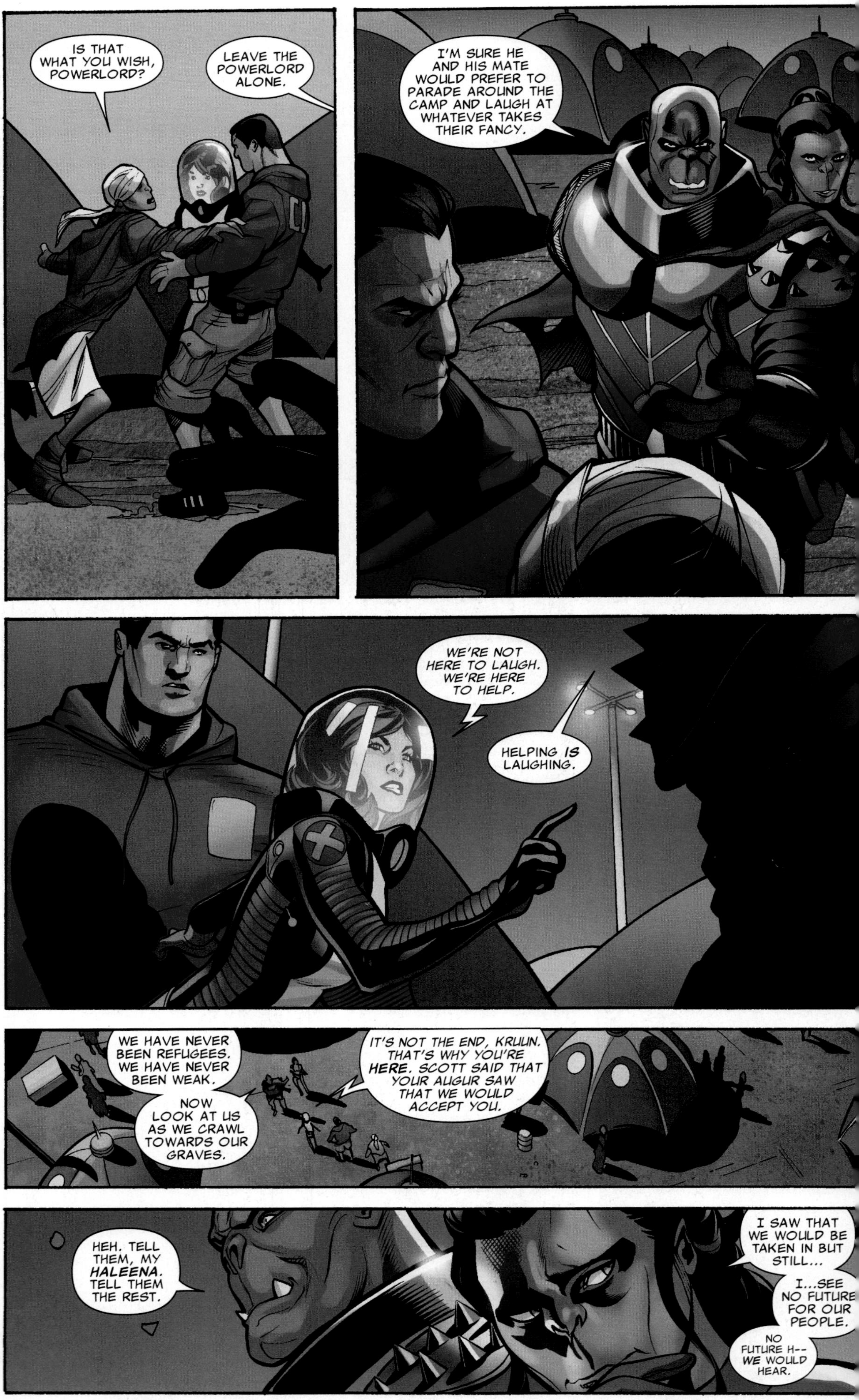

IS THAT WHAT YOU WISH, POWERLORD?
LEAVE THE POWERLORD ALONE.
I'M SURE HE AND HIS MATE WOULD PREFER TO PARADE AROUND THE CAMP AND LAUGH AT WHATEVER TAKES THEIR FANCY.
WE'RE NOT HERE TO LAUGH. WE'RE HERE TO HELP.
HELPING IS LAUGHING.
WE HAVE NEVER BEEN REFUGEES. WE HAVE NEVER BEEN WEAK.
NOW LOOK AT US AS WE CRAWL TOWARDS OUR GRAVES.
IT'S NOT THE END, KRUUN. THAT'S WHY YOU'RE HERE. SCOTT SAID THAT YOUR AUGUR SAW THAT WE WOULD ACCEPT YOU.
HEH. TELL THEM, MY HALEENA. TELL THEM THE REST.
I SAW THAT WE WOULD BE TAKEN IN BUT STILL...
I...SEE NO FUTURE FOR OUR PEOPLE.
NO FUTURE H-- WE WOULD HEAR.

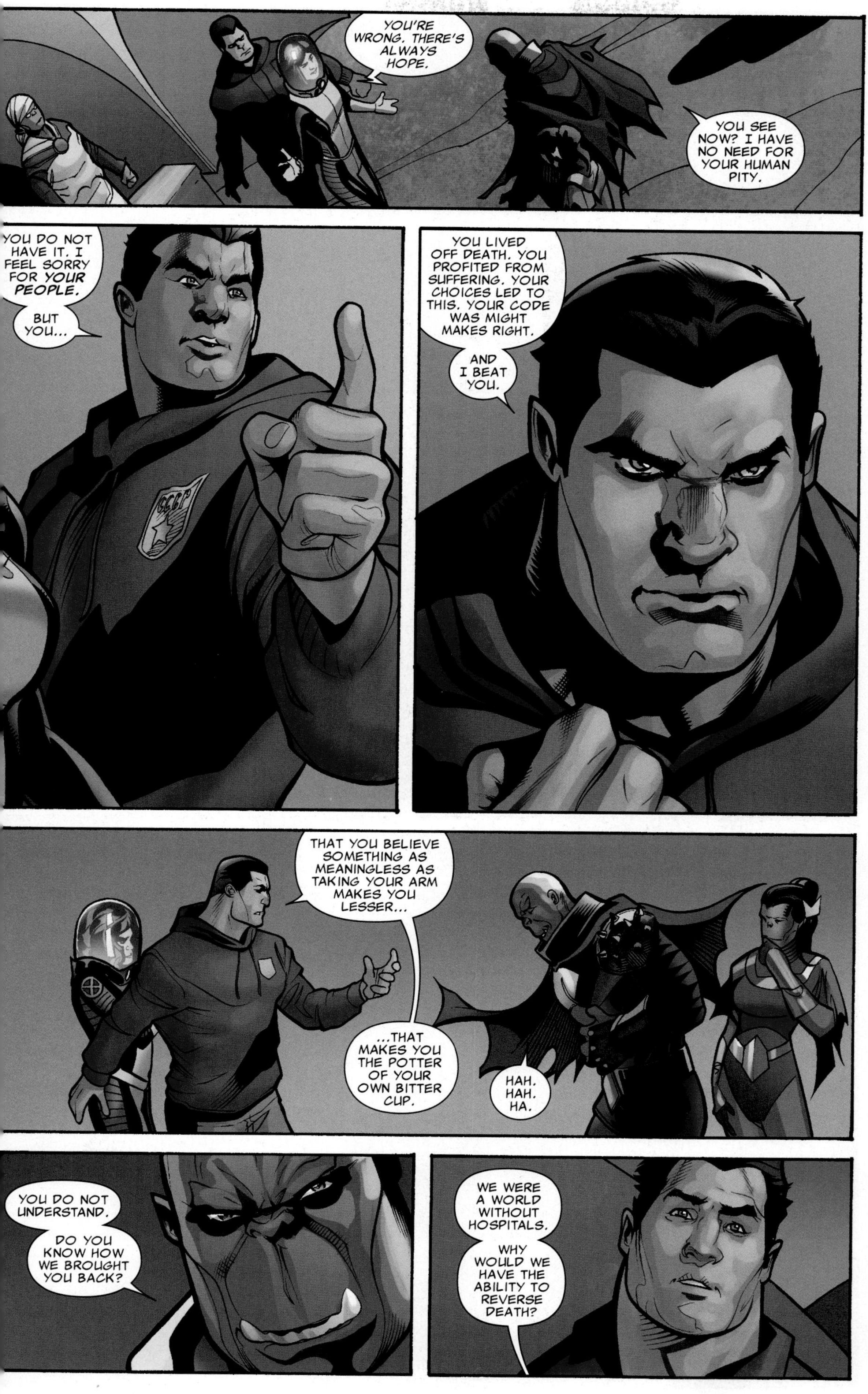
YOU'RE WRONG. THERE'S ALWAYS HOPE.
YOU SEE NOW? I HAVE NO NEED FOR YOUR HUMAN PITY.
YOU DO NOT HAVE IT. I FEEL SORRY FOR *YOUR PEOPLE.*
BUT YOU...
YOU LIVED OFF DEATH. YOU PROFITED FROM SUFFERING. YOUR CHOICES LED TO THIS. YOUR CODE WAS MIGHT MAKES RIGHT.
AND I BEAT YOU.
THAT YOU BELIEVE SOMETHING AS MEANINGLESS AS TAKING YOUR ARM MAKES YOU LESSER...
...THAT MAKES YOU THE POTTER OF YOUR OWN BITTER CUP.
HAH. HAH. HA.
YOU DO NOT UNDERSTAND.
DO YOU KNOW HOW WE BROUGHT YOU BACK?
WE WERE A WORLD WITHOUT HOSPITALS.
WHY WOULD WE HAVE THE ABILITY TO REVERSE DEATH?

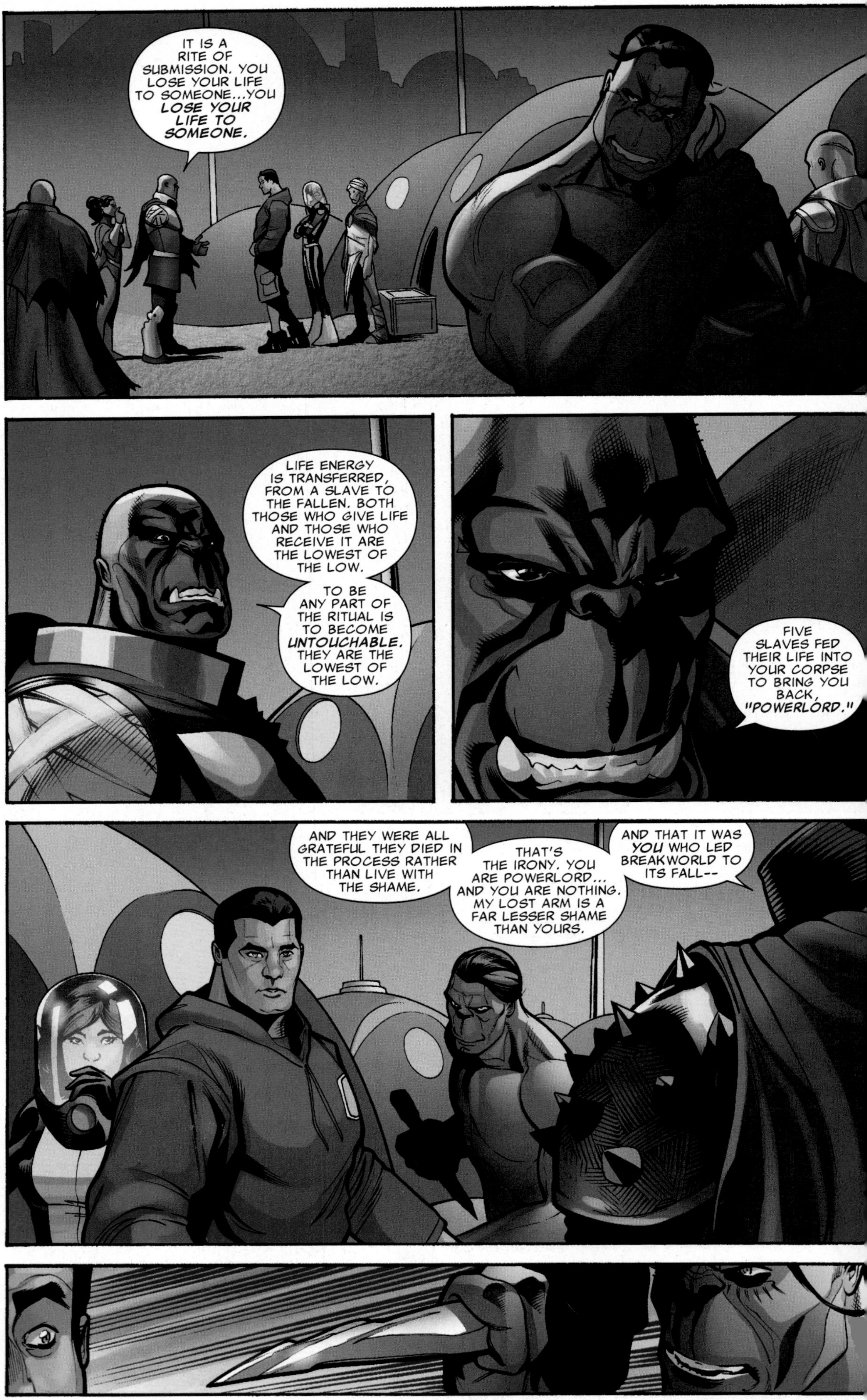
IT IS A RITE OF SUBMISSION. YOU LOSE YOUR LIFE TO SOMEONE...YOU *LOSE YOUR LIFE TO SOMEONE.*
LIFE ENERGY IS TRANSFERRED, FROM A SLAVE TO THE FALLEN. BOTH THOSE WHO GIVE LIFE AND THOSE WHO RECEIVE IT ARE THE LOWEST OF THE LOW.
TO BE ANY PART OF THE RITUAL IS TO BECOME *UNTOUCHABLE.* THEY ARE THE LOWEST OF THE LOW.
FIVE SLAVES FED THEIR LIFE INTO YOUR CORPSE TO BRING YOU BACK, *"POWERLORD."*
AND THEY WERE ALL GRATEFUL THEY DIED IN THE PROCESS RATHER THAN LIVE WITH THE SHAME.
THAT'S THE IRONY. YOU ARE POWERLORD... AND YOU ARE NOTHING. MY LOST ARM IS A FAR LESSER SHAME THAN YOURS.
AND THAT IT WAS *YOU* WHO LED BREAKWORLD TO ITS FALL--

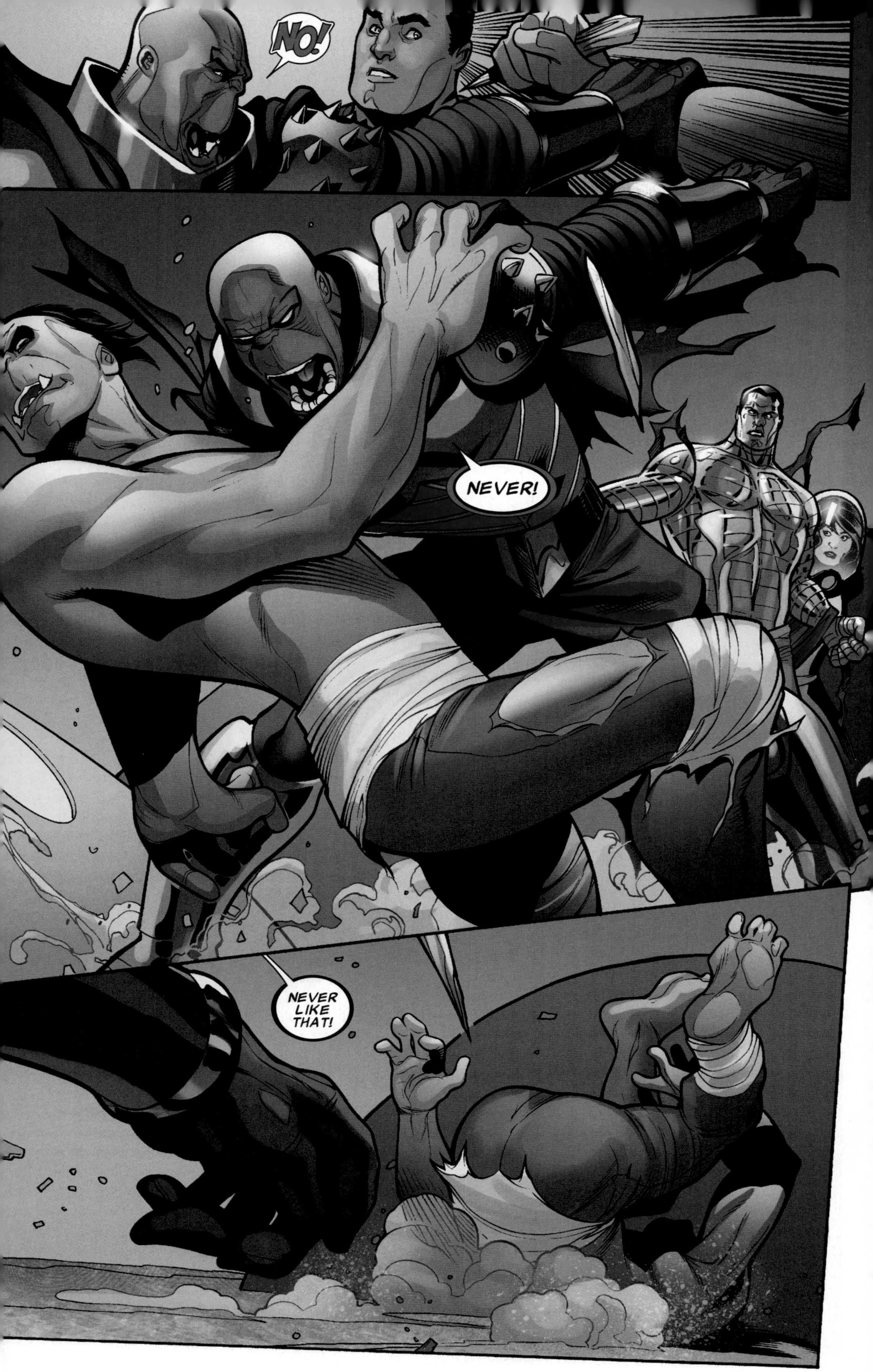
NO!
NEVER!
NEVER LIKE THAT!

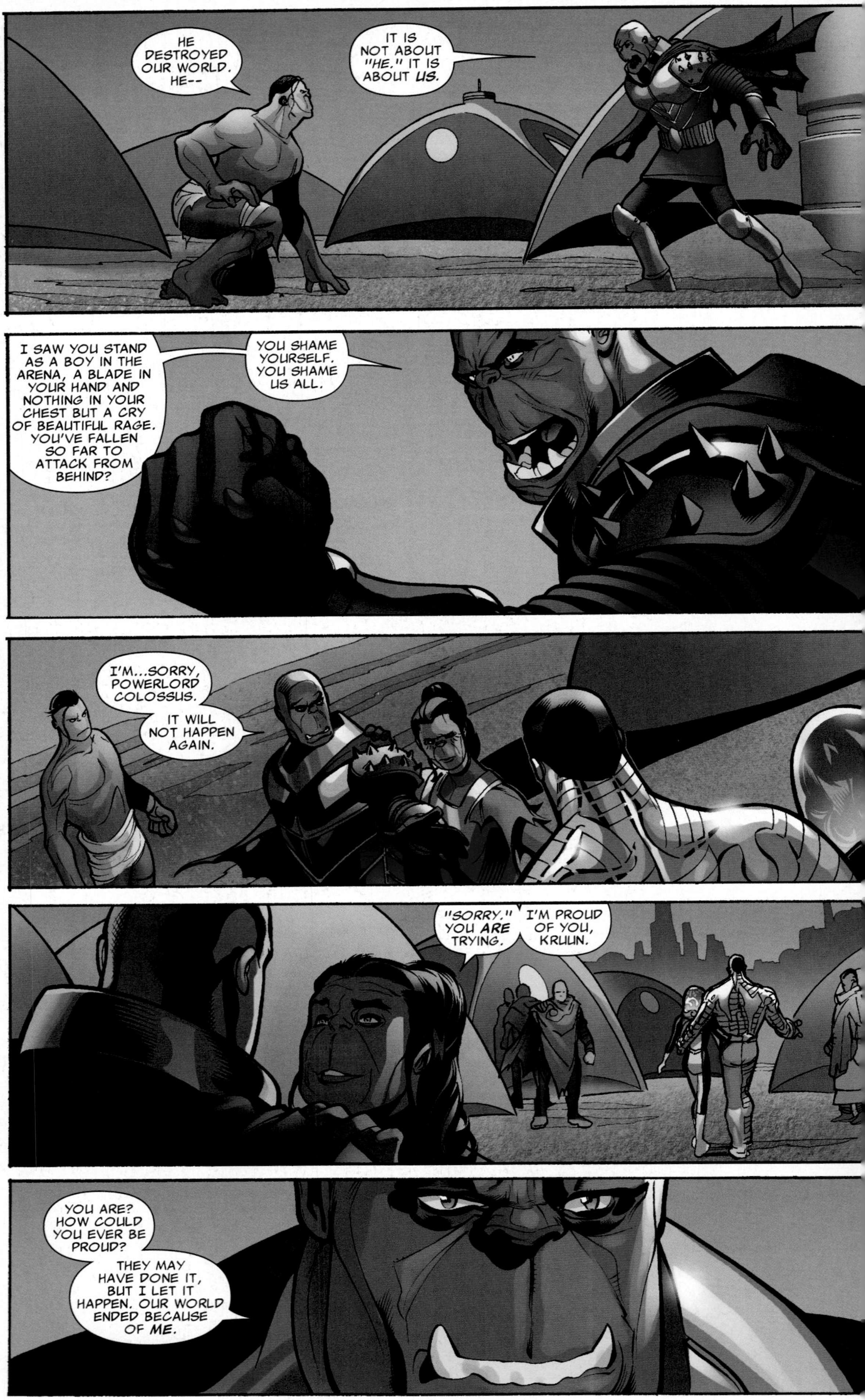

HE DESTROYED OUR WORLD. HE--
IT IS NOT ABOUT "HE." IT IS ABOUT US.
I SAW YOU STAND AS A BOY IN THE ARENA, A BLADE IN YOUR HAND AND NOTHING IN YOUR CHEST BUT A CRY OF BEAUTIFUL RAGE. YOU'VE FALLEN SO FAR TO ATTACK FROM BEHIND?
YOU SHAME YOURSELF. YOU SHAME US ALL.
I'M...SORRY, POWERLORD COLOSSUS.
IT WILL NOT HAPPEN AGAIN.
"SORRY." YOU ARE TRYING.
I'M PROUD OF YOU, KRUUN.
YOU ARE? HOW COULD YOU EVER BE PROUD?
THEY MAY HAVE DONE IT, BUT I LET IT HAPPEN. OUR WORLD ENDED BECAUSE OF ME.

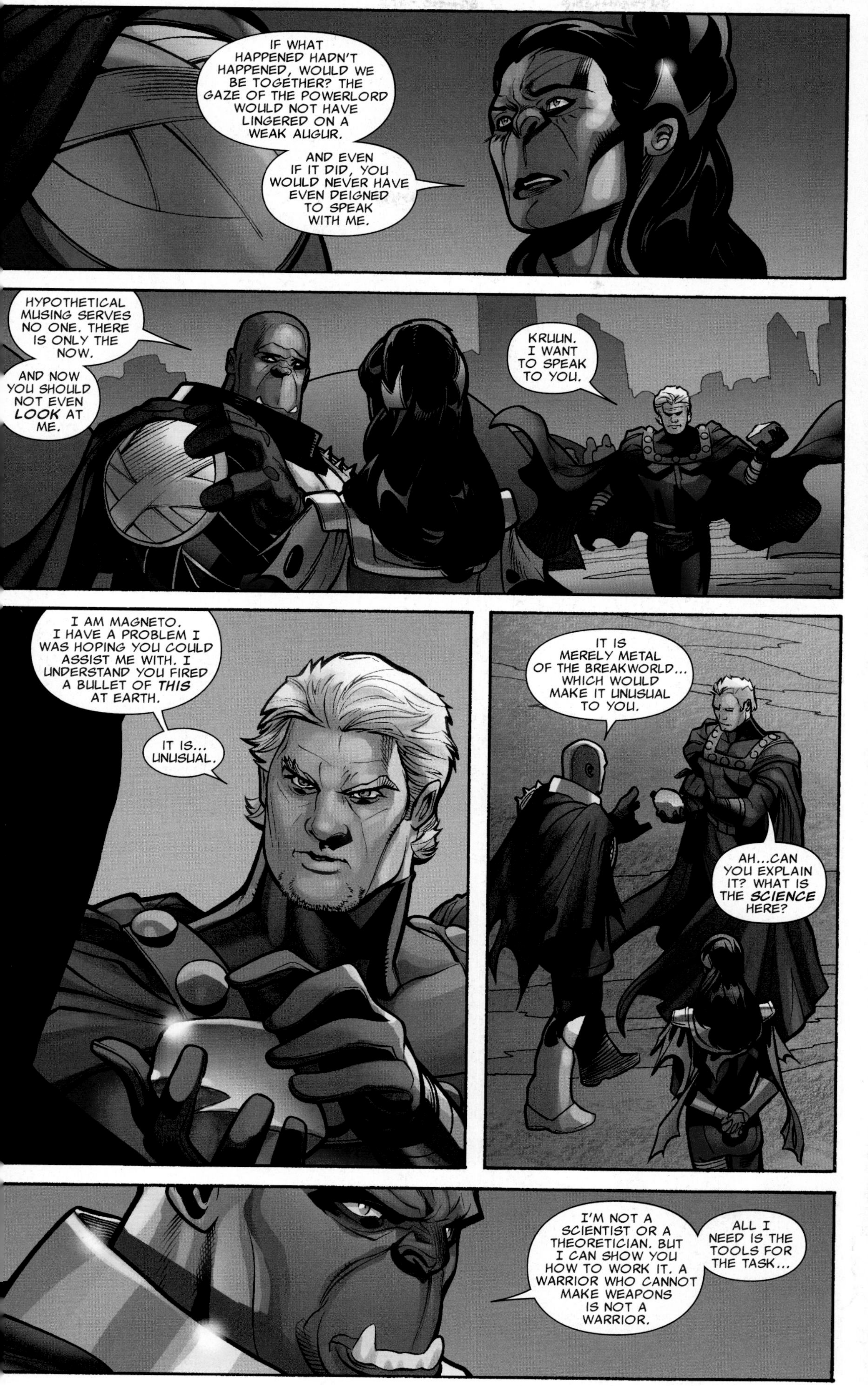
IF WHAT HAPPENED HADN'T HAPPENED, WOULD WE BE TOGETHER? THE GAZE OF THE POWERLORD WOULD NOT HAVE LINGERED ON A WEAK AUGUR.
AND EVEN IF IT DID, YOU WOULD NEVER HAVE EVEN DEIGNED TO SPEAK WITH ME.
HYPOTHETICAL MUSING SERVES NO ONE. THERE IS ONLY THE NOW.
AND NOW YOU SHOULD NOT EVEN LOOK AT ME.
KRUUN. I WANT TO SPEAK TO YOU.
I AM MAGNETO. I HAVE A PROBLEM I WAS HOPING YOU COULD ASSIST ME WITH. I UNDERSTAND YOU FIRED A BULLET OF THIS AT EARTH.
IT IS... UNUSUAL.
IT IS MERELY METAL OF THE BREAKWORLD... WHICH WOULD MAKE IT UNUSUAL TO YOU.
AH...CAN YOU EXPLAIN IT? WHAT IS THE SCIENCE HERE?
I'M NOT A SCIENTIST OR A THEORETICIAN. BUT I CAN SHOW YOU HOW TO WORK IT. A WARRIOR WHO CANNOT MAKE WEAPONS IS NOT A WARRIOR.
ALL I NEED IS THE TOOLS FOR THE TASK...

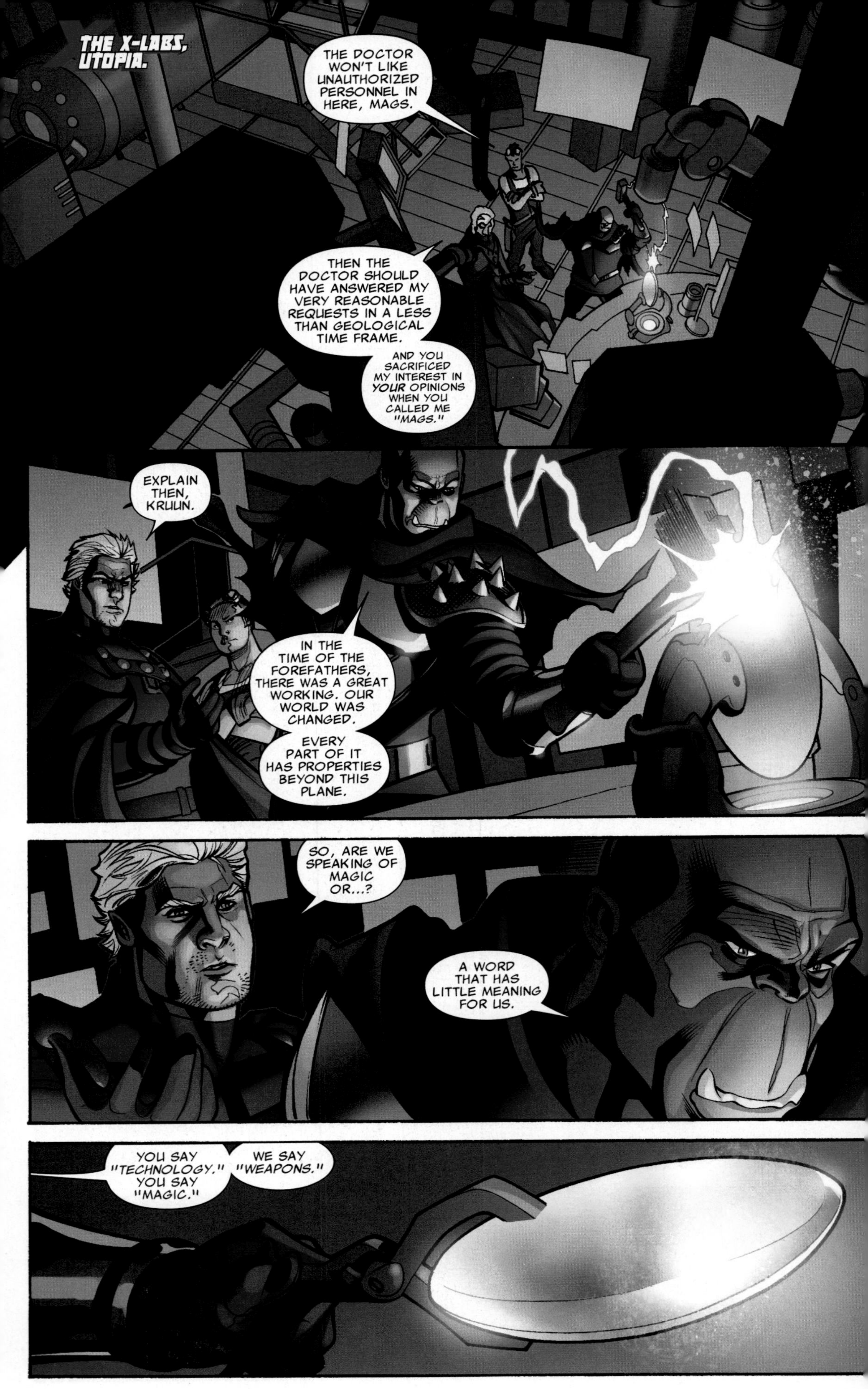
THE X-LABS, UTOPIA.
THE DOCTOR WON'T LIKE UNAUTHORIZED PERSONNEL IN HERE, MAGS.
THEN THE DOCTOR SHOULD HAVE ANSWERED MY VERY REASONABLE REQUESTS IN A LESS THAN GEOLOGICAL TIME FRAME.
AND YOU SACRIFICED MY INTEREST IN YOUR OPINIONS WHEN YOU CALLED ME "MAGS."
EXPLAIN THEN, KRUUN.
IN THE TIME OF THE FOREFATHERS, THERE WAS A GREAT WORKING. OUR WORLD WAS CHANGED.
EVERY PART OF IT HAS PROPERTIES BEYOND THIS PLANE.
SO, ARE WE SPEAKING OF MAGIC OR...?
A WORD THAT HAS LITTLE MEANING FOR US.
YOU SAY "TECHNOLOGY." YOU SAY "MAGIC."
WE SAY "WEAPONS."

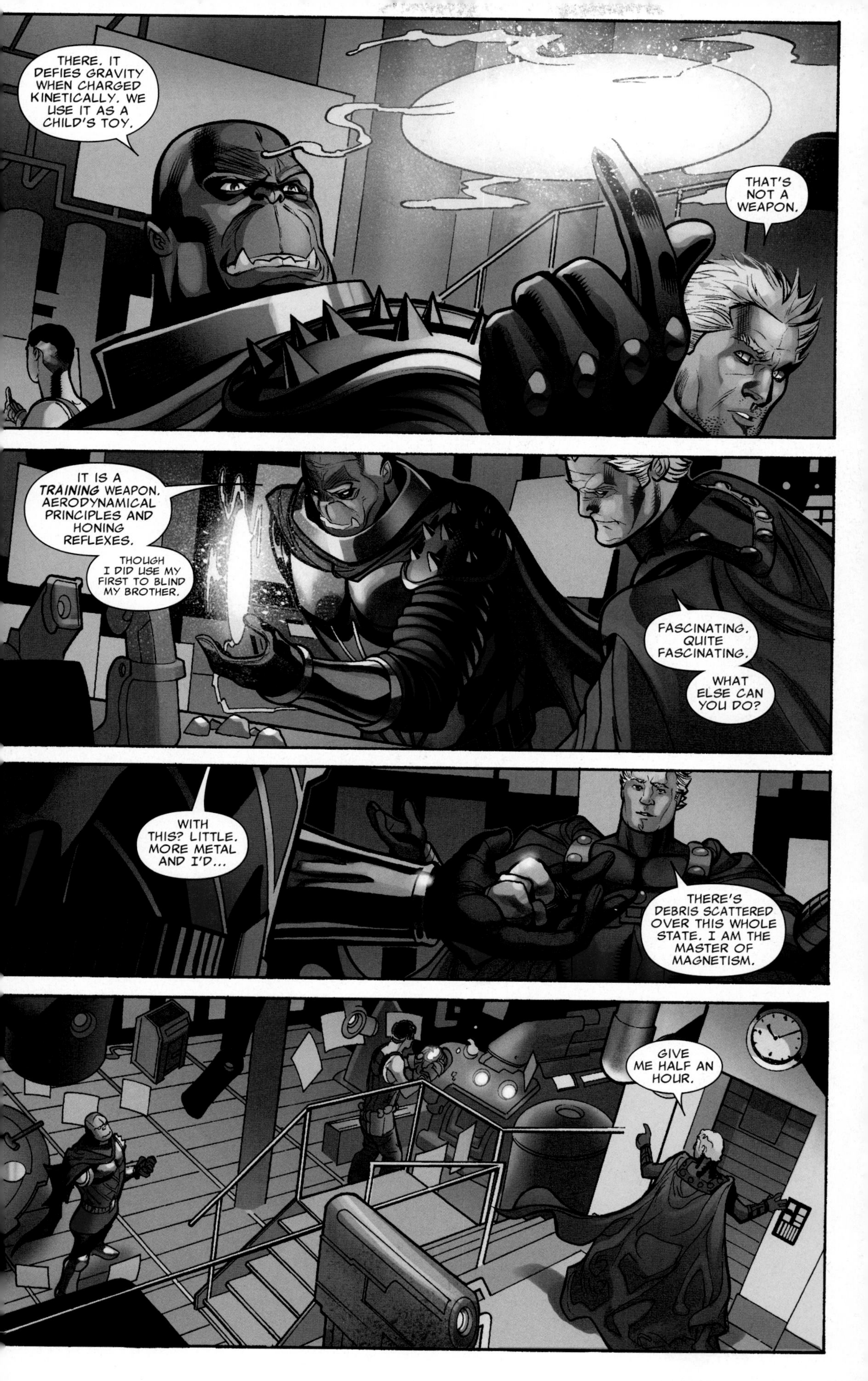
THERE. IT DEFIES GRAVITY WHEN CHARGED KINETICALLY. WE USE IT AS A CHILD'S TOY.
THAT'S NOT A WEAPON.
IT IS A TRAINING WEAPON. AERODYNAMICAL PRINCIPLES AND HONING REFLEXES.
THOUGH I DID USE MY FIRST TO BLIND MY BROTHER.
FASCINATING. QUITE FASCINATING.
WHAT ELSE CAN YOU DO?
WITH THIS? LITTLE. MORE METAL AND I'D...
THERE'S DEBRIS SCATTERED OVER THIS WHOLE STATE. I AM THE MASTER OF MAGNETISM.
GIVE ME HALF AN HOUR.

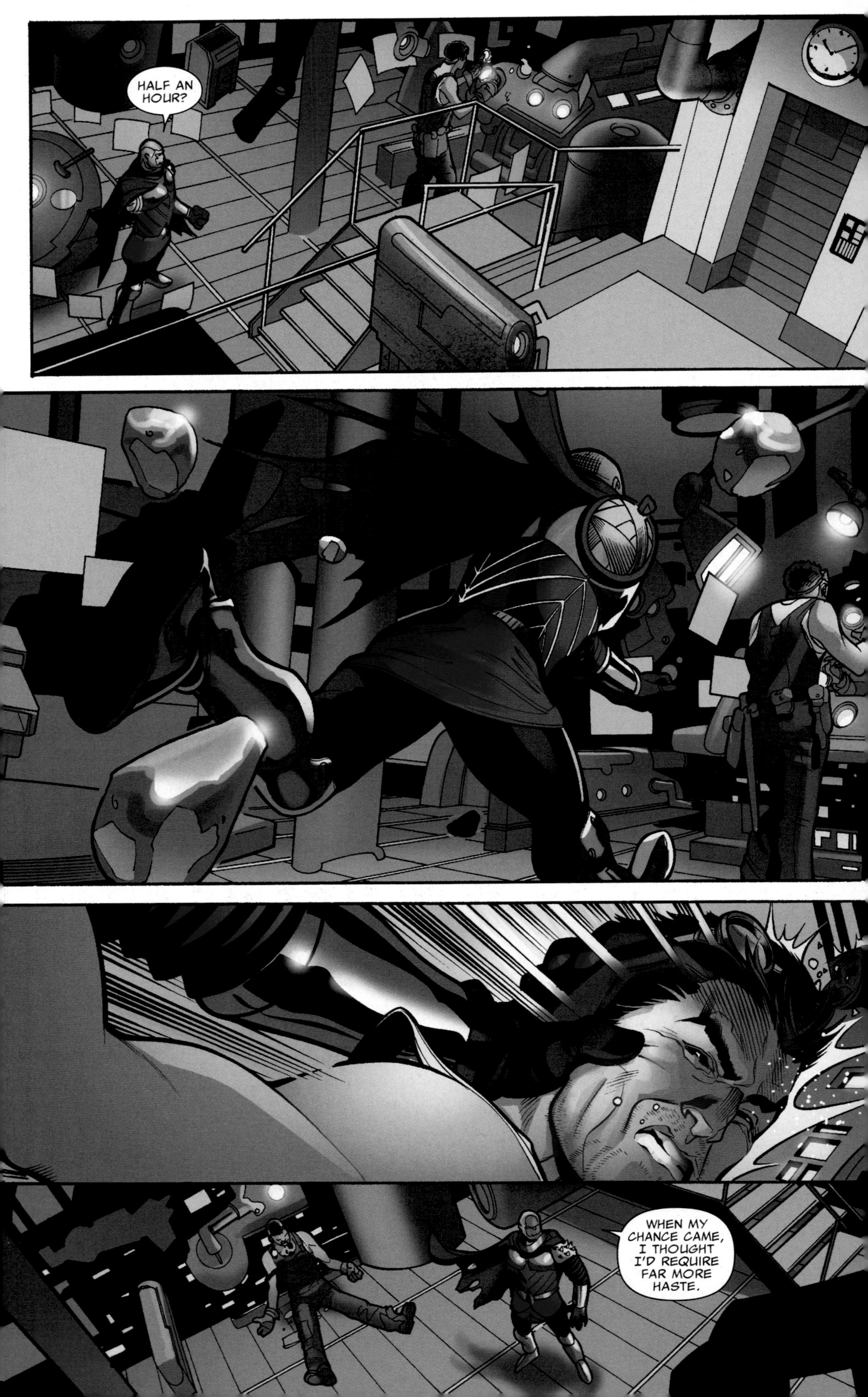
HALF AN HOUR?
WHEN MY CHANCE CAME, I THOUGHT I'D REQUIRE FAR MORE HASTE.

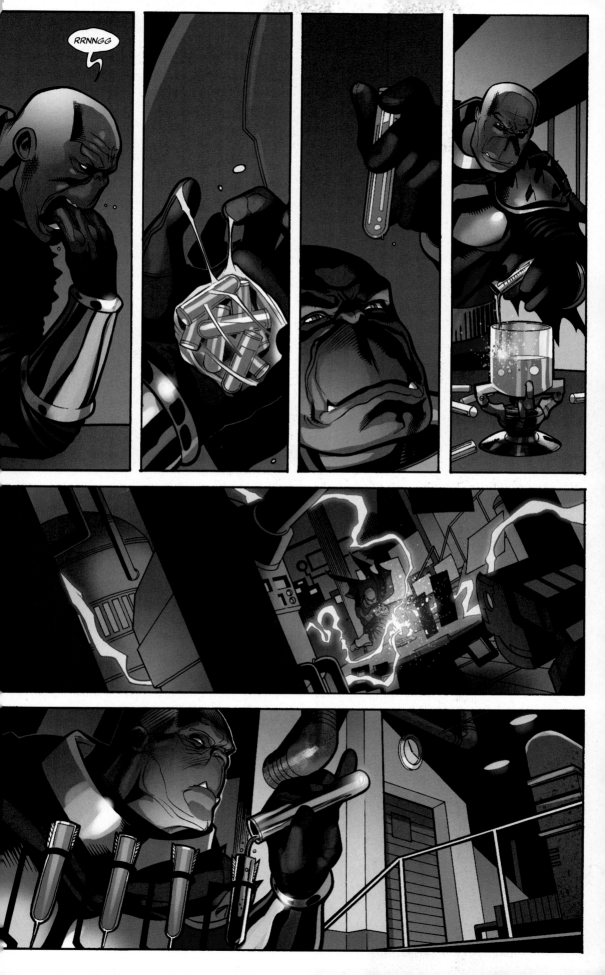

RRNNGG

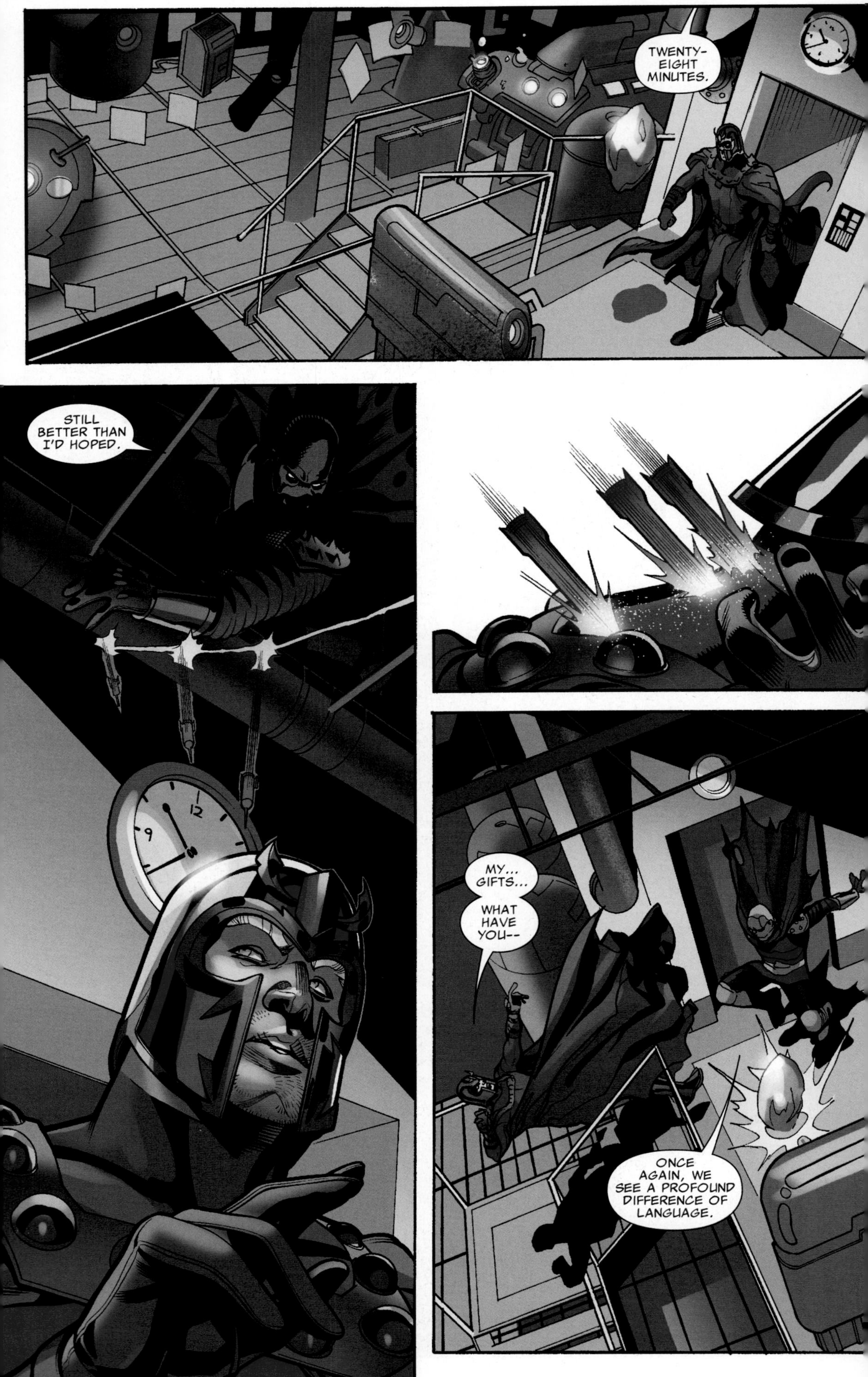
TWENTY-EIGHT MINUTES.
STILL BETTER THAN I'D HOPED.
MY... GIFTS...
WHAT HAVE YOU--
ONCE AGAIN, WE SEE A PROFOUND DIFFERENCE OF LANGUAGE.

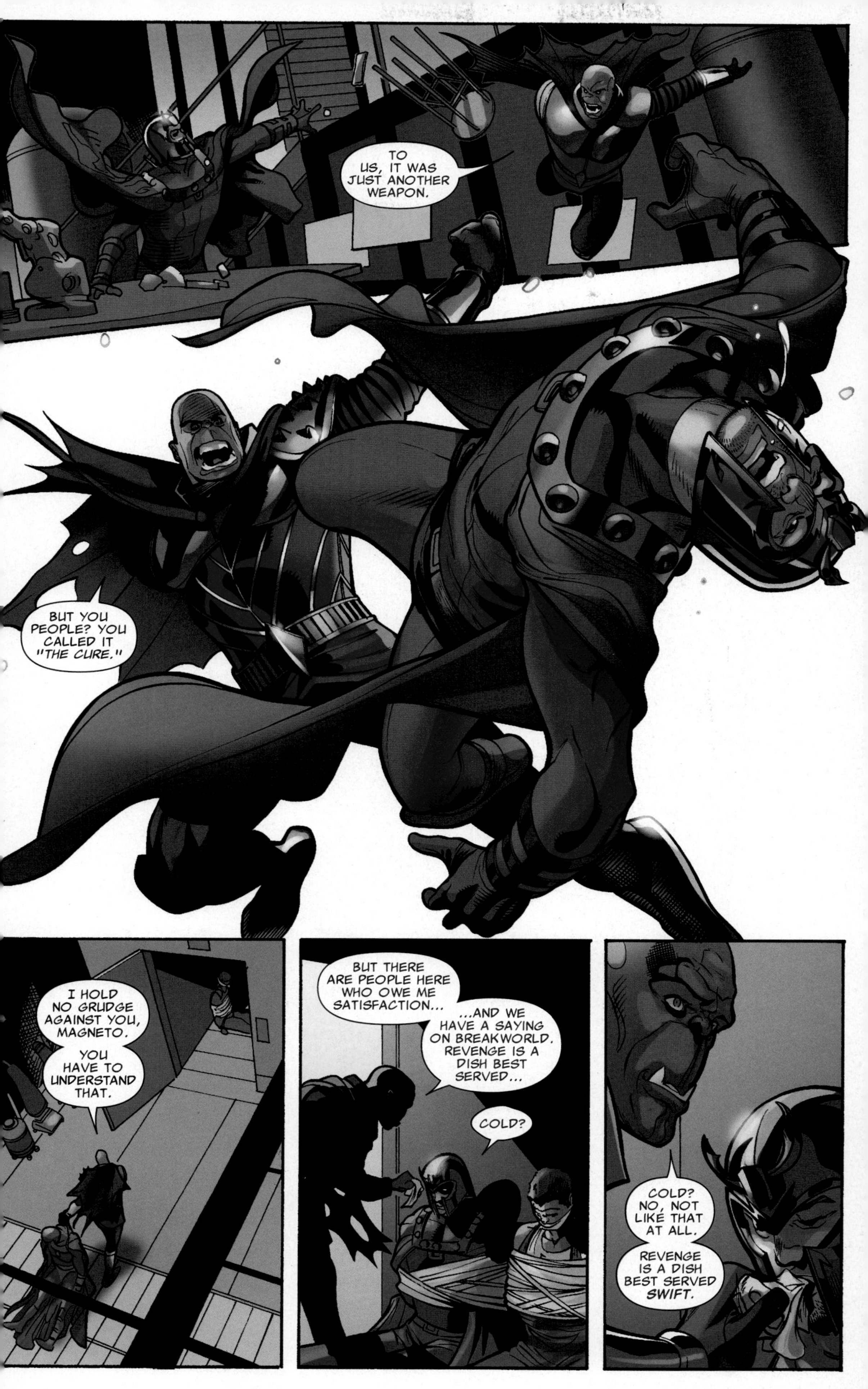
TO US, IT WAS JUST ANOTHER WEAPON.
BUT YOU PEOPLE? YOU CALLED IT "THE CURE."
I HOLD NO GRUDGE AGAINST YOU, MAGNETO.
YOU HAVE TO UNDERSTAND THAT.
BUT THERE ARE PEOPLE HERE WHO OWE ME SATISFACTION...
...AND WE HAVE A SAYING ON BREAKWORLD. REVENGE IS A DISH BEST SERVED...
COLD?
COLD? NO, NOT LIKE THAT AT ALL.
REVENGE IS A DISH BEST SERVED *SWIFT*.

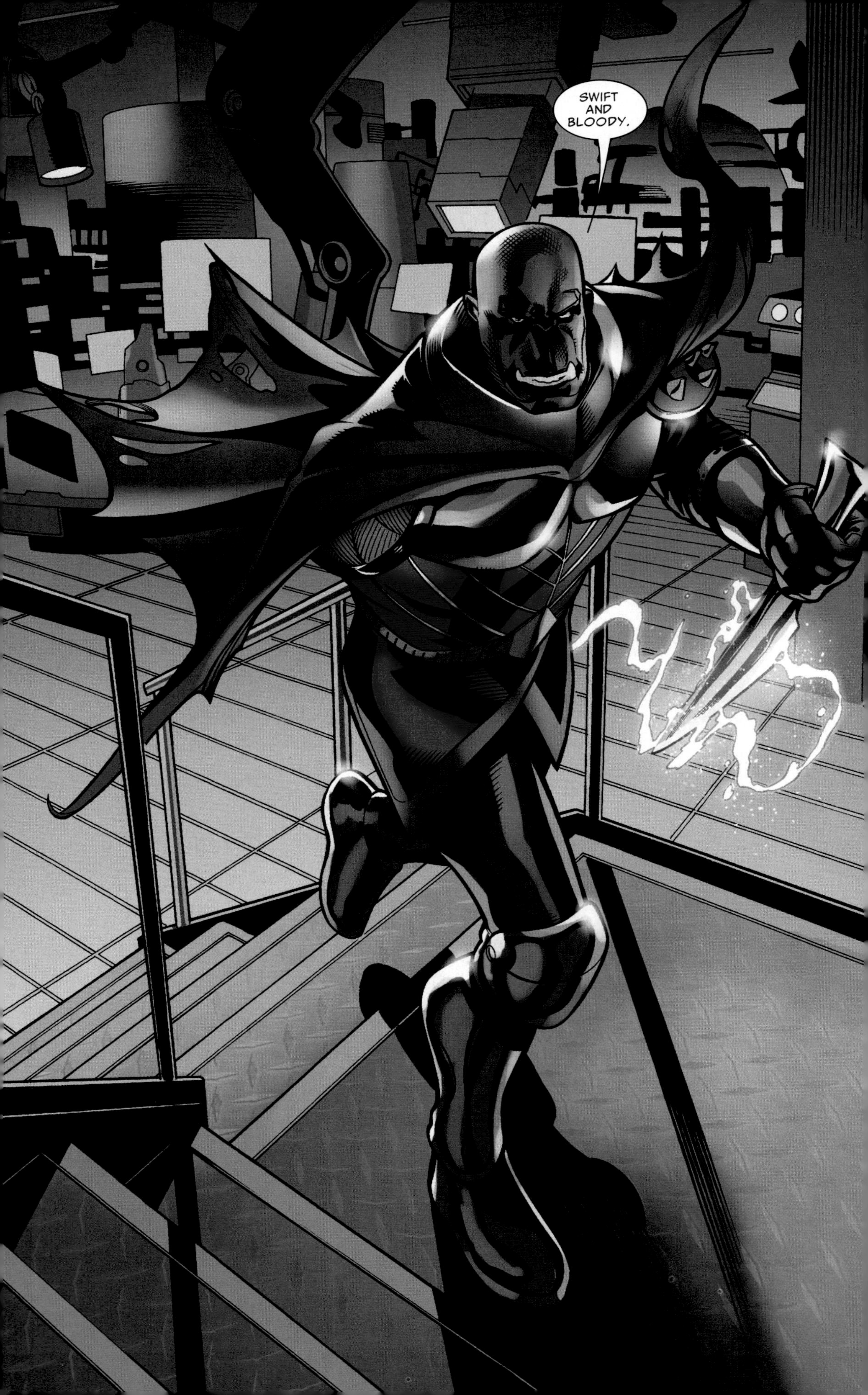
SWIFT AND BLOODY.

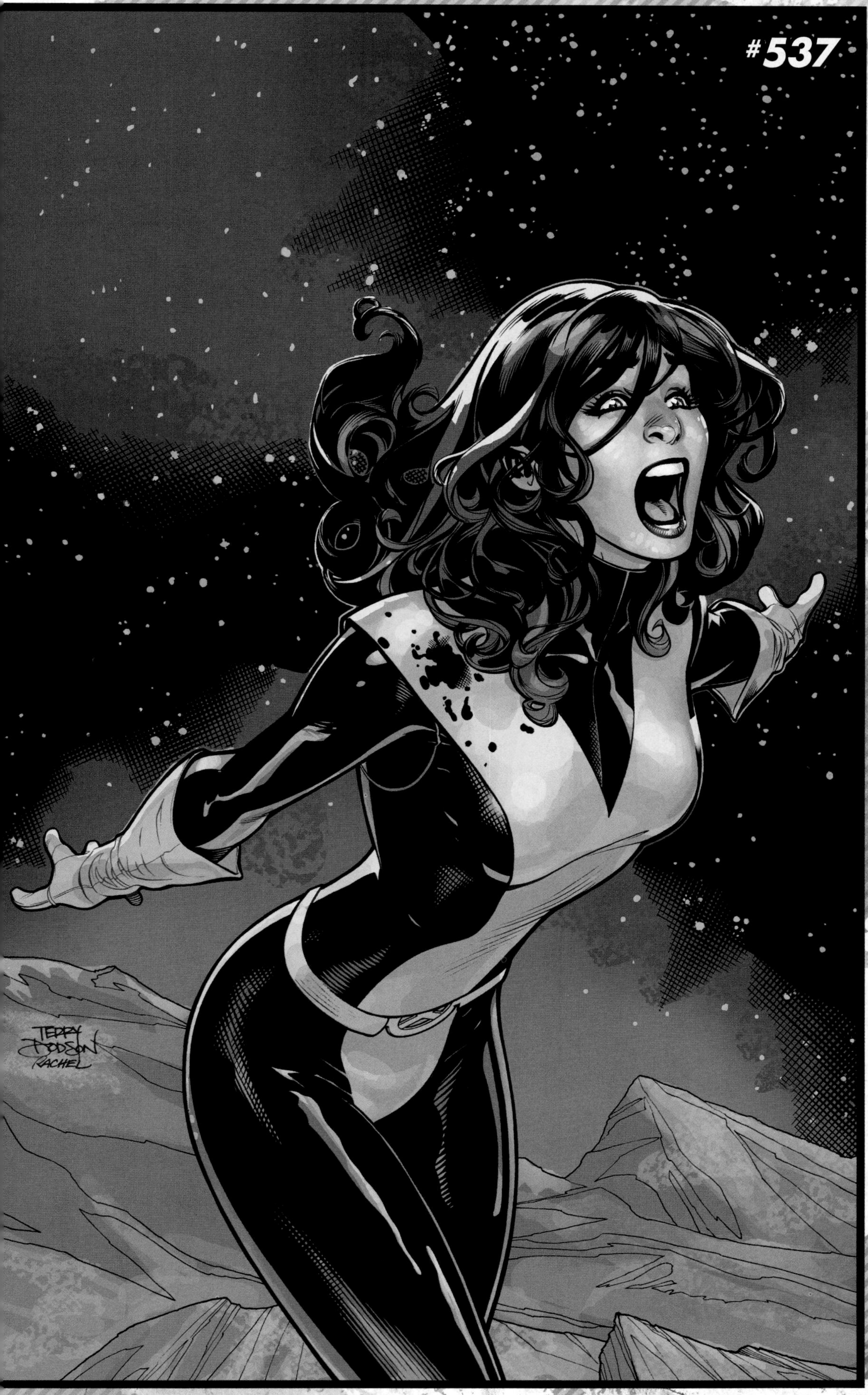
#537
TERRY DODSON
RACHEL

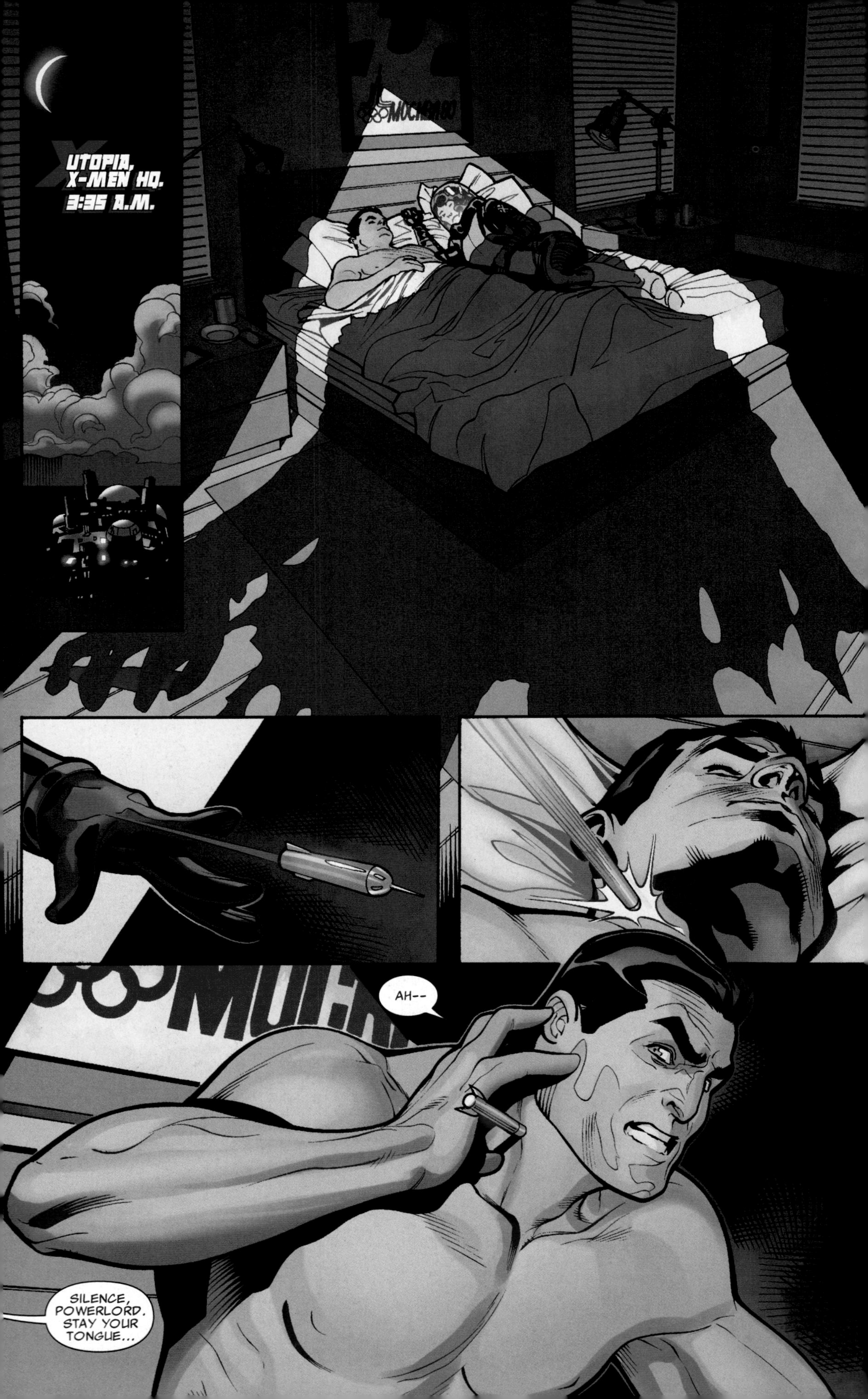
UTOPIA, X-MEN HQ. 3:35 A.M.
AH--
SILENCE, POWERLORD. STAY YOUR TONGUE...

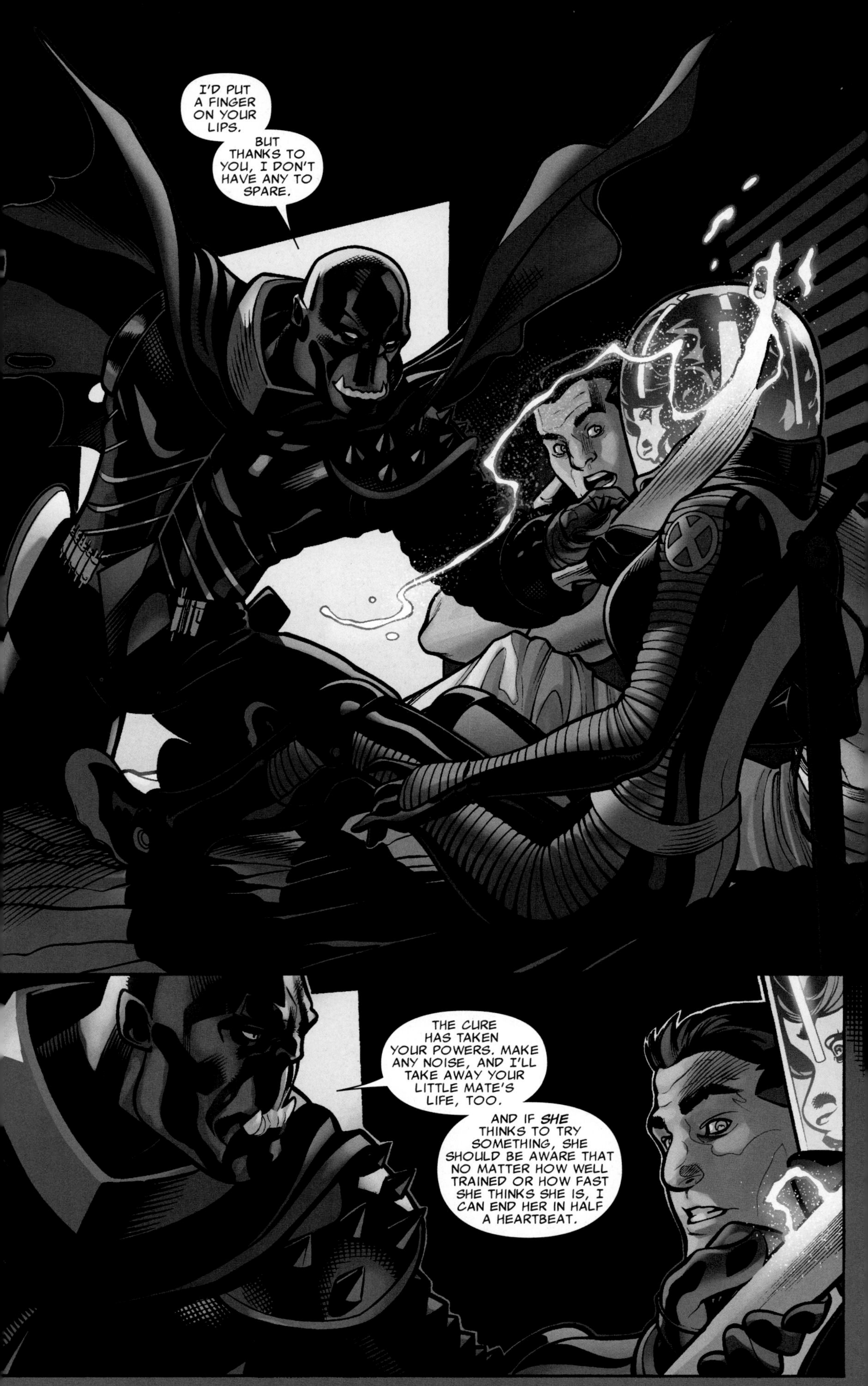
I'D PUT A FINGER ON YOUR LIPS.
BUT THANKS TO YOU, I DON'T HAVE ANY TO SPARE.
THE CURE HAS TAKEN YOUR POWERS. MAKE ANY NOISE, AND I'LL TAKE AWAY YOUR LITTLE MATE'S LIFE, TOO.
AND IF SHE THINKS TO TRY SOMETHING, SHE SHOULD BE AWARE THAT NO MATTER HOW WELL TRAINED OR HOW FAST SHE THINKS SHE IS, I CAN END HER IN HALF A HEARTBEAT.

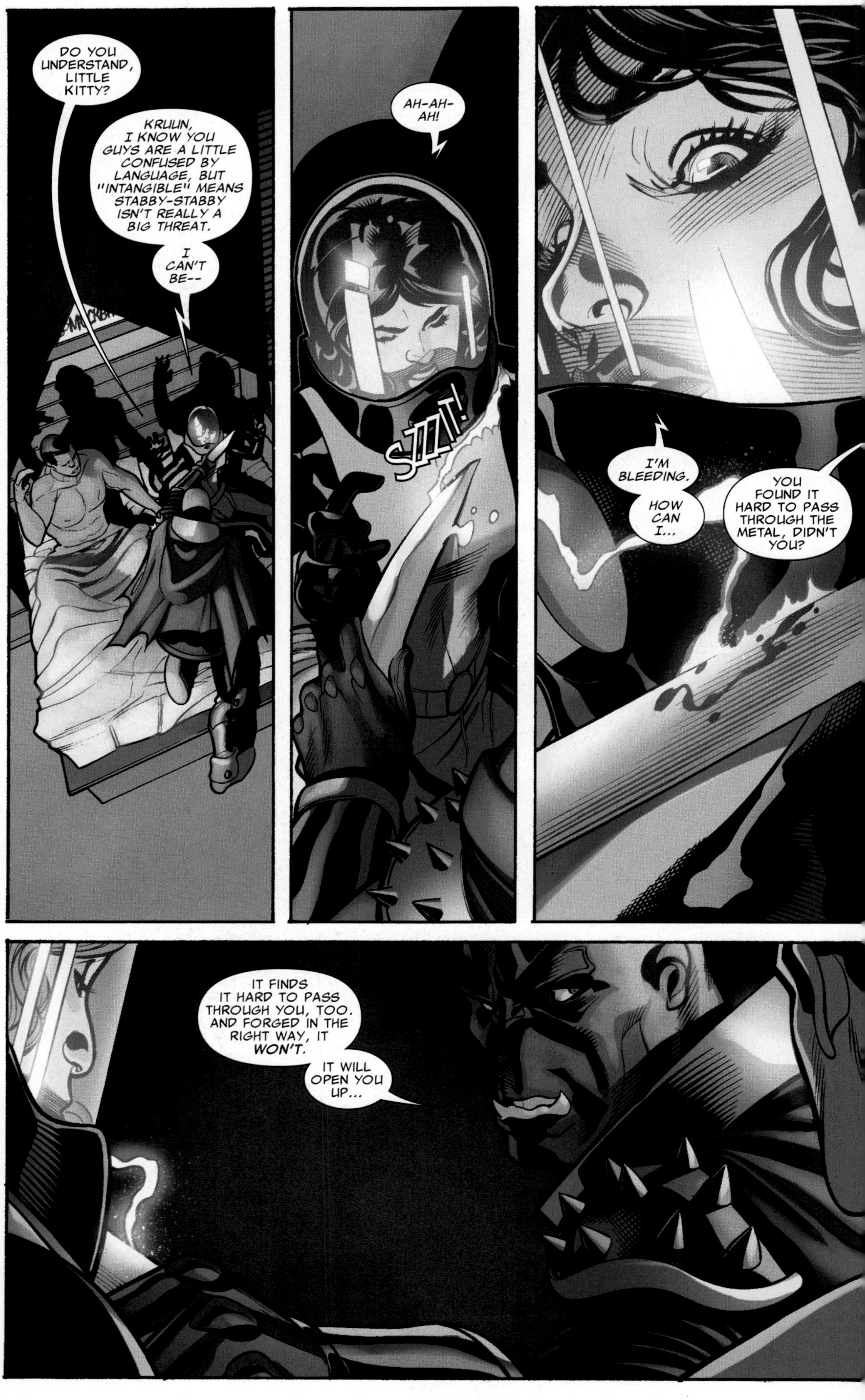
DO YOU UNDERSTAND, LITTLE KITTY?
KRUUN, I KNOW YOU GUYS ARE A LITTLE CONFUSED BY LANGUAGE, BUT "INTANGIBLE" MEANS STABBY-STABBY ISN'T REALLY A BIG THREAT.
I CAN'T BE--
AH-AH-AH!
SZZT!
I'M BLEEDING.
HOW CAN I...
YOU FOUND IT HARD TO PASS THROUGH THE METAL, DIDN'T YOU?
IT FINDS IT HARD TO PASS THROUGH YOU, TOO. AND FORGED IN THE RIGHT WAY, IT *WON'T*.
IT WILL OPEN YOU UP...

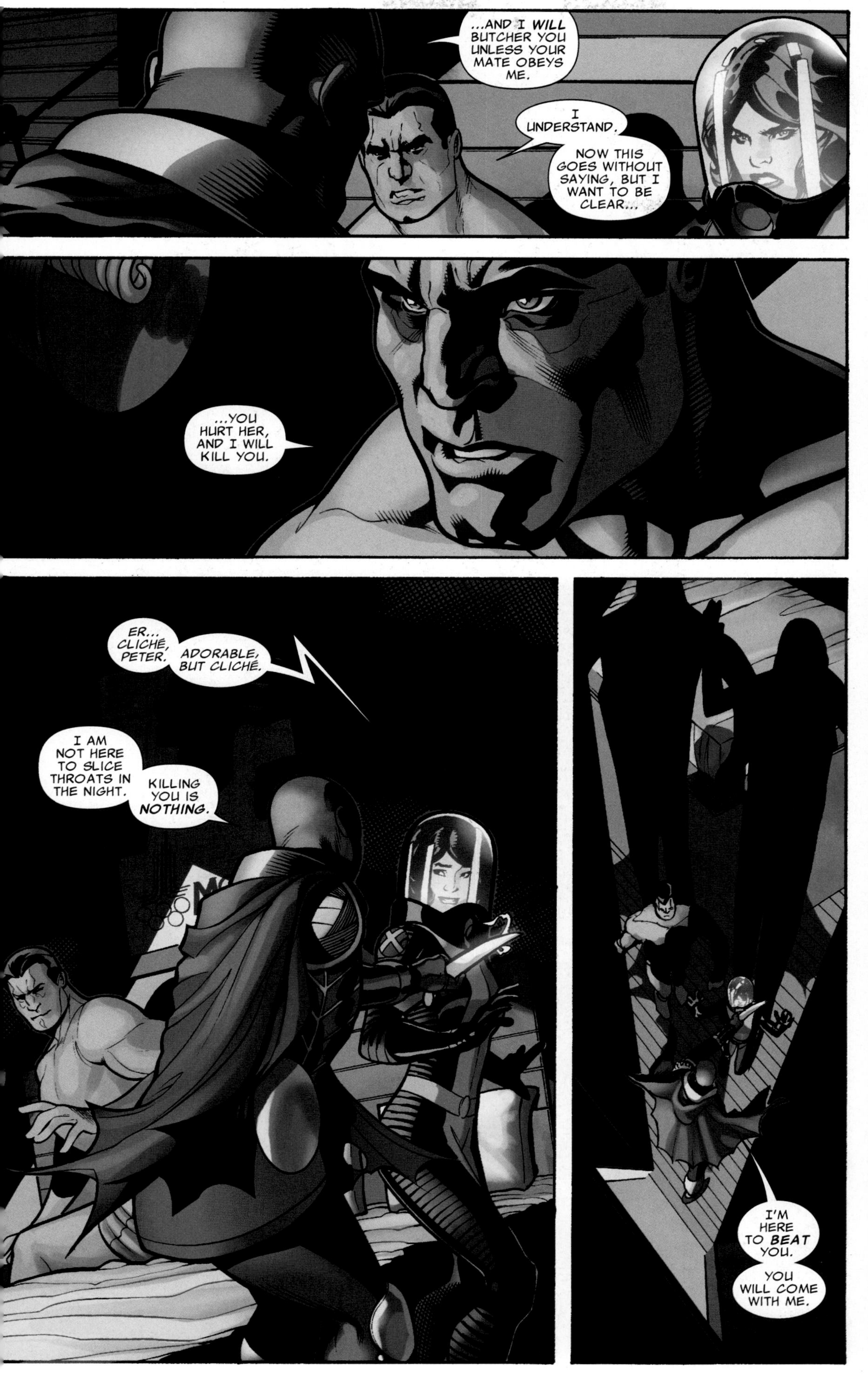
...AND I *WILL* BUTCHER YOU UNLESS YOUR MATE OBEYS ME.
I UNDERSTAND.
NOW THIS GOES WITHOUT SAYING, BUT I WANT TO BE CLEAR...
...YOU HURT HER, AND I WILL KILL YOU.
ER... CLICHÉ, PETER.
ADORABLE, BUT CLICHÉ.
I AM NOT HERE TO SLICE THROATS IN THE NIGHT.
KILLING YOU IS ***NOTHING***.
I'M HERE TO ***BEAT*** YOU.
YOU WILL COME WITH ME.

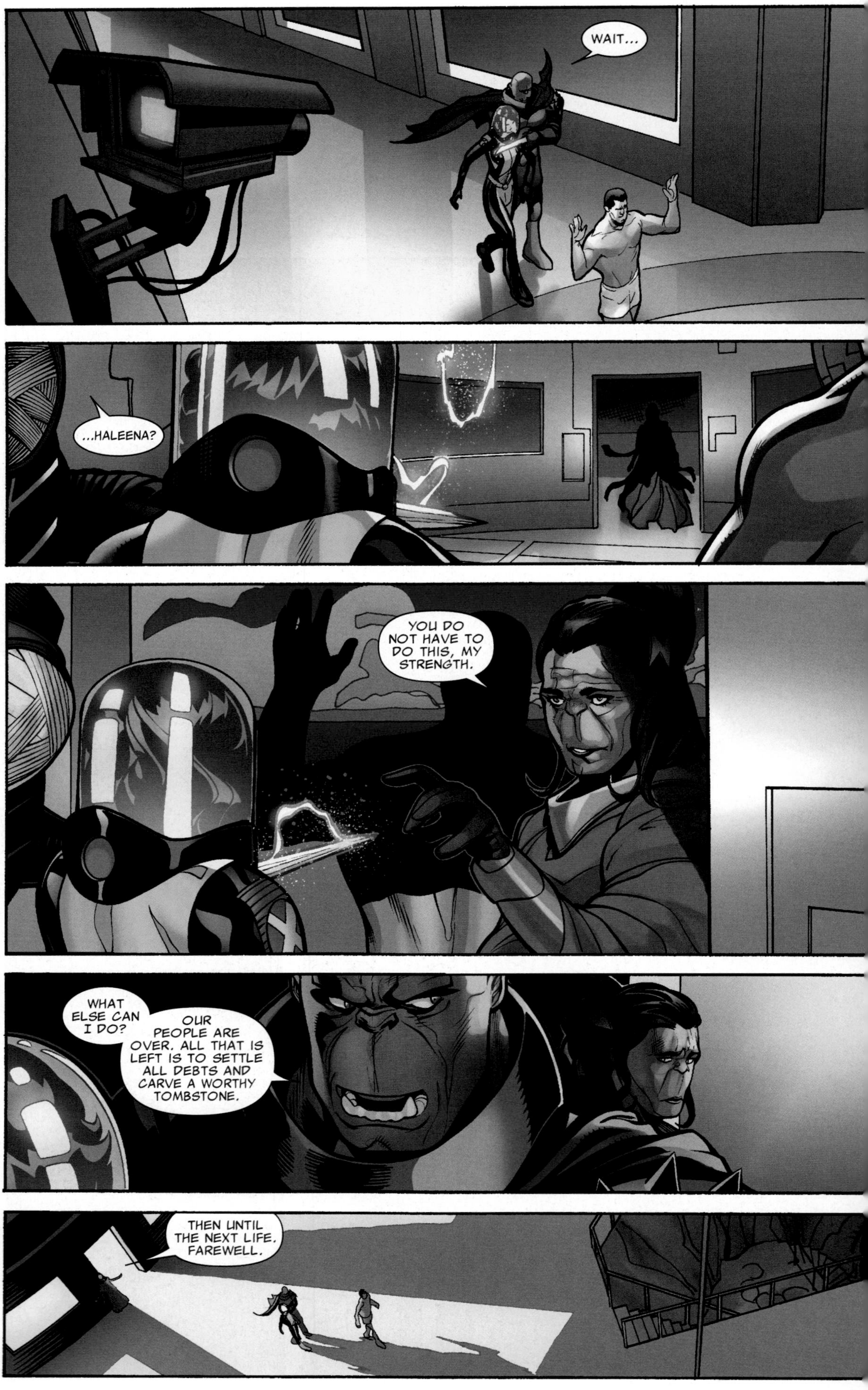
WAIT...
...HALEENA?
YOU DO NOT HAVE TO DO THIS, MY STRENGTH.
WHAT ELSE CAN I DO?
OUR PEOPLE ARE OVER. ALL THAT IS LEFT IS TO SETTLE ALL DEBTS AND CARVE A WORTHY TOMBSTONE.
THEN UNTIL THE NEXT LIFE. FAREWELL.

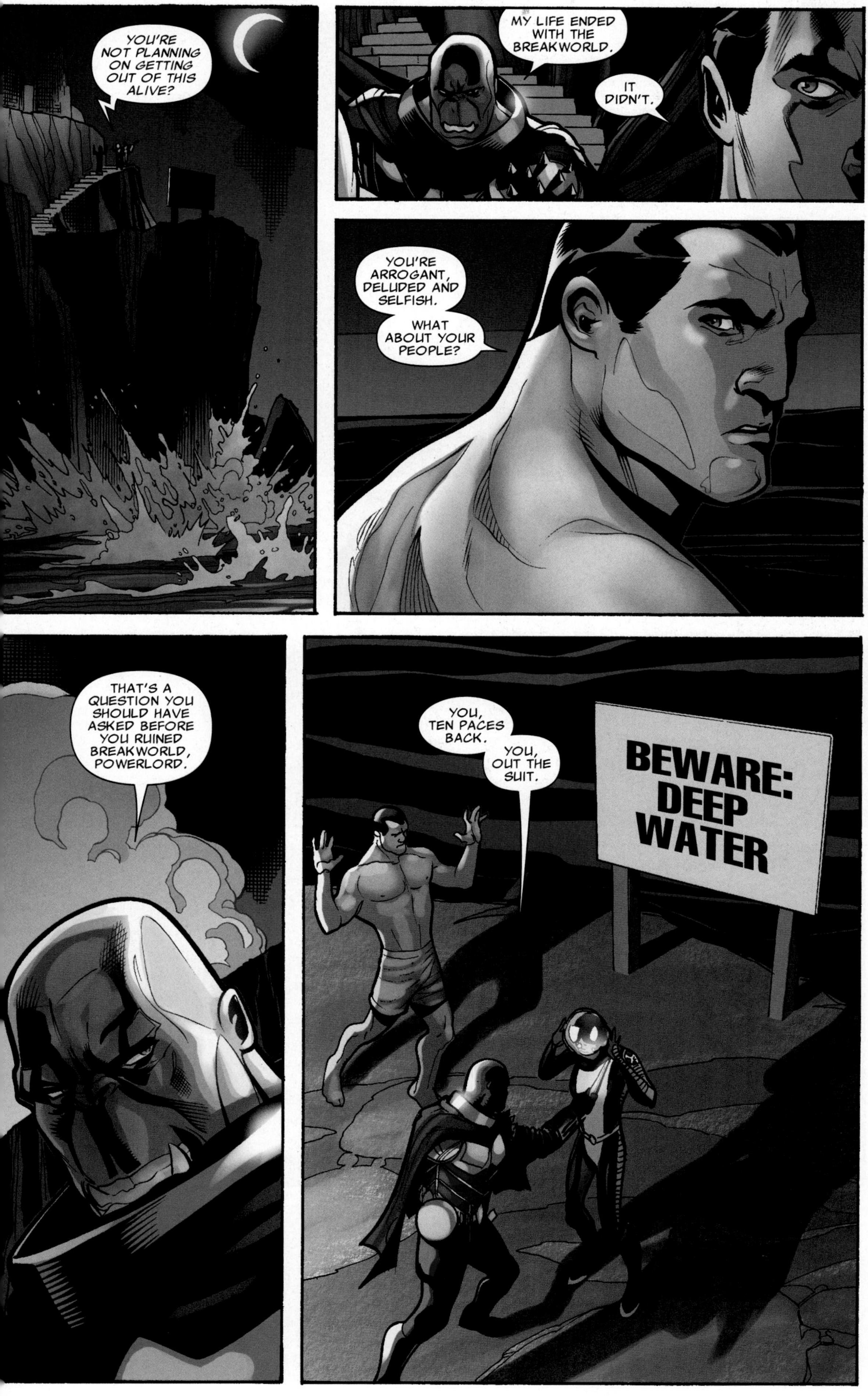
YOU'RE NOT PLANNING ON GETTING OUT OF THIS ALIVE?
MY LIFE ENDED WITH THE BREAKWORLD.
IT DIDN'T.
YOU'RE ARROGANT, DELUDED AND SELFISH.
WHAT ABOUT YOUR PEOPLE?
THAT'S A QUESTION YOU SHOULD HAVE ASKED BEFORE YOU RUINED BREAKWORLD, POWERLORD.
YOU, TEN PACES BACK.
YOU, OUT THE SUIT.
BEWARE: DEEP WATER

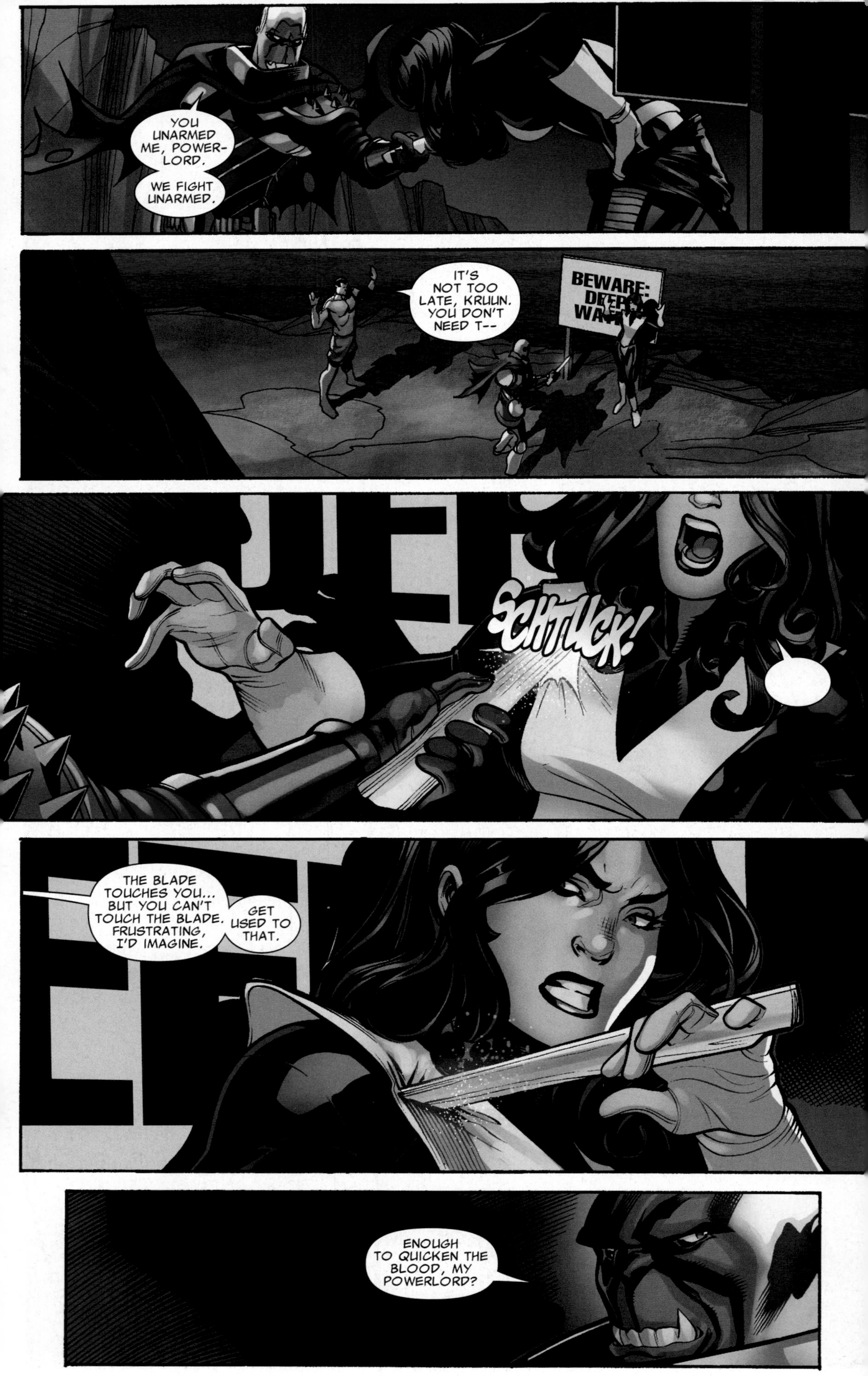

YOU UNARMED ME, POWER-LORD.
WE FIGHT UNARMED.
IT'S NOT TOO LATE, KRULN. YOU DON'T NEED T--
BEWARE:
SCHTUCK!
THE BLADE TOUCHES YOU... BUT YOU CAN'T TOUCH THE BLADE. FRUSTRATING, I'D IMAGINE.
GET USED TO THAT.
ENOUGH TO QUICKEN THE BLOOD, MY POWERLORD?

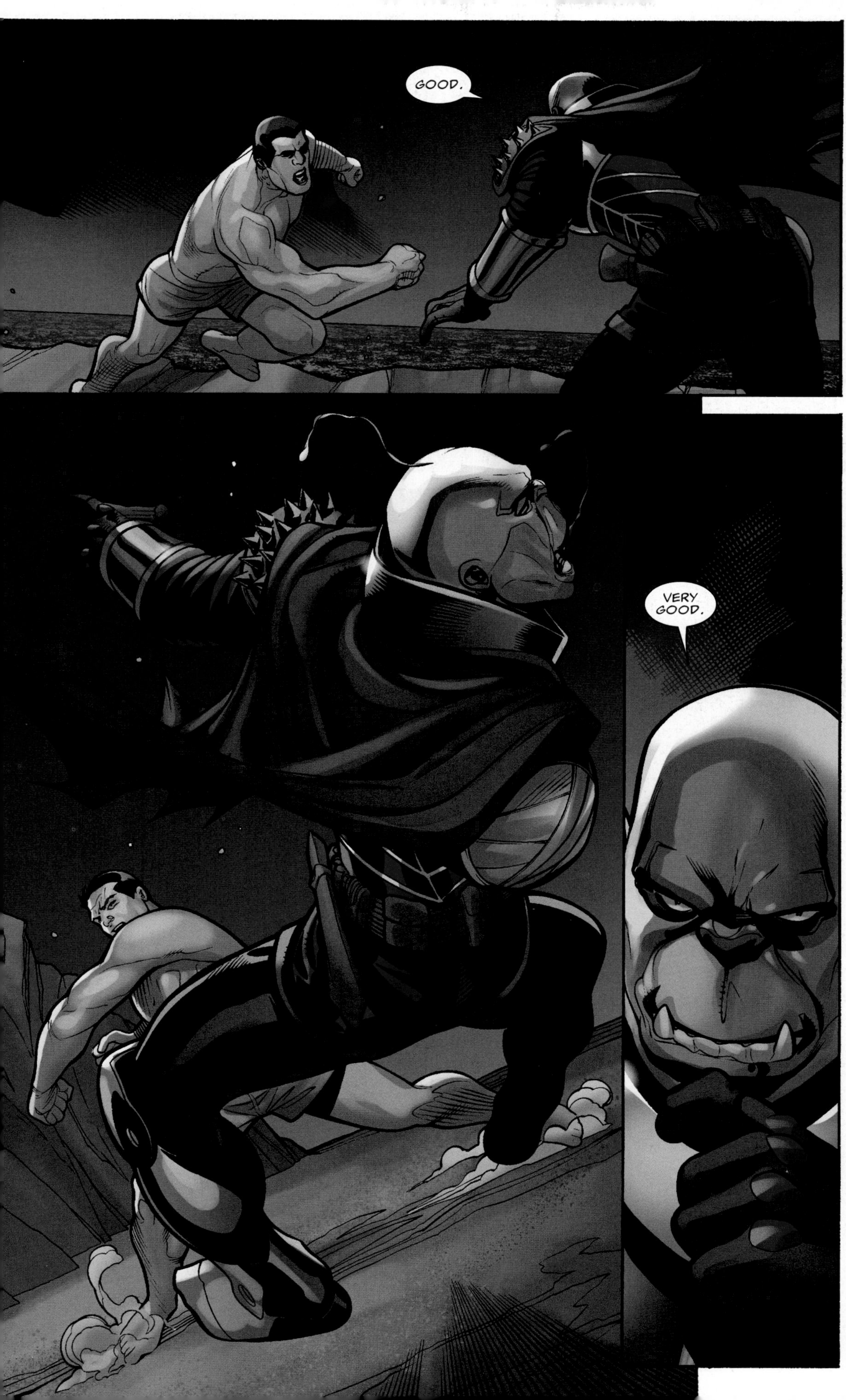
GOOD.
VERY GOOD.

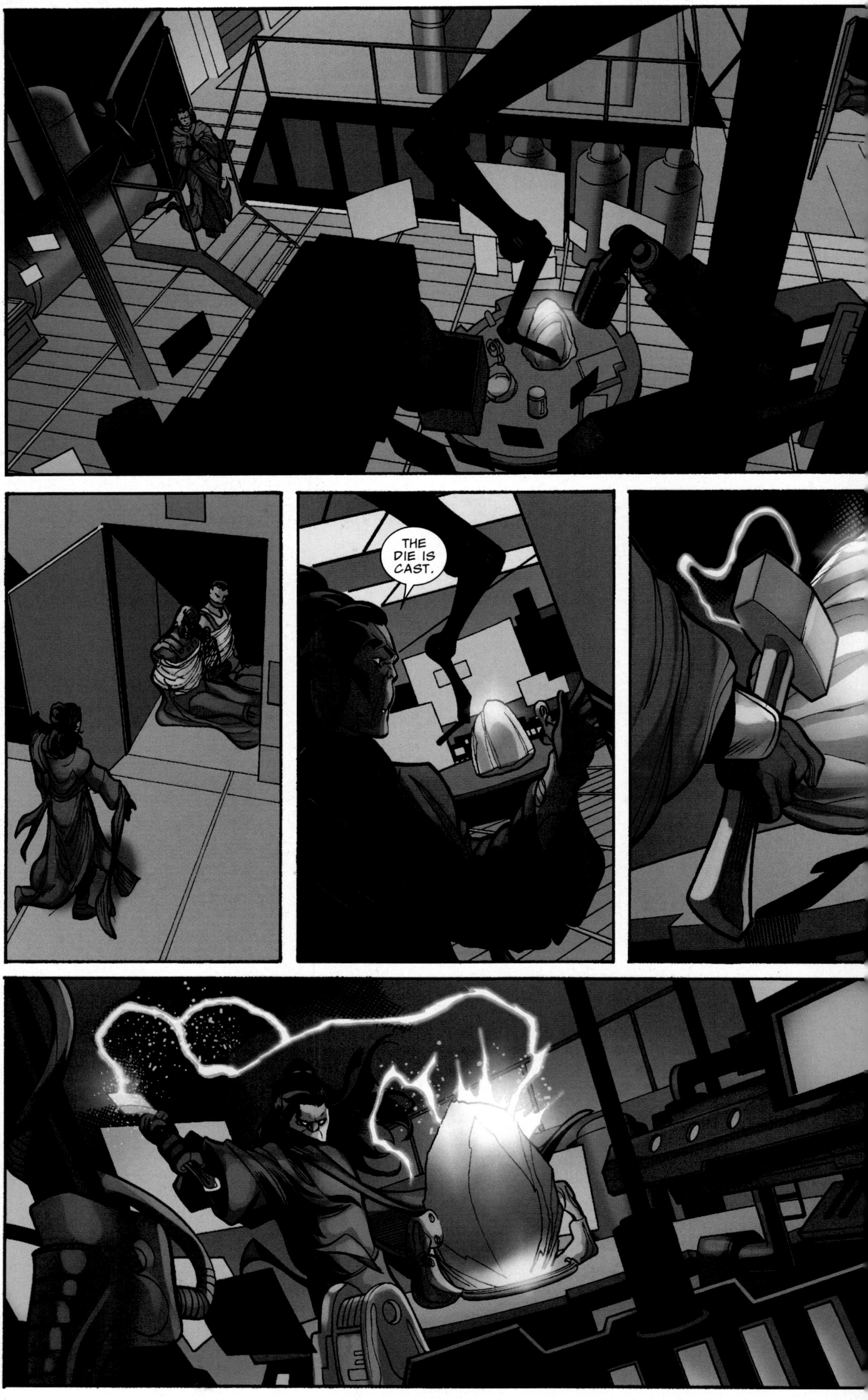
THE DIE IS CAST.

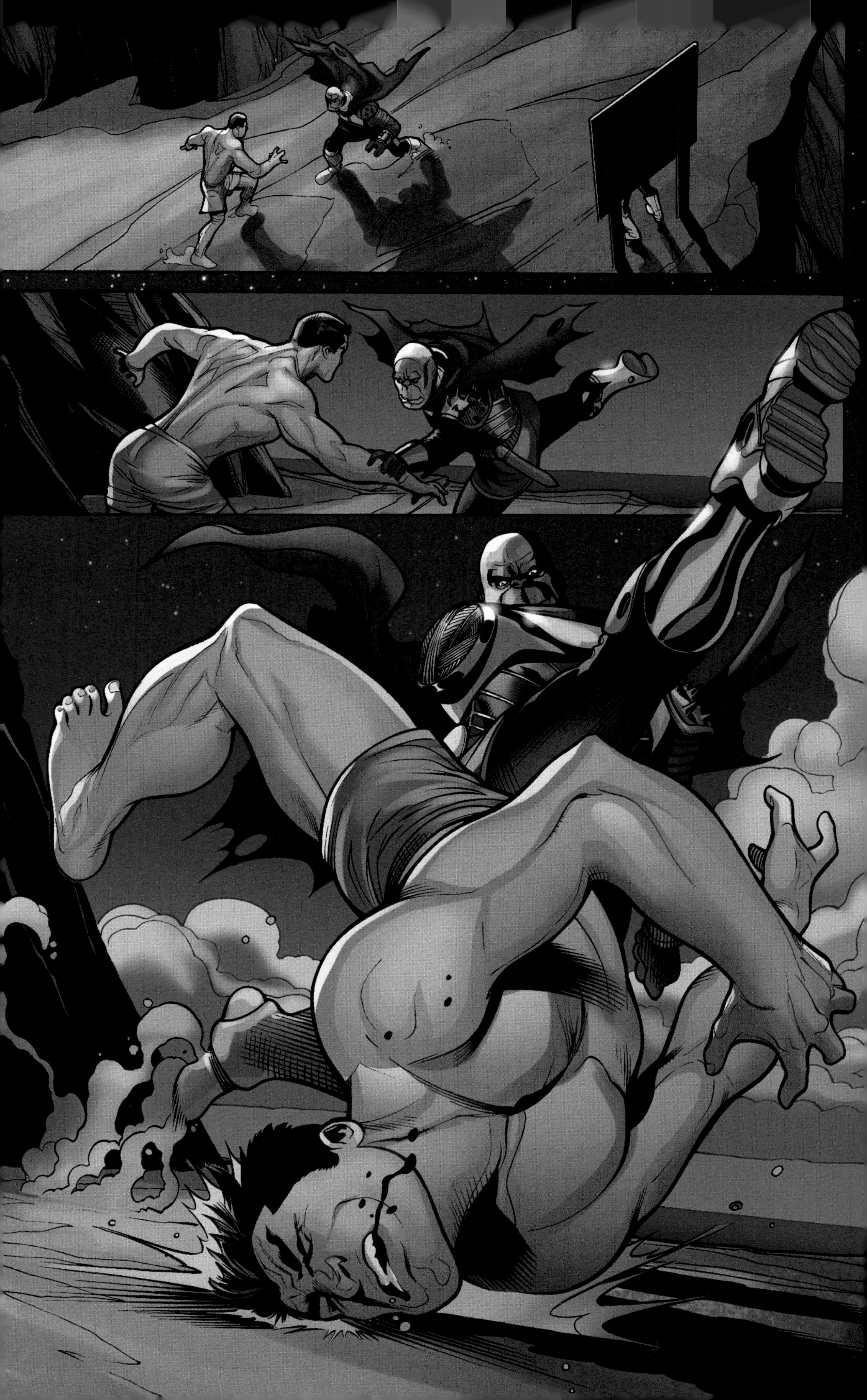

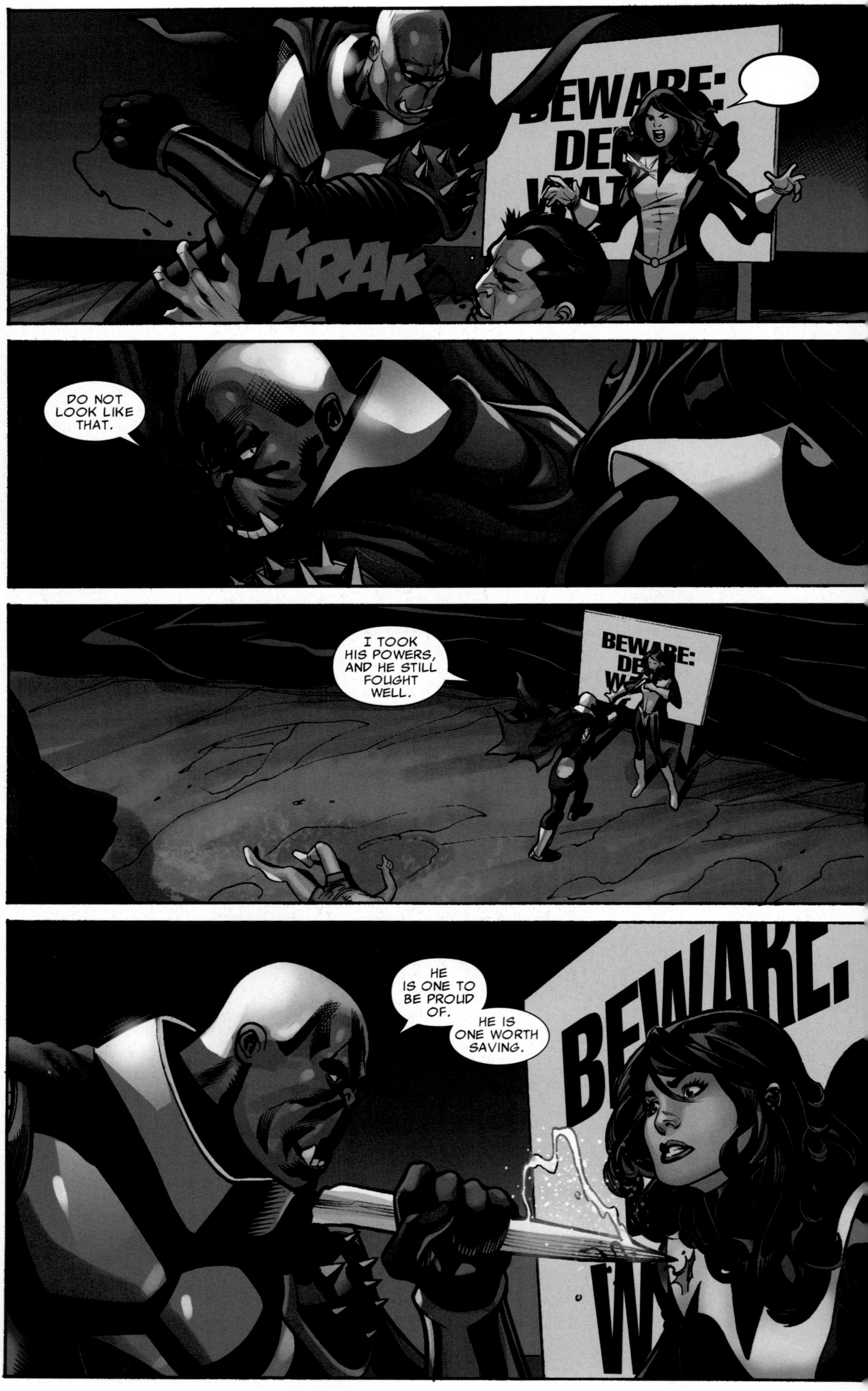
KRAK
BEWARE:
DO NOT LOOK LIKE THAT.
I TOOK HIS POWERS, AND HE STILL FOUGHT WELL.
BEWARE:
HE IS ONE TO BE PROUD OF.
HE IS ONE WORTH SAVING.
BEWARE.

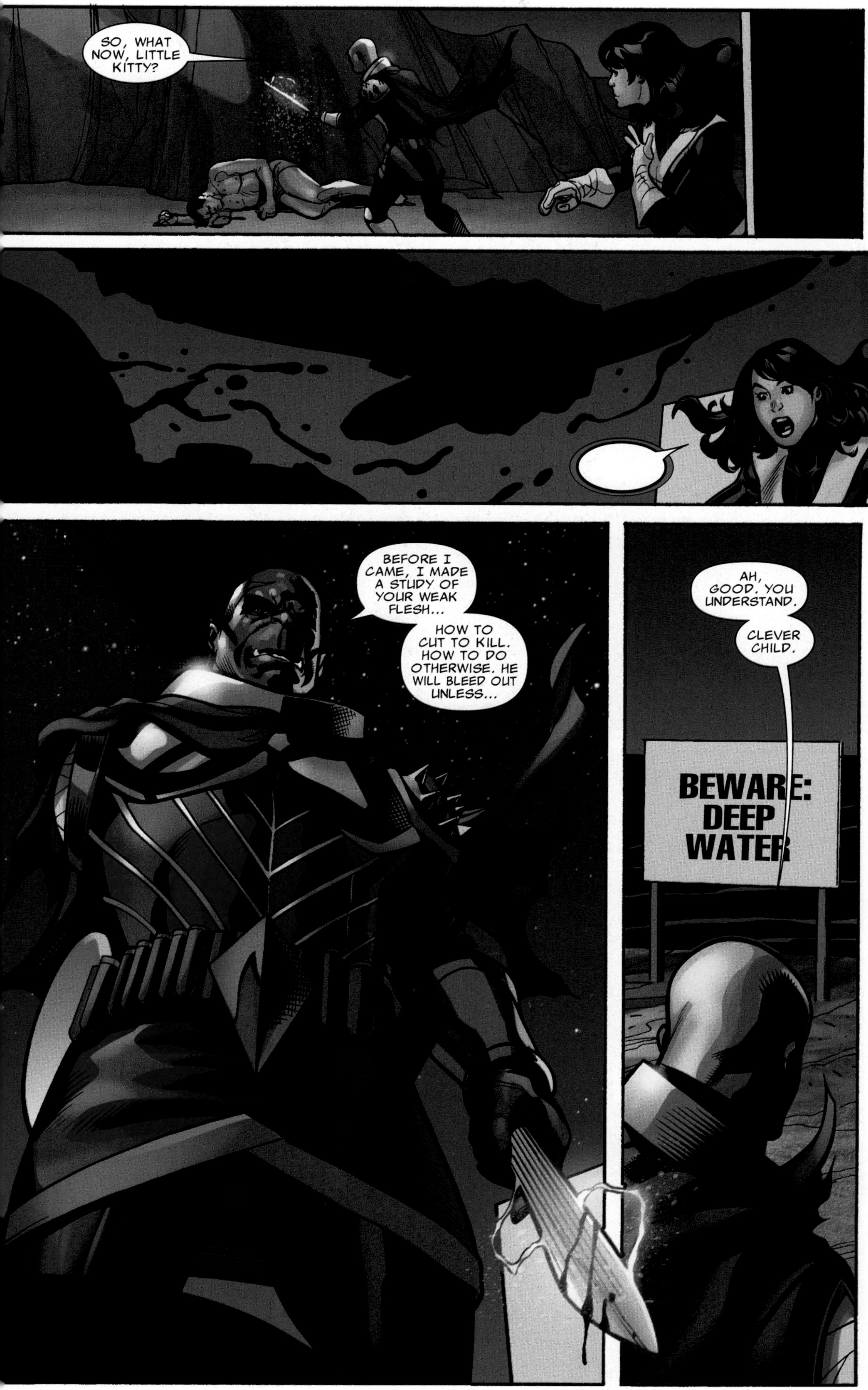
SO, WHAT NOW, LITTLE KITTY?
BEFORE I CAME, I MADE A STUDY OF YOUR WEAK FLESH...
HOW TO CUT TO KILL. HOW TO DO OTHERWISE. HE WILL BLEED OUT UNLESS...
AH, GOOD. YOU UNDERSTAND.
CLEVER CHILD.
BEWARE: DEEP WATER

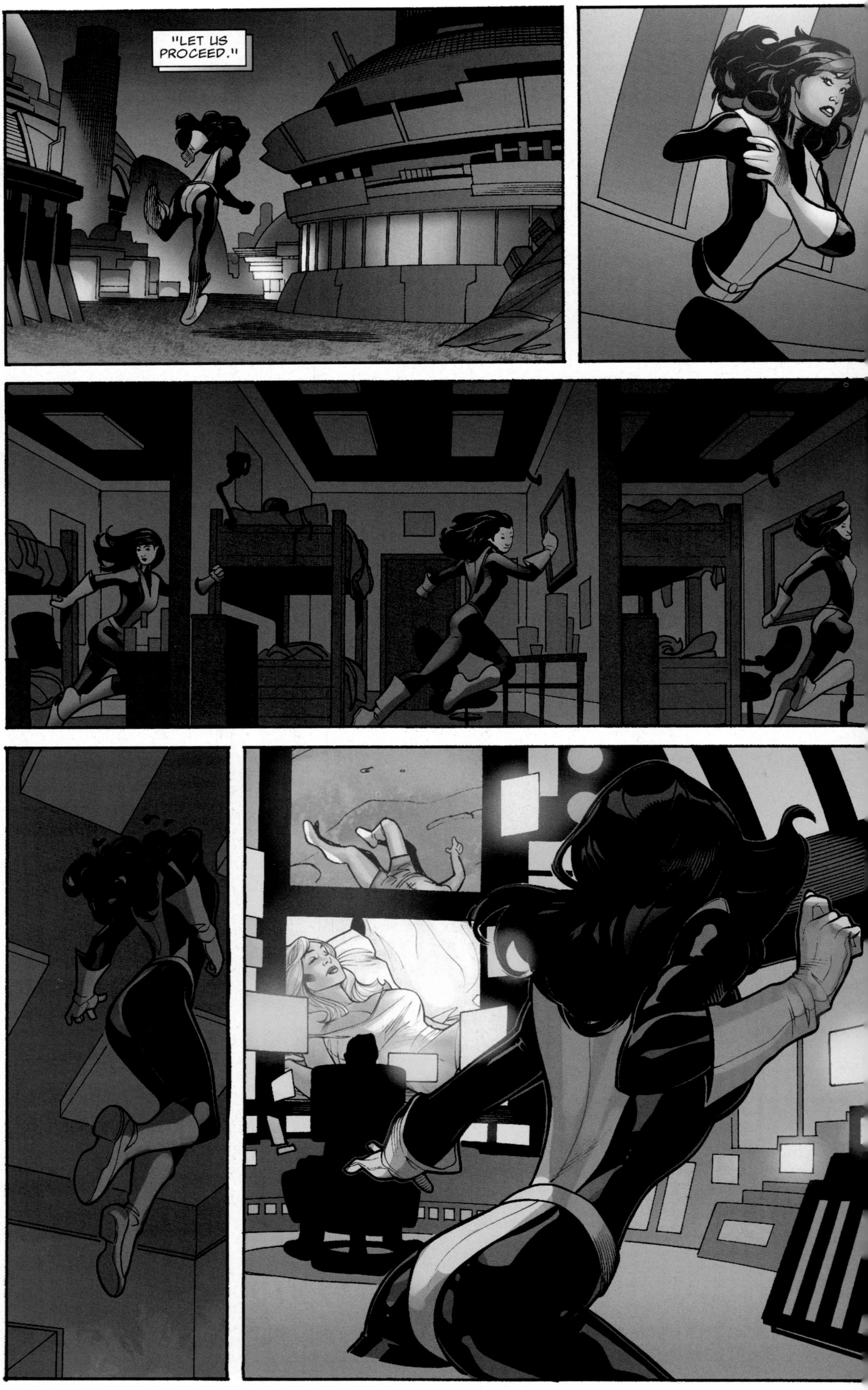
"LET US PROCEED."

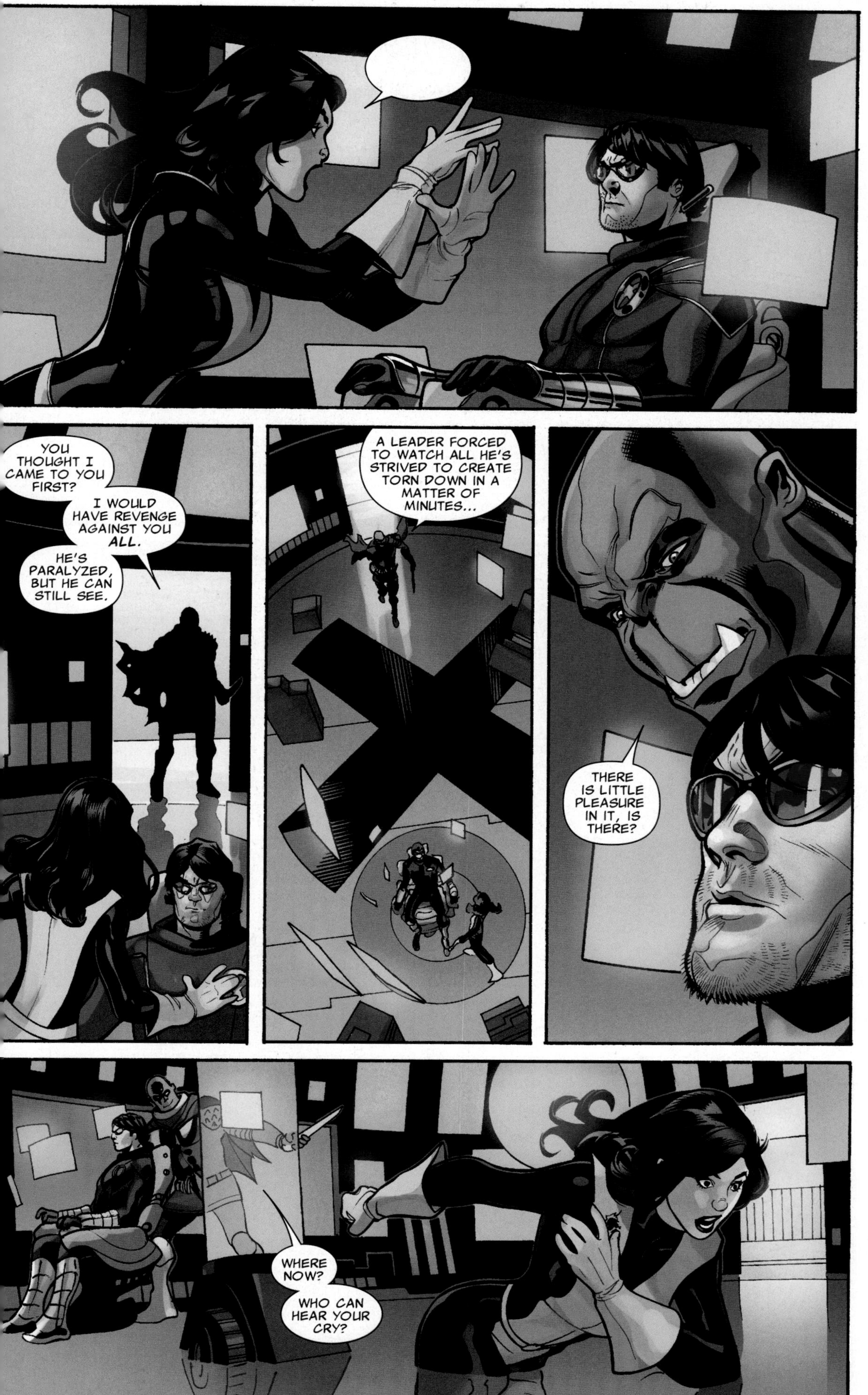
YOU THOUGHT I CAME TO YOU FIRST?
I WOULD HAVE REVENGE AGAINST YOU ALL.
HE'S PARALYZED, BUT HE CAN STILL SEE.
A LEADER FORCED TO WATCH ALL HE'S STRIVED TO CREATE TORN DOWN IN A MATTER OF MINUTES...
THERE IS LITTLE PLEASURE IN IT, IS THERE?
WHERE NOW?
WHO CAN HEAR YOUR CRY?

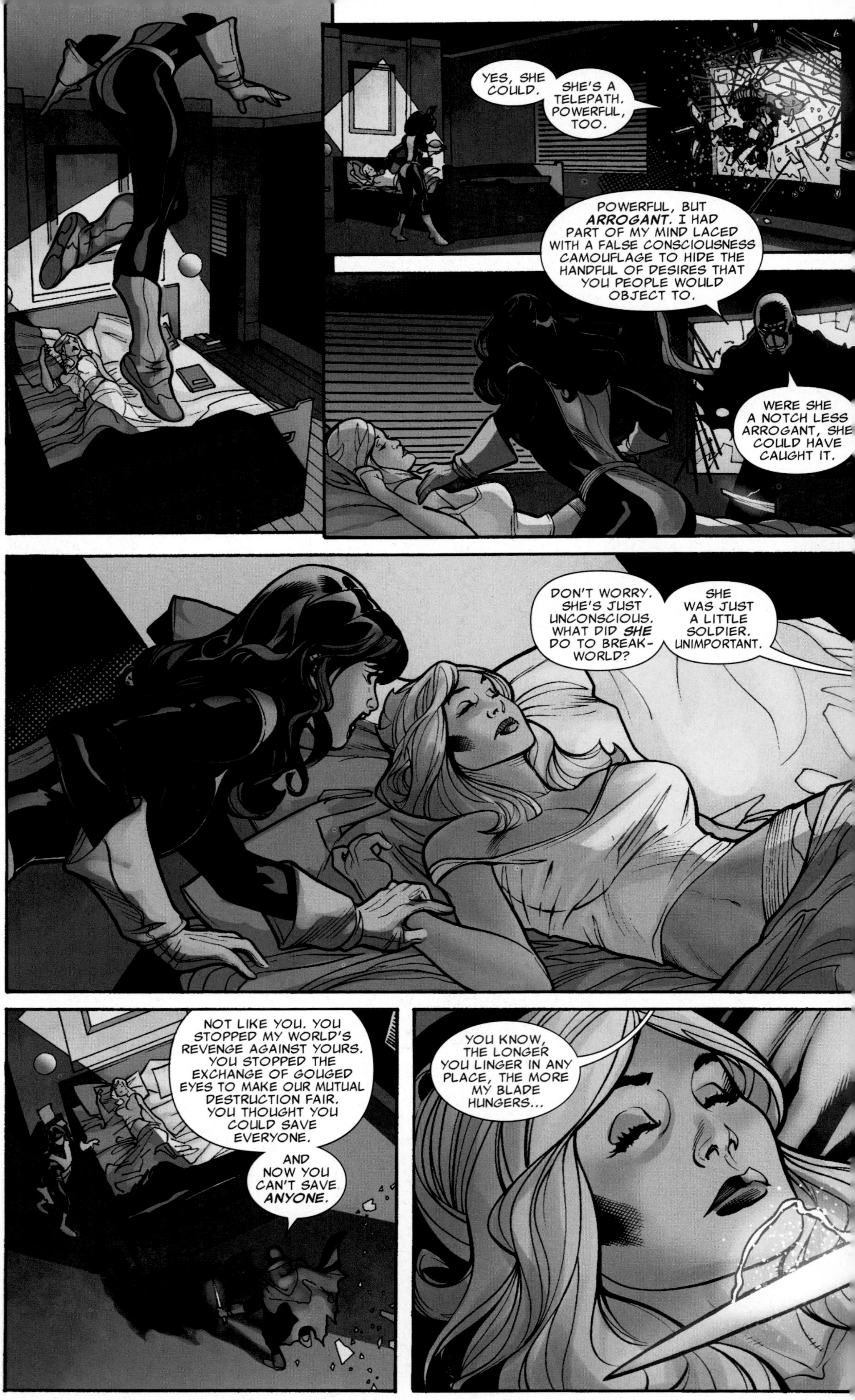
YES, SHE COULD.
SHE'S A TELEPATH. POWERFUL, TOO.
POWERFUL, BUT ARROGANT. I HAD PART OF MY MIND LACED WITH A FALSE CONSCIOUSNESS CAMOUFLAGE TO HIDE THE HANDFUL OF DESIRES THAT YOU PEOPLE WOULD OBJECT TO.
WERE SHE A NOTCH LESS ARROGANT, SHE COULD HAVE CAUGHT IT.
DON'T WORRY. SHE'S JUST UNCONSCIOUS. WHAT DID SHE DO TO BREAKWORLD?
SHE WAS JUST A LITTLE SOLDIER. UNIMPORTANT.
NOT LIKE YOU. YOU STOPPED MY WORLD'S REVENGE AGAINST YOURS. YOU STOPPED THE EXCHANGE OF GOUGED EYES TO MAKE OUR MUTUAL DESTRUCTION FAIR. YOU THOUGHT YOU COULD SAVE EVERYONE.
AND NOW YOU CAN'T SAVE ANYONE.
YOU KNOW, THE LONGER YOU LINGER IN ANY PLACE, THE MORE MY BLADE HUNGERS...

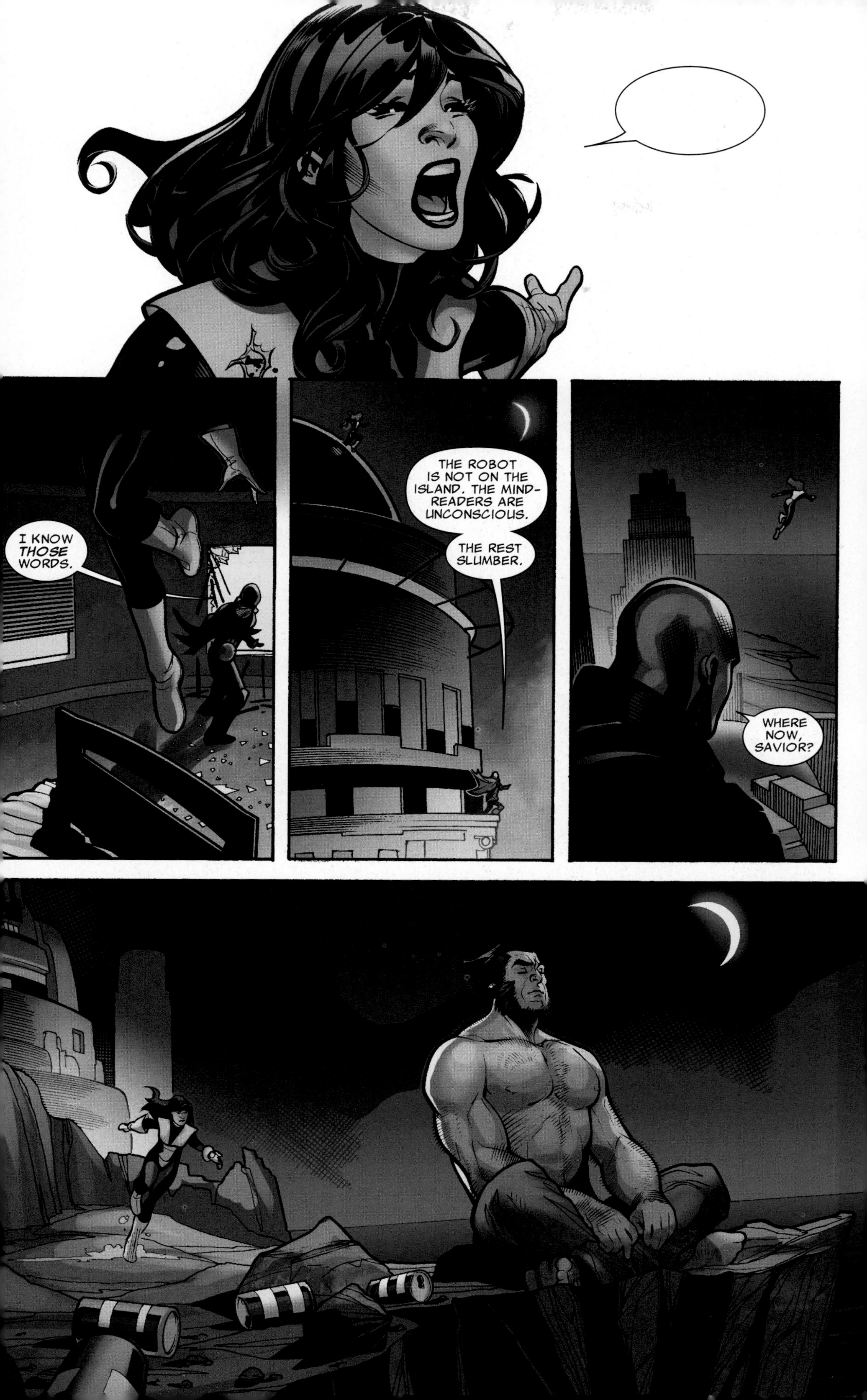
I KNOW *THOSE* WORDS.
THE ROBOT IS NOT ON THE ISLAND. THE MIND-READERS ARE UNCONSCIOUS.
THE REST SLUMBER.
WHERE NOW, SAVIOR?

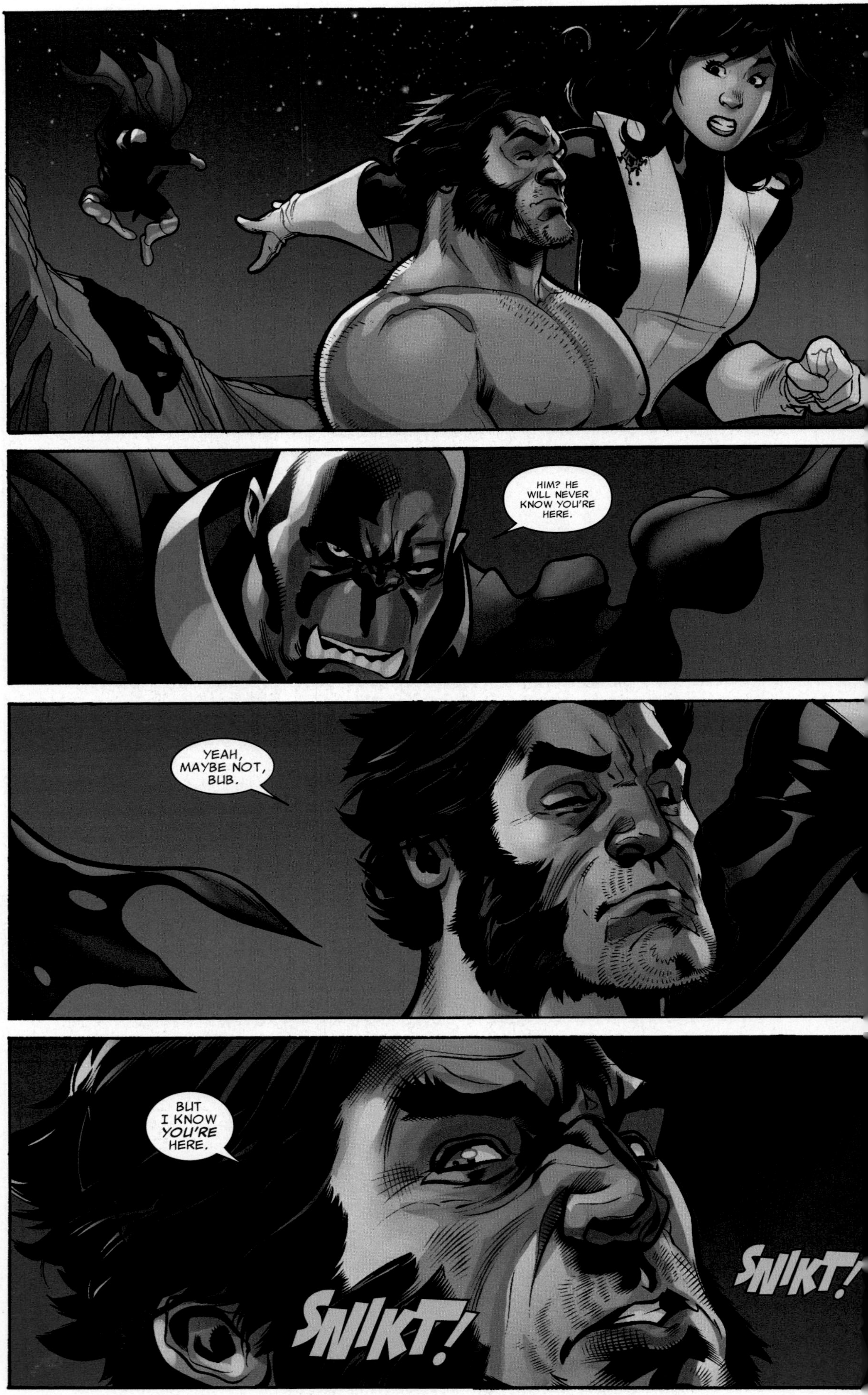
HIM? HE WILL NEVER KNOW YOU'RE HERE.
YEAH, MAYBE NOT, BUB.
BUT I KNOW YOU'RE HERE.
SNIKT!
SNIKT!

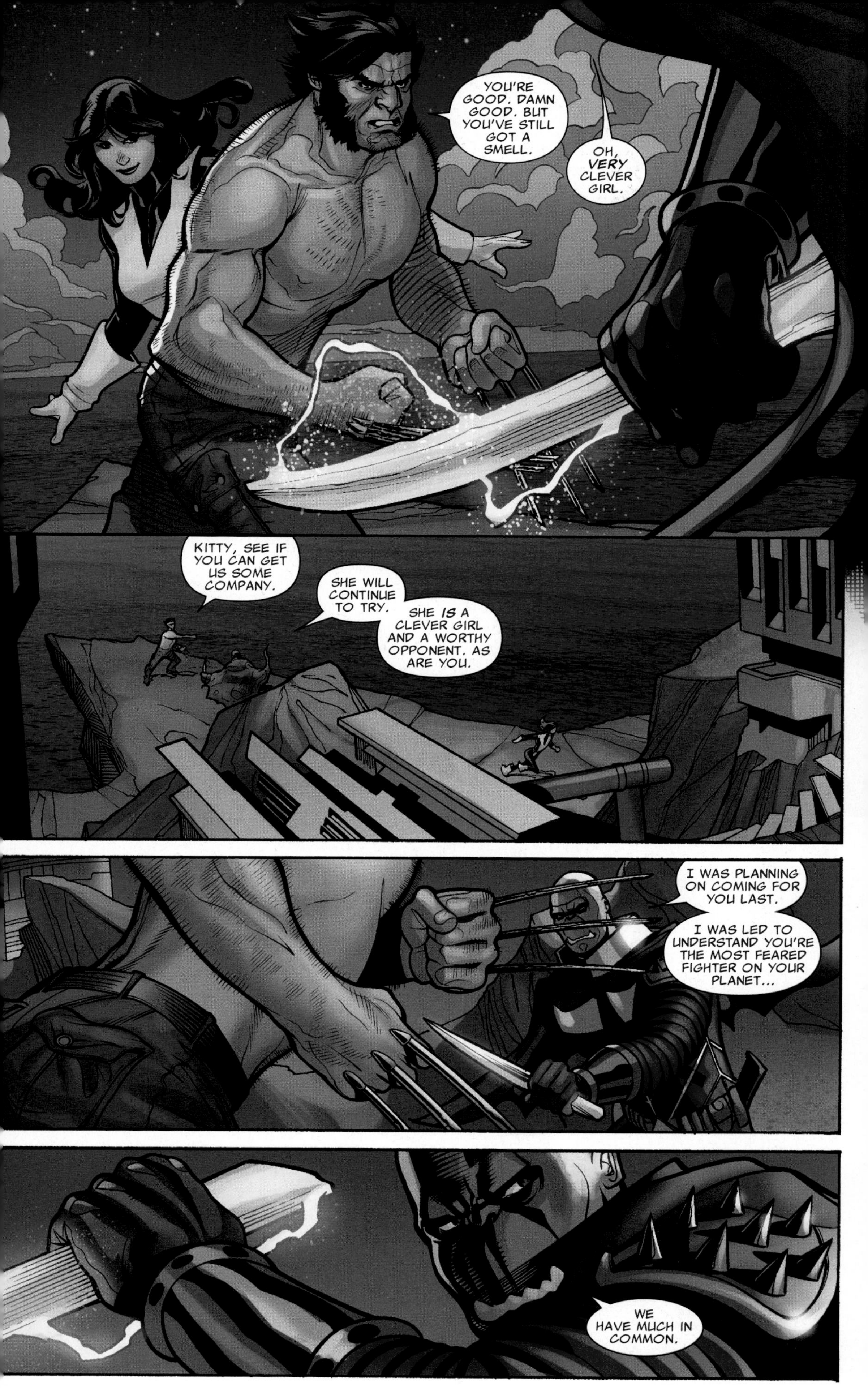
YOU'RE GOOD. DAMN GOOD. BUT YOU'VE STILL GOT A SMELL.
OH, VERY CLEVER GIRL.
KITTY, SEE IF YOU CAN GET US SOME COMPANY.
SHE WILL CONTINUE TO TRY.
SHE IS A CLEVER GIRL AND A WORTHY OPPONENT. AS ARE YOU.
I WAS PLANNING ON COMING FOR YOU LAST.
I WAS LED TO UNDERSTAND YOU'RE THE MOST FEARED FIGHTER ON YOUR PLANET...
WE HAVE MUCH IN COMMON.

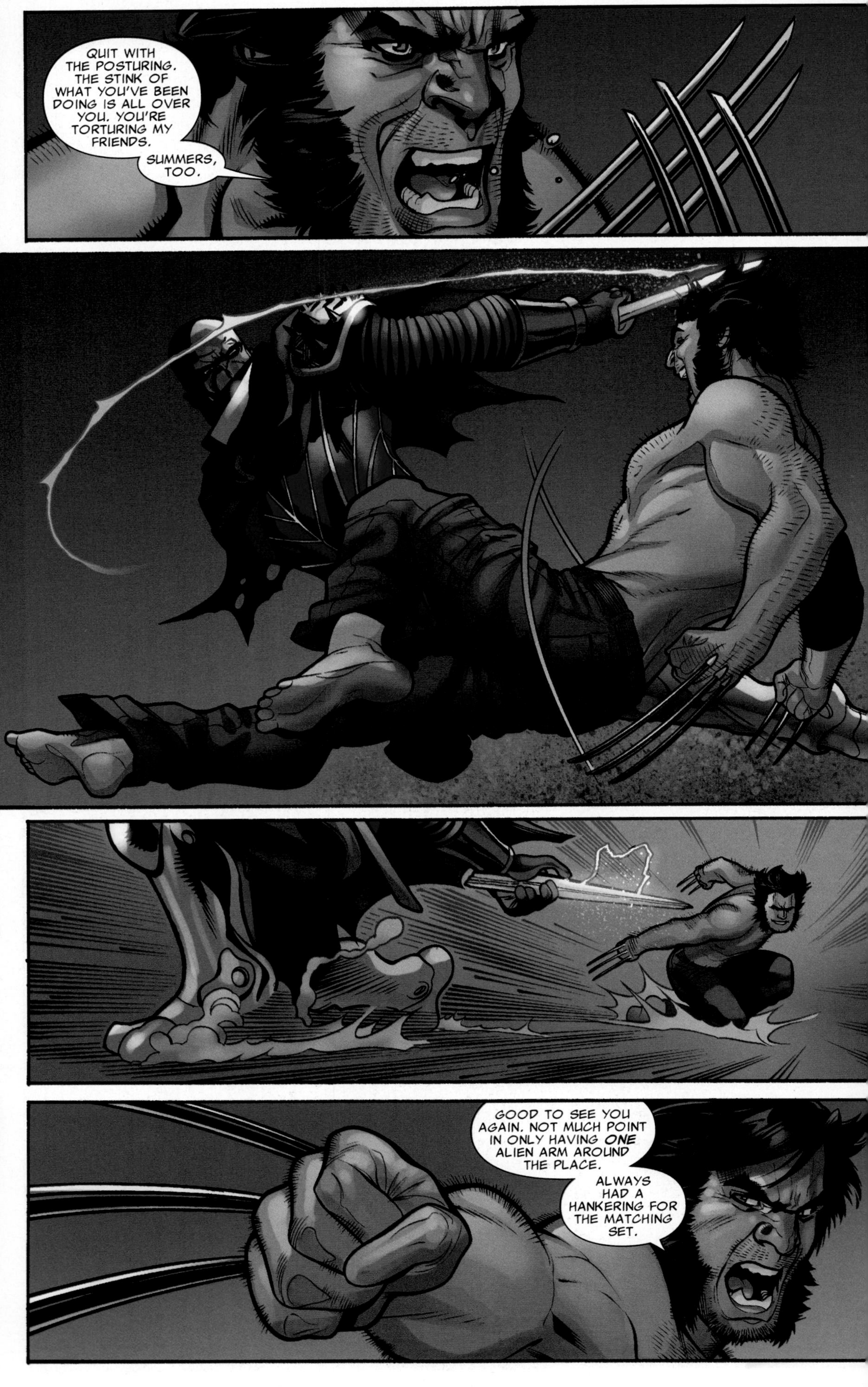
QUIT WITH THE POSTURING. THE STINK OF WHAT YOU'VE BEEN DOING IS ALL OVER YOU. YOU'RE TORTURING MY FRIENDS.
SUMMERS, TOO.
GOOD TO SEE YOU AGAIN. NOT MUCH POINT IN ONLY HAVING *ONE* ALIEN ARM AROUND THE PLACE.
ALWAYS HAD A HANKERING FOR THE MATCHING SET.

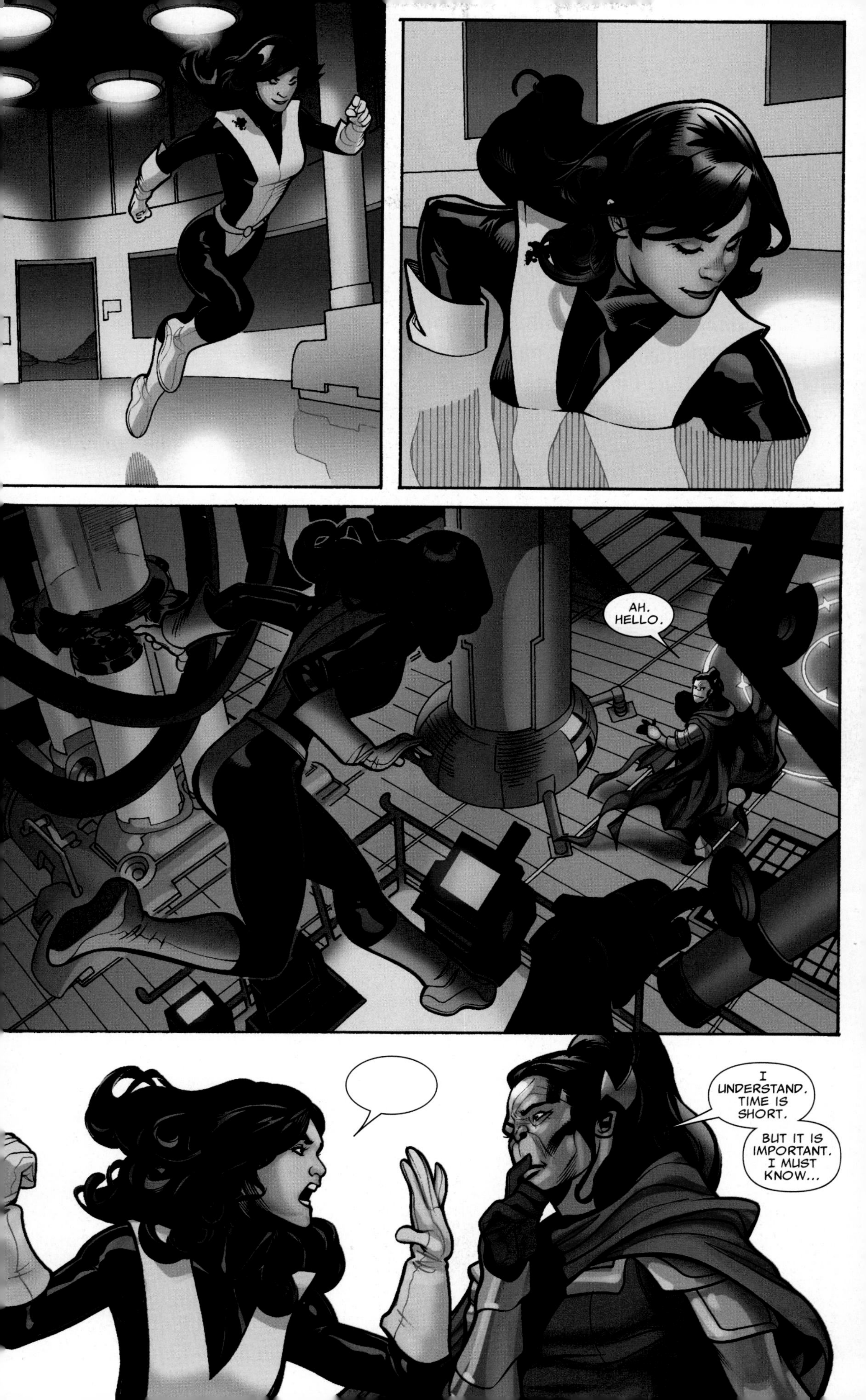
AH. HELLO.
I UNDERSTAND. TIME IS SHORT.
BUT IT IS IMPORTANT. I MUST KNOW...

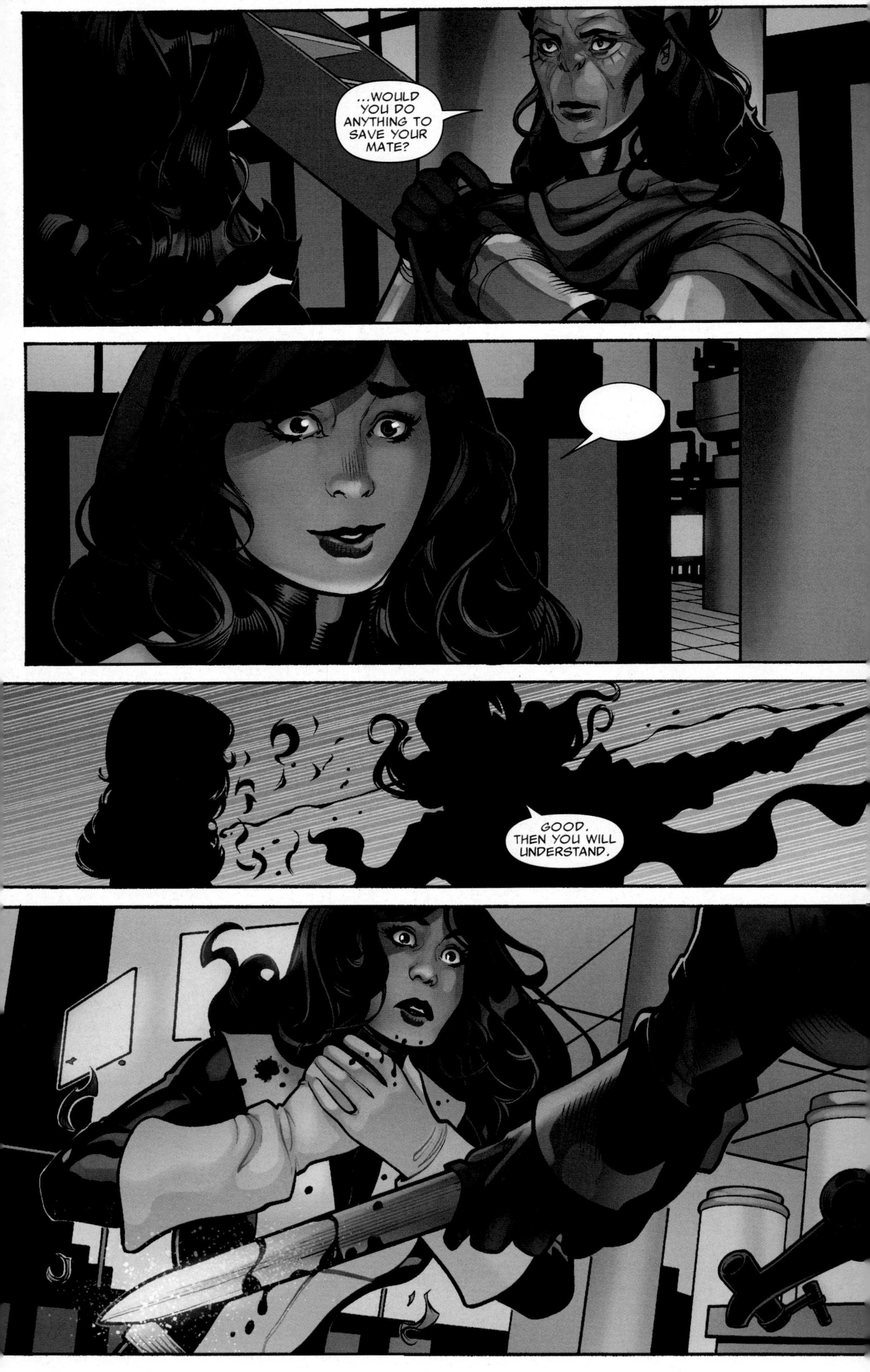
...WOULD YOU DO ANYTHING TO SAVE YOUR MATE?
GOOD. THEN YOU WILL UNDERSTAND.

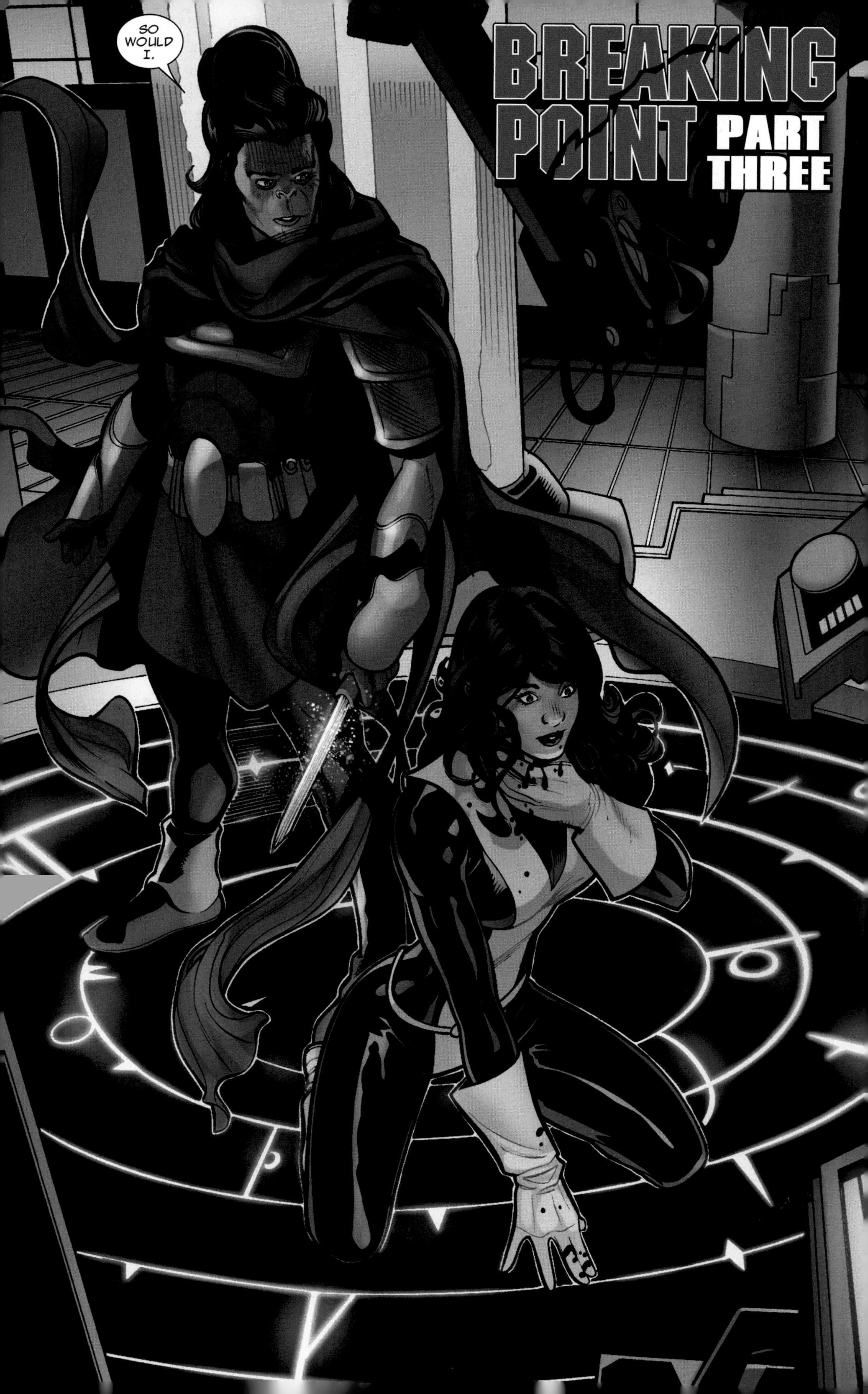
SO WOULD I.
BREAKING POINT PART THREE

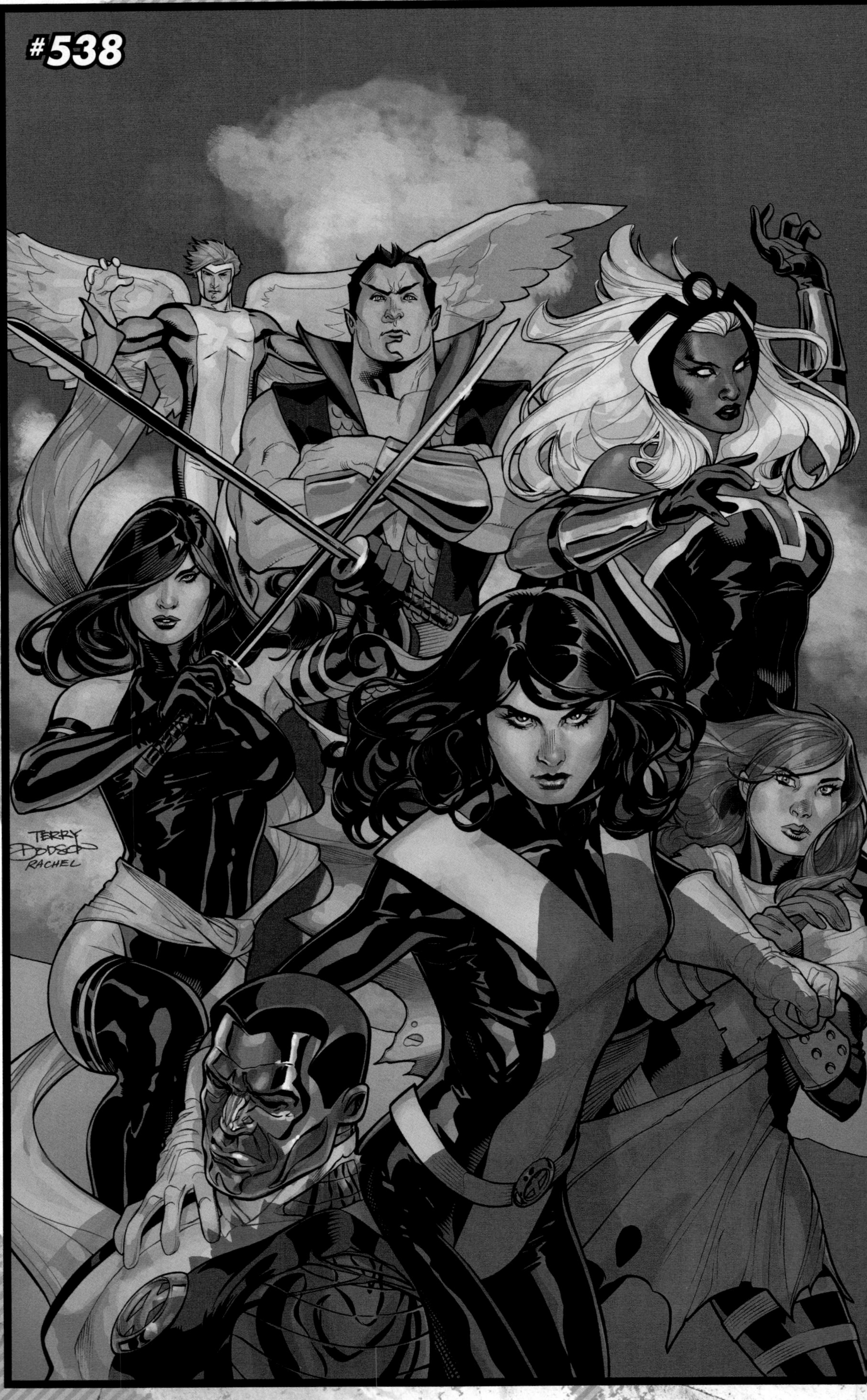
#538
TERRY
DODSON
RACHEL

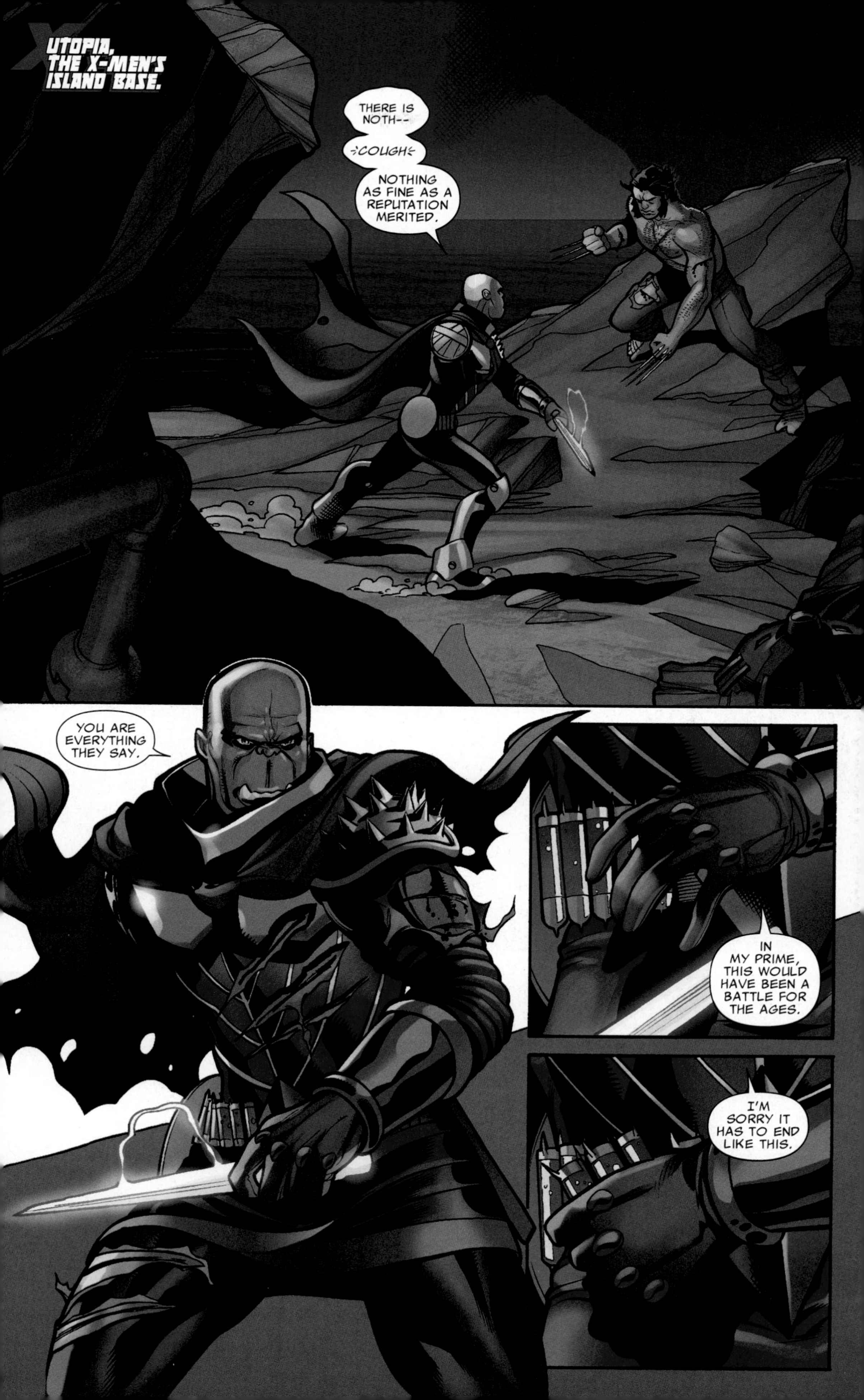
UTOPIA, THE X-MEN'S ISLAND BASE.
THERE IS NOTH--
COUGH
NOTHING AS FINE AS A REPUTATION MERITED.
YOU ARE EVERYTHING THEY SAY.
IN MY PRIME, THIS WOULD HAVE BEEN A BATTLE FOR THE AGES.
I'M SORRY IT HAS TO END LIKE THIS.

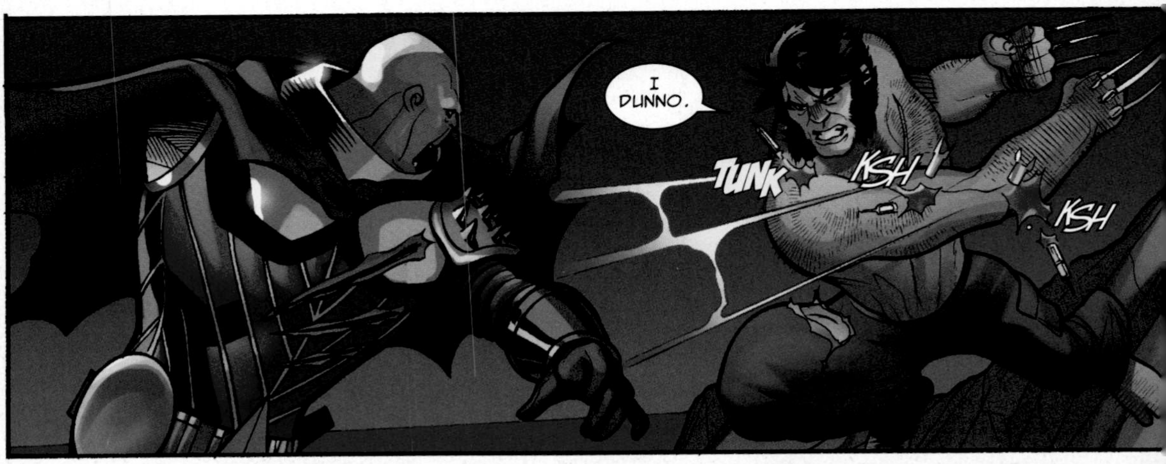
I DUNNO.
TUNK
KSH
KSH

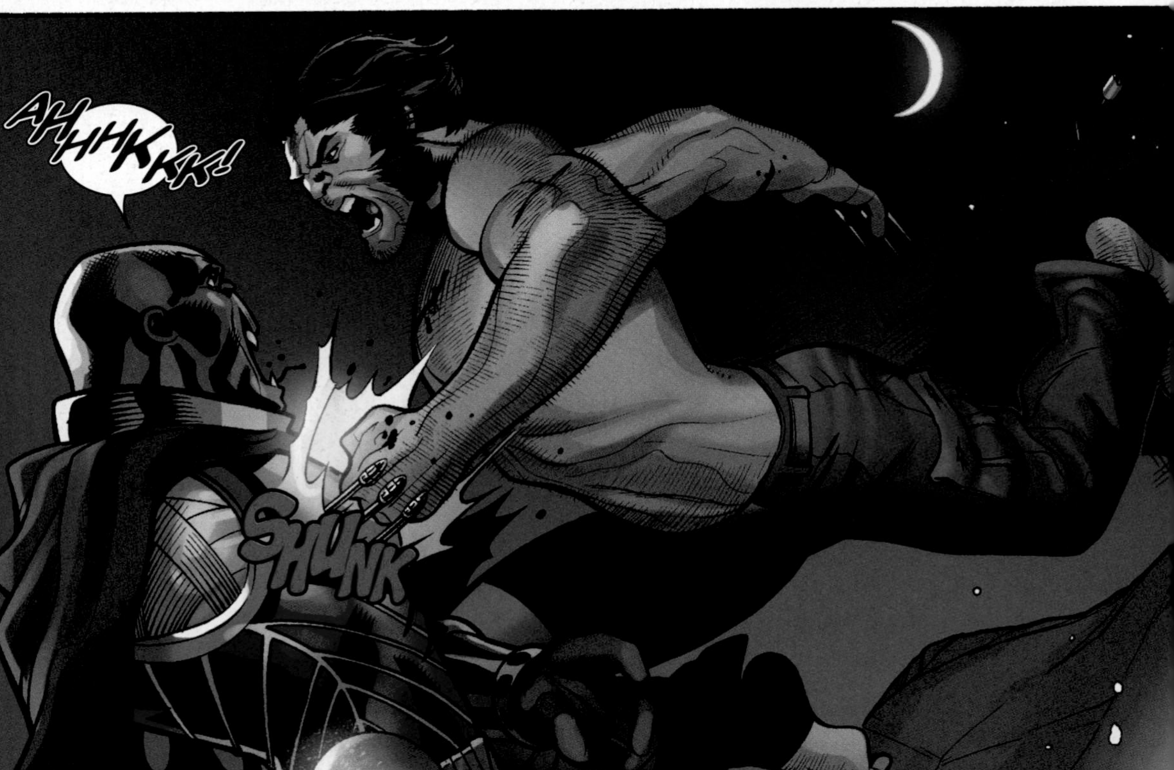
AHHHKKK!
SHUNK

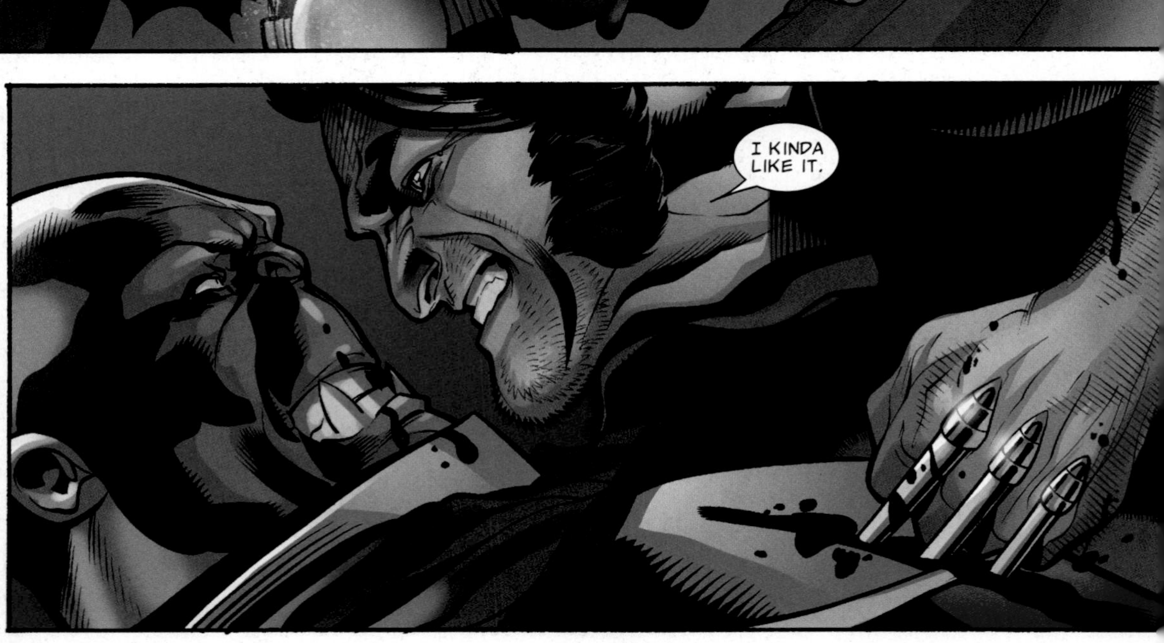
I KINDA LIKE IT.

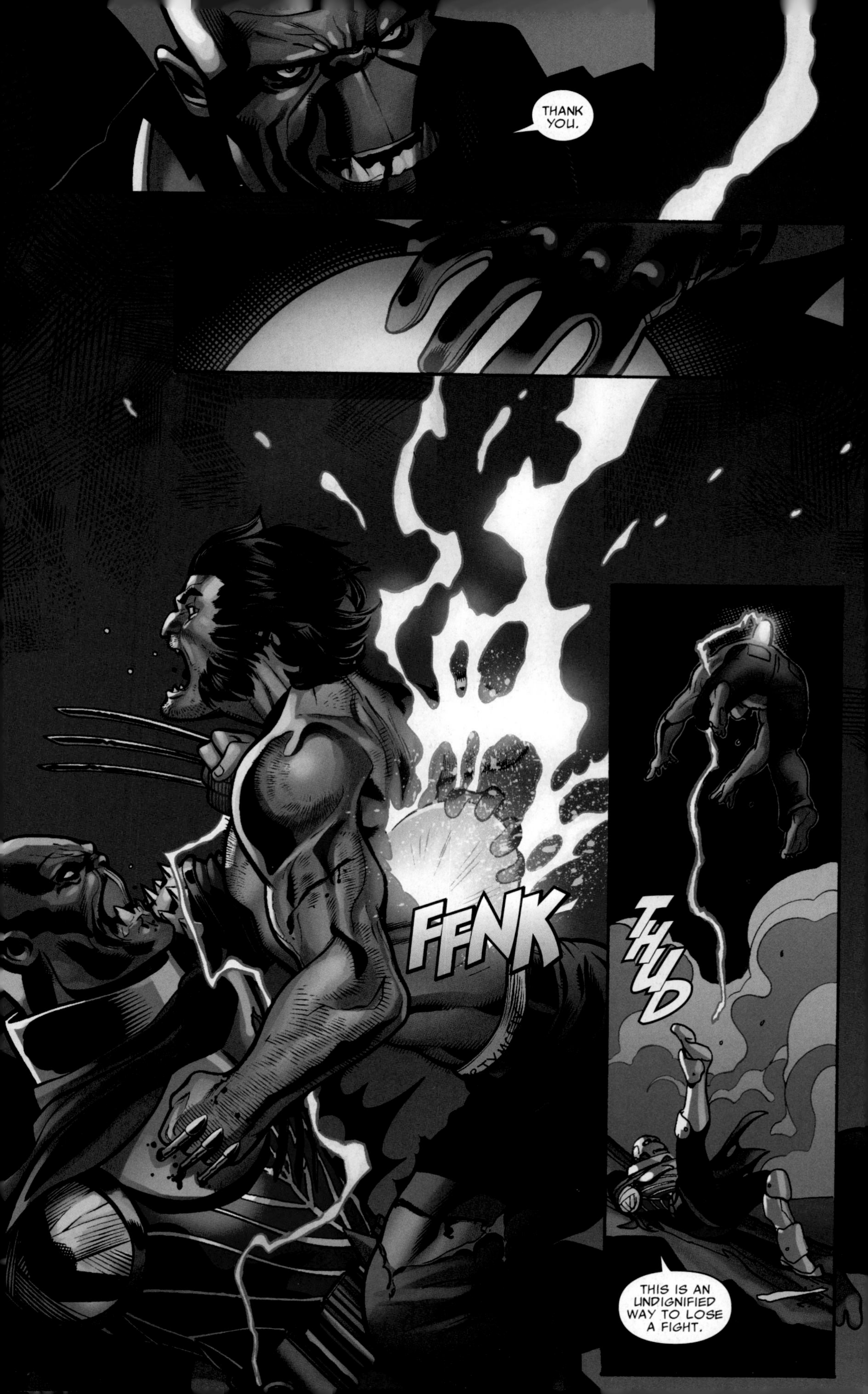
THANK YOU.
FFNK
THUD
THIS IS AN UNDIGNIFIED WAY TO LOSE A FIGHT.

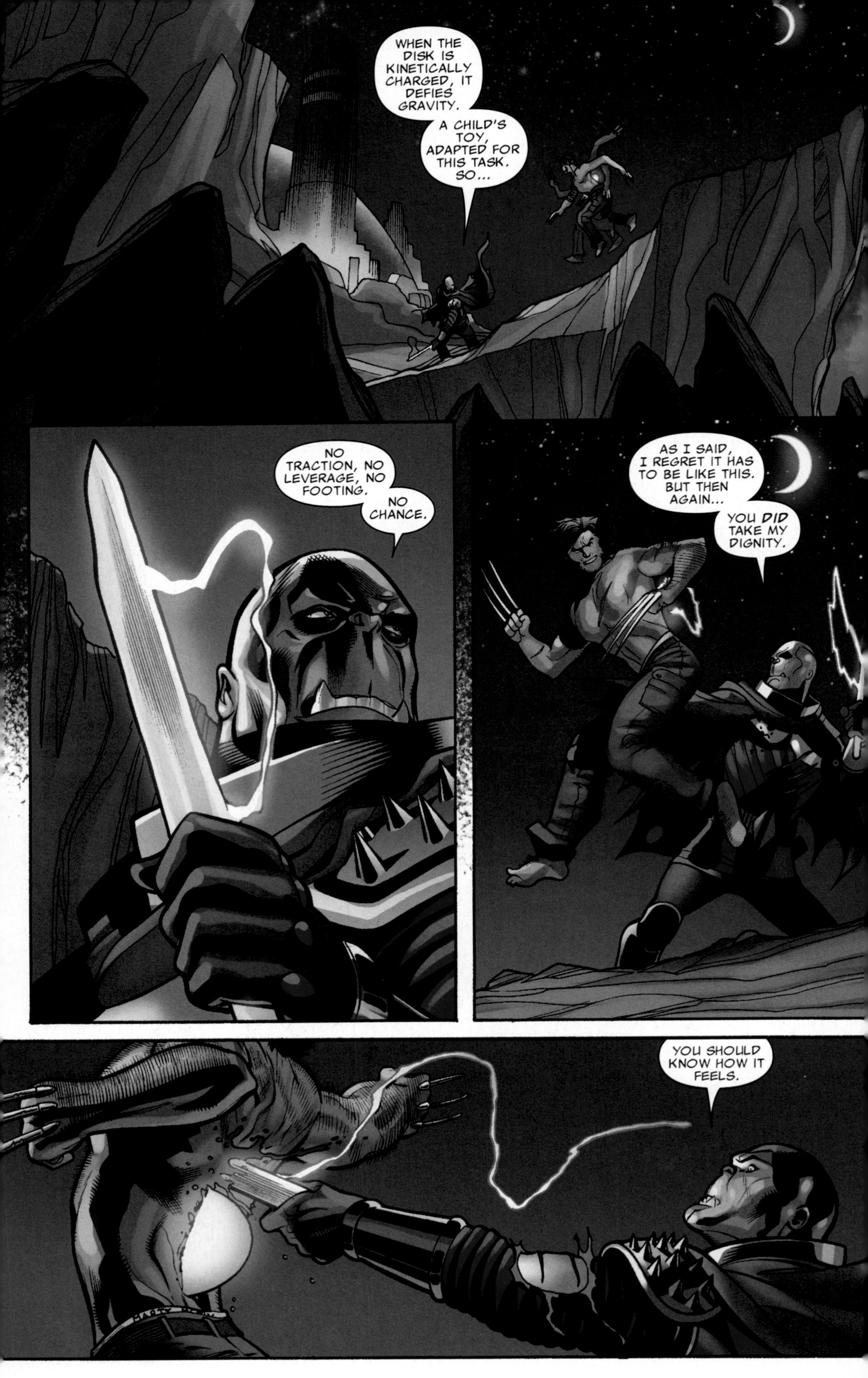
WHEN THE DISK IS KINETICALLY CHARGED, IT DEFIES GRAVITY.
A CHILD'S TOY, ADAPTED FOR THIS TASK. SO...
NO TRACTION, NO LEVERAGE, NO FOOTING.
NO CHANCE.
AS I SAID, I REGRET IT HAS TO BE LIKE THIS. BUT THEN AGAIN...
YOU DID TAKE MY DIGNITY.
YOU SHOULD KNOW HOW IT FEELS.

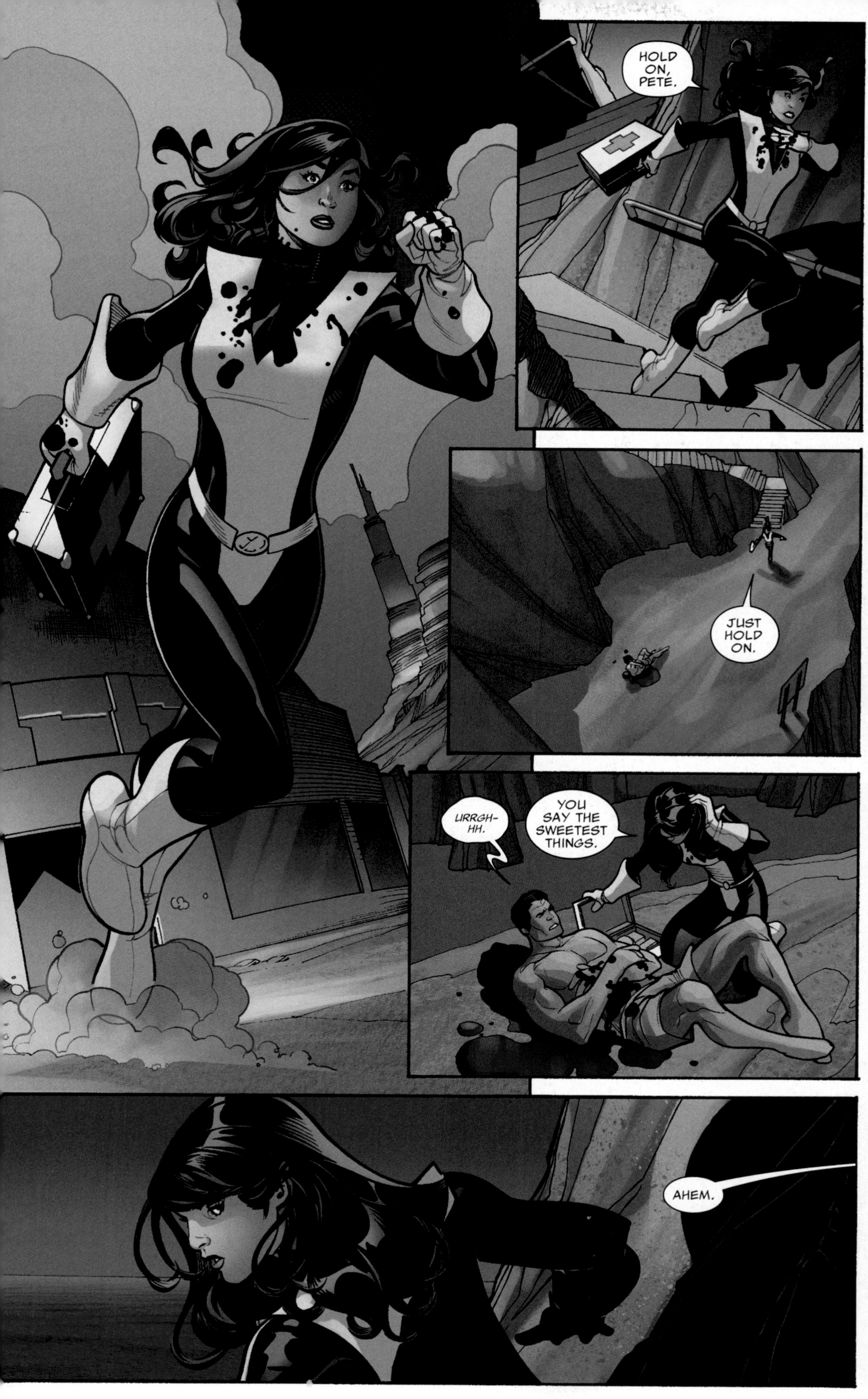
HOLD ON, PETE.
JUST HOLD ON.
URRGH-HH.
YOU SAY THE SWEETEST THINGS.
AHEM.

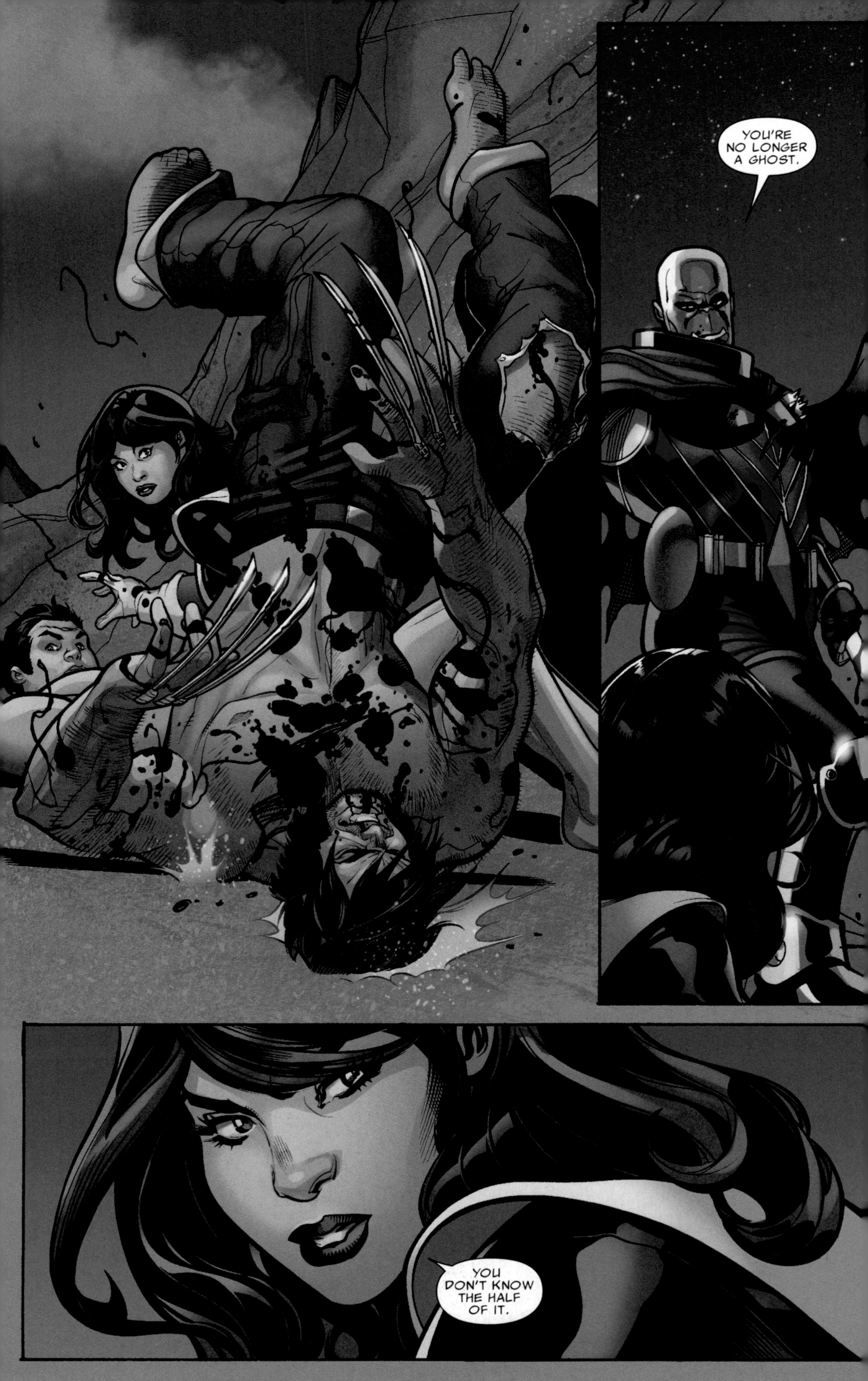
YOU'RE NO LONGER A GHOST.
YOU DON'T KNOW THE HALF OF IT.

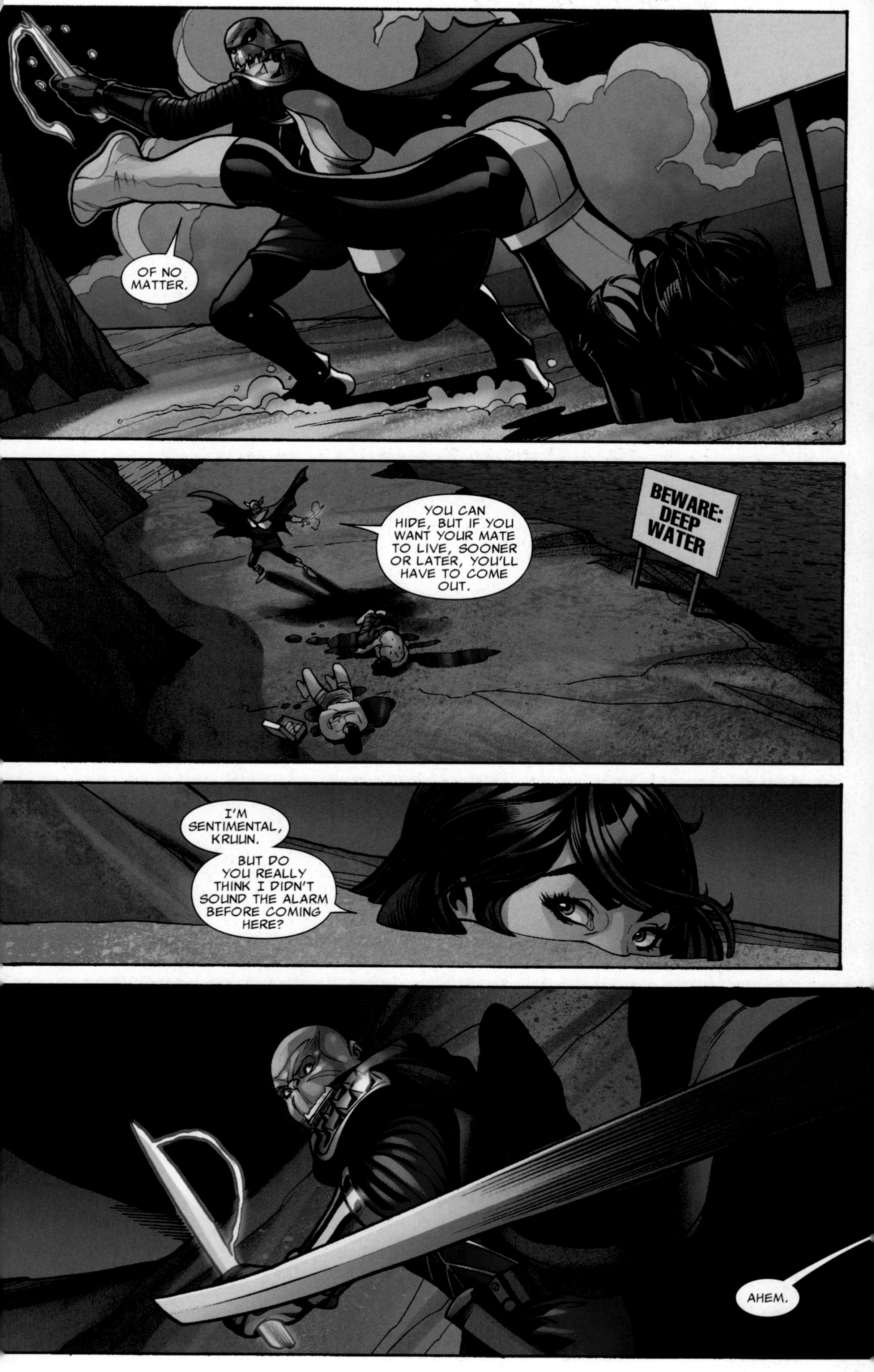
OF NO MATTER.
YOU CAN HIDE, BUT IF YOU WANT YOUR MATE TO LIVE, SOONER OR LATER, YOU'LL HAVE TO COME OUT.
BEWARE: DEEP WATER
I'M SENTIMENTAL, KRUUN.
BUT DO YOU REALLY THINK I DIDN'T SOUND THE ALARM BEFORE COMING HERE?
AHEM.

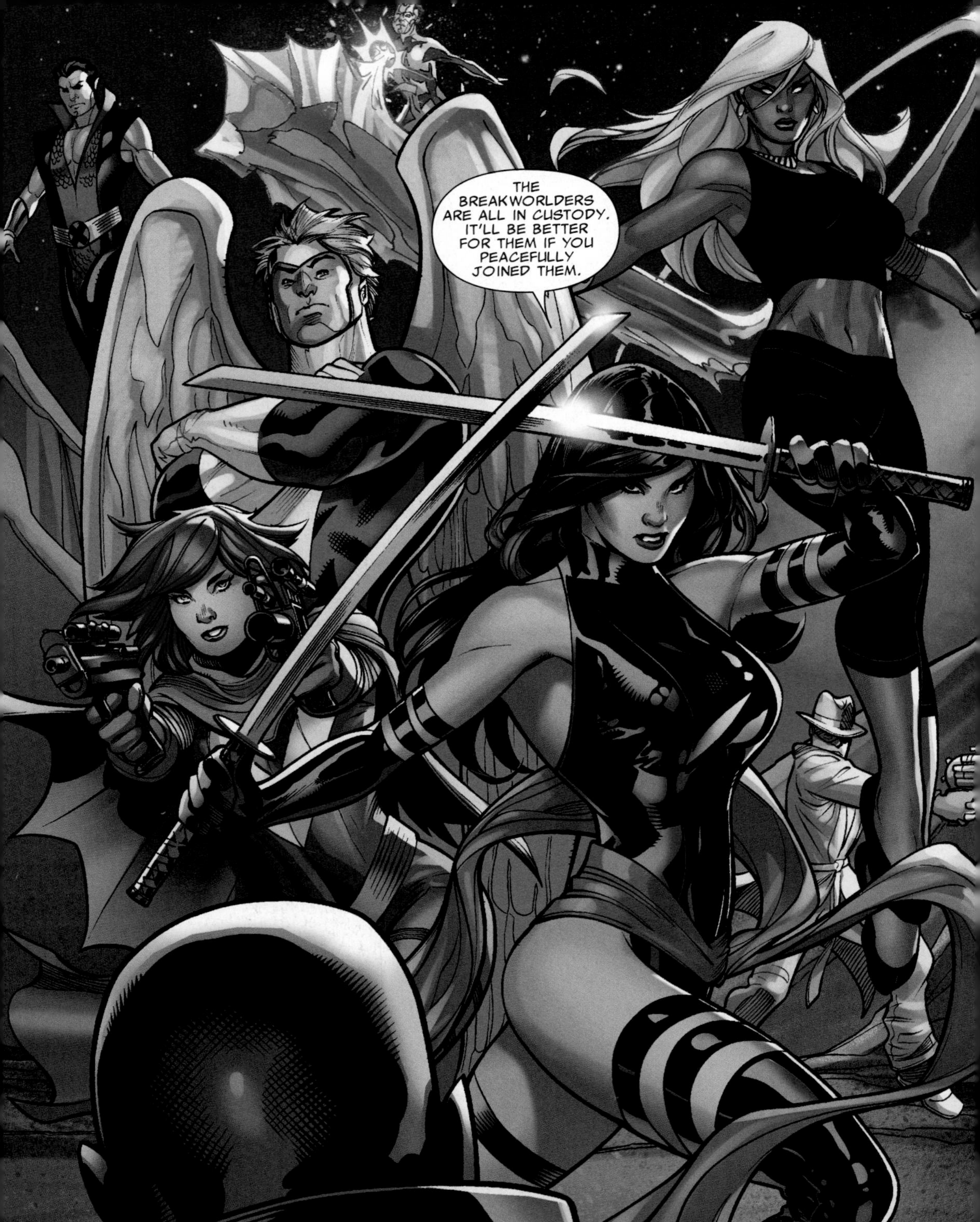
THE BREAKWORLDERS ARE ALL IN CUSTODY. IT'LL BE BETTER FOR THEM IF YOU PEACEFULLY JOINED THEM.

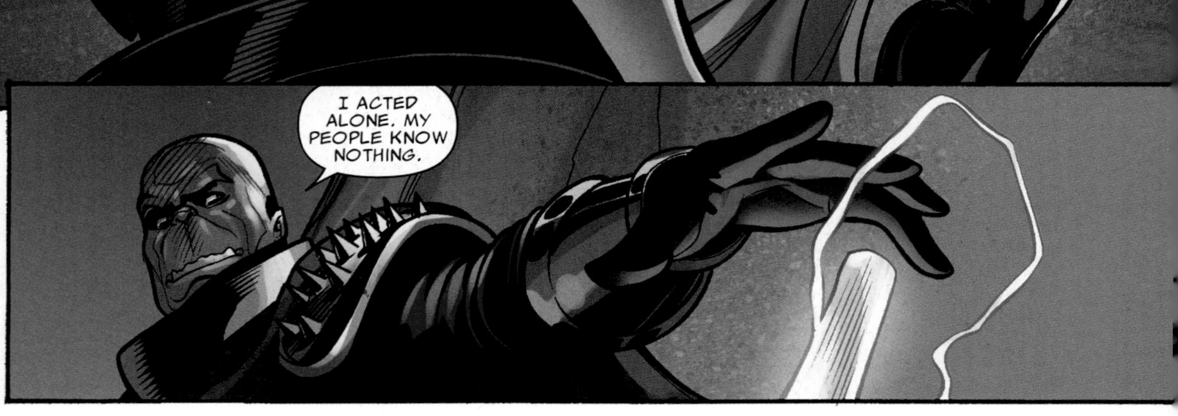
I ACTED ALONE. MY PEOPLE KNOW NOTHING.

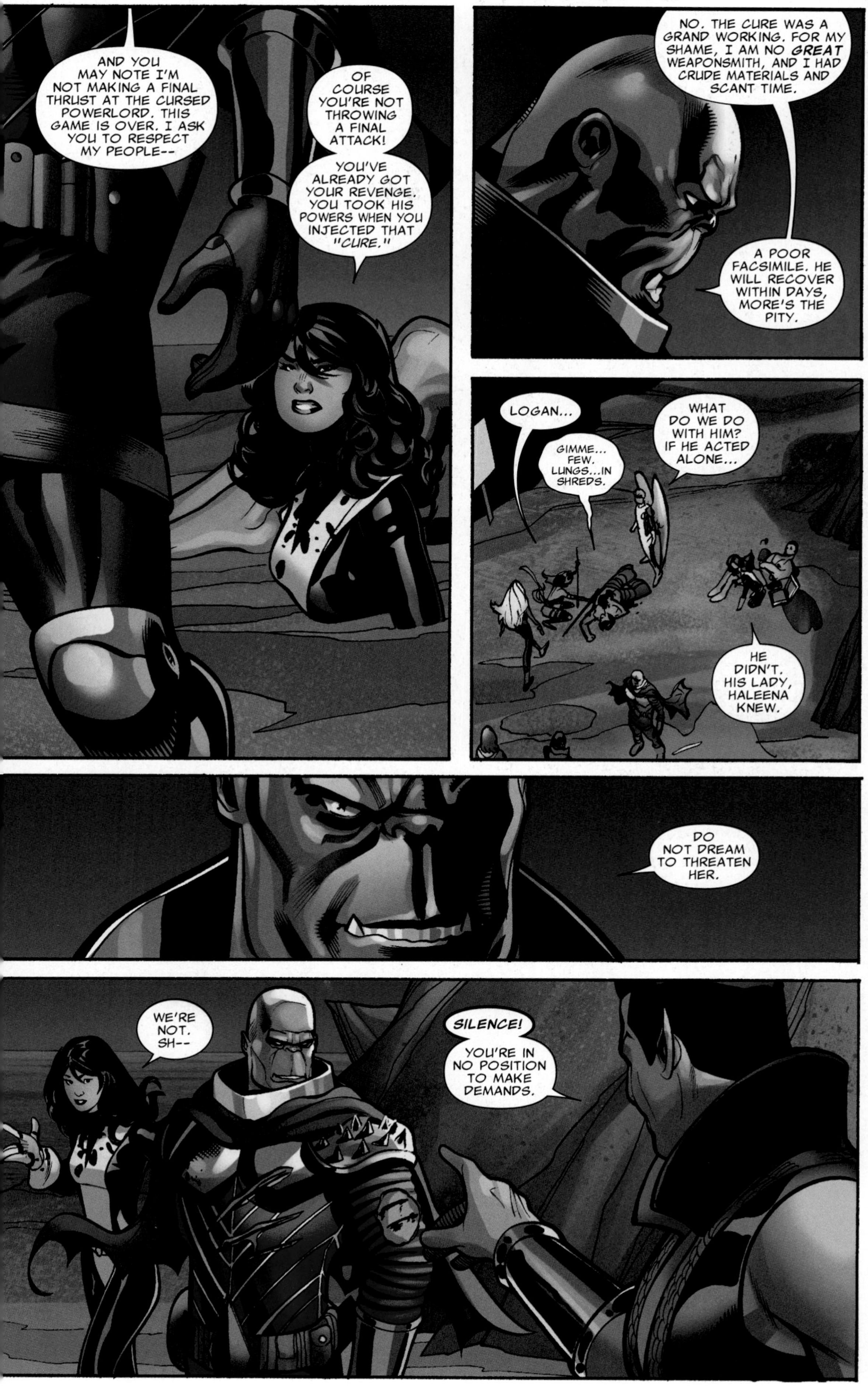
AND YOU MAY NOTE I'M NOT MAKING A FINAL THRUST AT THE CURSED POWERLORD. THIS GAME IS OVER. I ASK YOU TO RESPECT MY PEOPLE--
OF COURSE YOU'RE NOT THROWING A FINAL ATTACK!
YOU'VE ALREADY GOT YOUR REVENGE. YOU TOOK HIS POWERS WHEN YOU INJECTED THAT "CURE."
NO. THE CURE WAS A GRAND WORKING. FOR MY SHAME, I AM NO GREAT WEAPONSMITH, AND I HAD CRUDE MATERIALS AND SCANT TIME.
A POOR FACSIMILE. HE WILL RECOVER WITHIN DAYS, MORE'S THE PITY.
LOGAN...
GIMME... FEW. LUNGS...IN SHREDS.
WHAT DO WE DO WITH HIM? IF HE ACTED ALONE...
HE DIDN'T. HIS LADY, HALEENA KNEW.
DO NOT DREAM TO THREATEN HER.
WE'RE NOT. SH--
SILENCE!
YOU'RE IN NO POSITION TO MAKE DEMANDS.

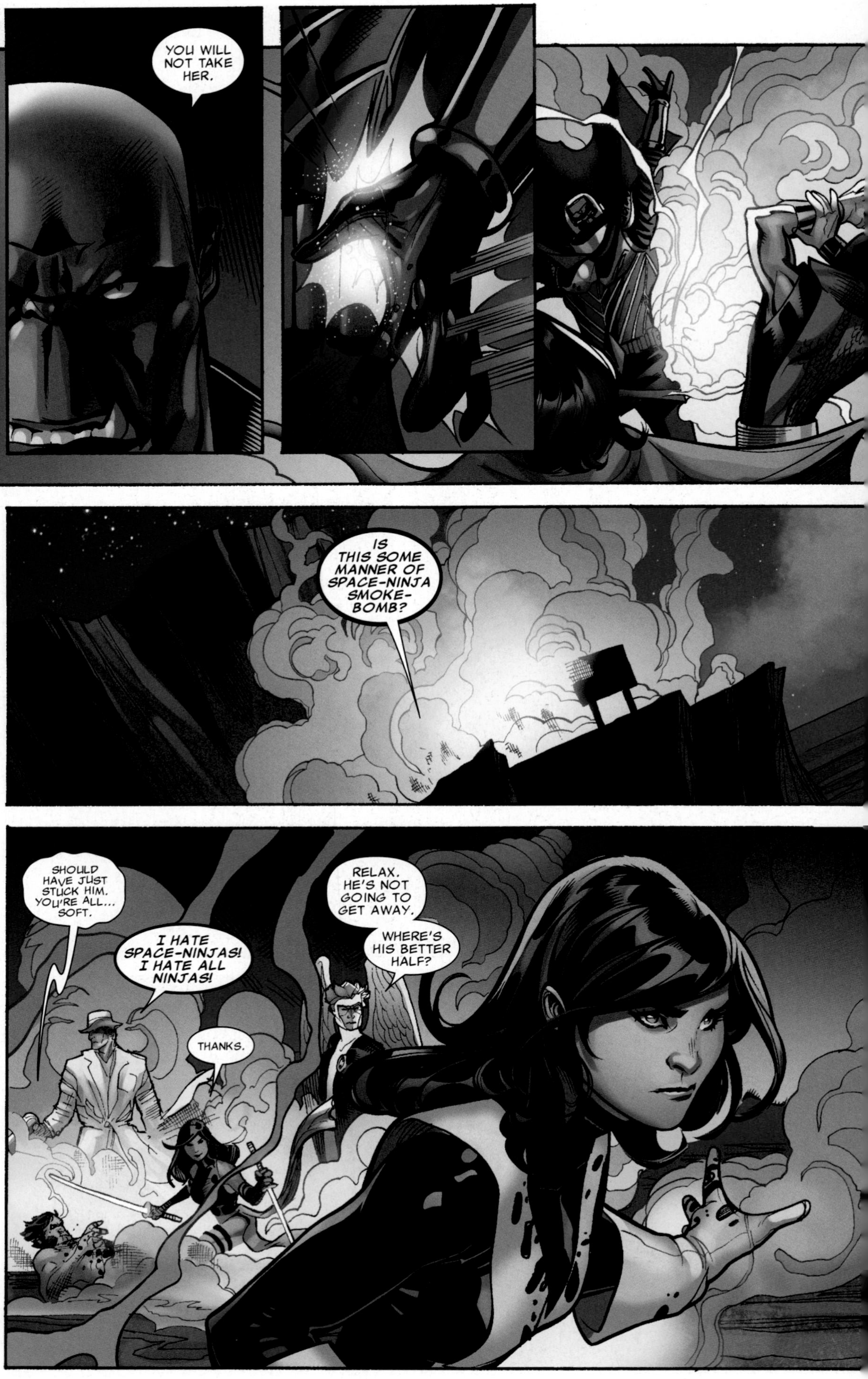
YOU WILL NOT TAKE HER.
IS THIS SOME MANNER OF SPACE-NINJA SMOKE-BOMB?
SHOULD HAVE JUST STUCK HIM. YOU'RE ALL... SOFT.
I HATE SPACE-NINJAS! I HATE ALL NINJAS!
THANKS.
RELAX. HE'S NOT GOING TO GET AWAY.
WHERE'S HIS BETTER HALF?

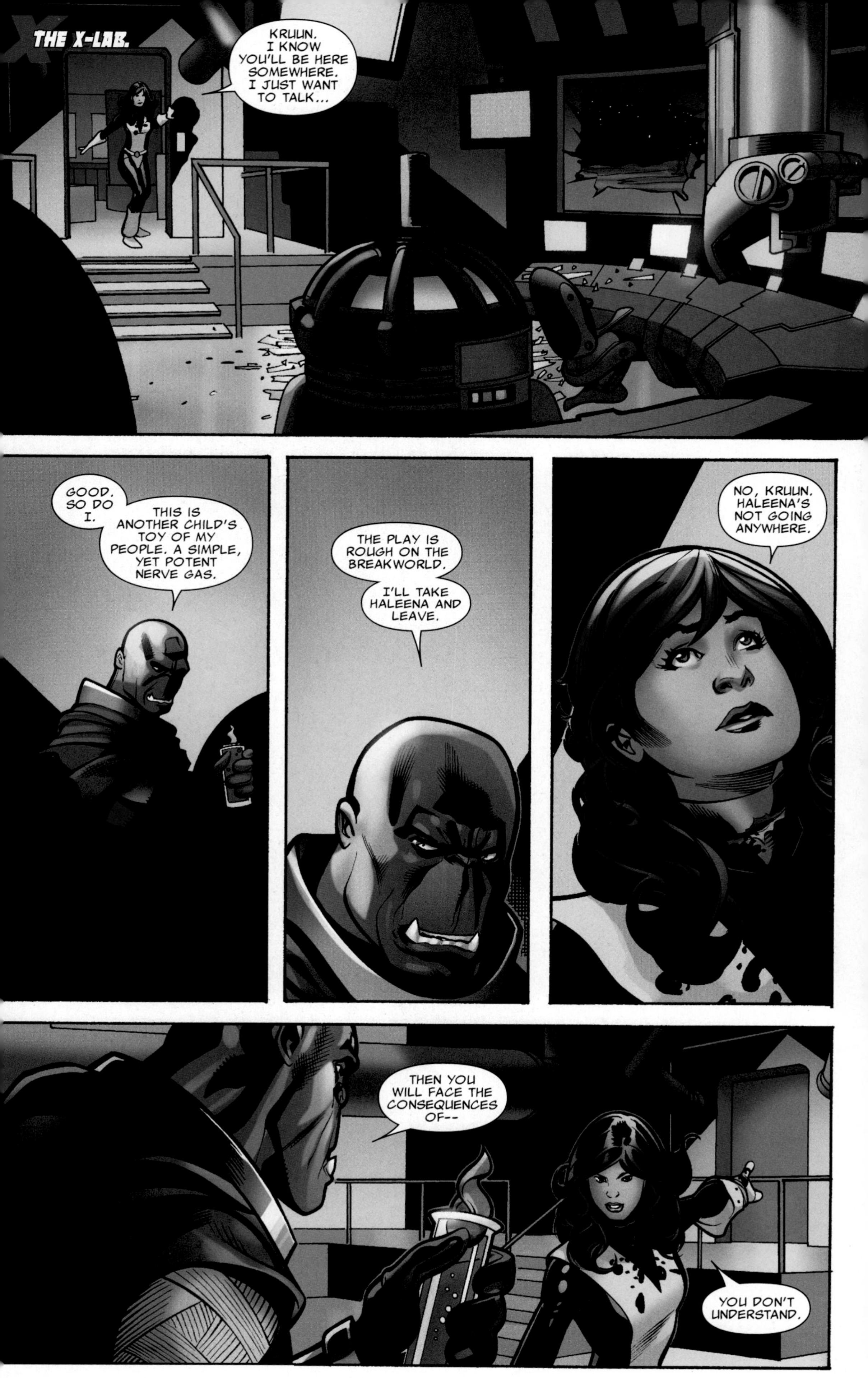
THE X-LAB.
KRULIN. I KNOW YOU'LL BE HERE SOMEWHERE. I JUST WANT TO TALK...
GOOD. SO DO I.
THIS IS ANOTHER CHILD'S TOY OF MY PEOPLE. A SIMPLE, YET POTENT NERVE GAS.
THE PLAY IS ROUGH ON THE BREAKWORLD.
I'LL TAKE HALEENA AND LEAVE.
NO, KRULIN. HALEENA'S NOT GOING ANYWHERE.
THEN YOU WILL FACE THE CONSEQUENCES OF--
YOU DON'T UNDERSTAND.

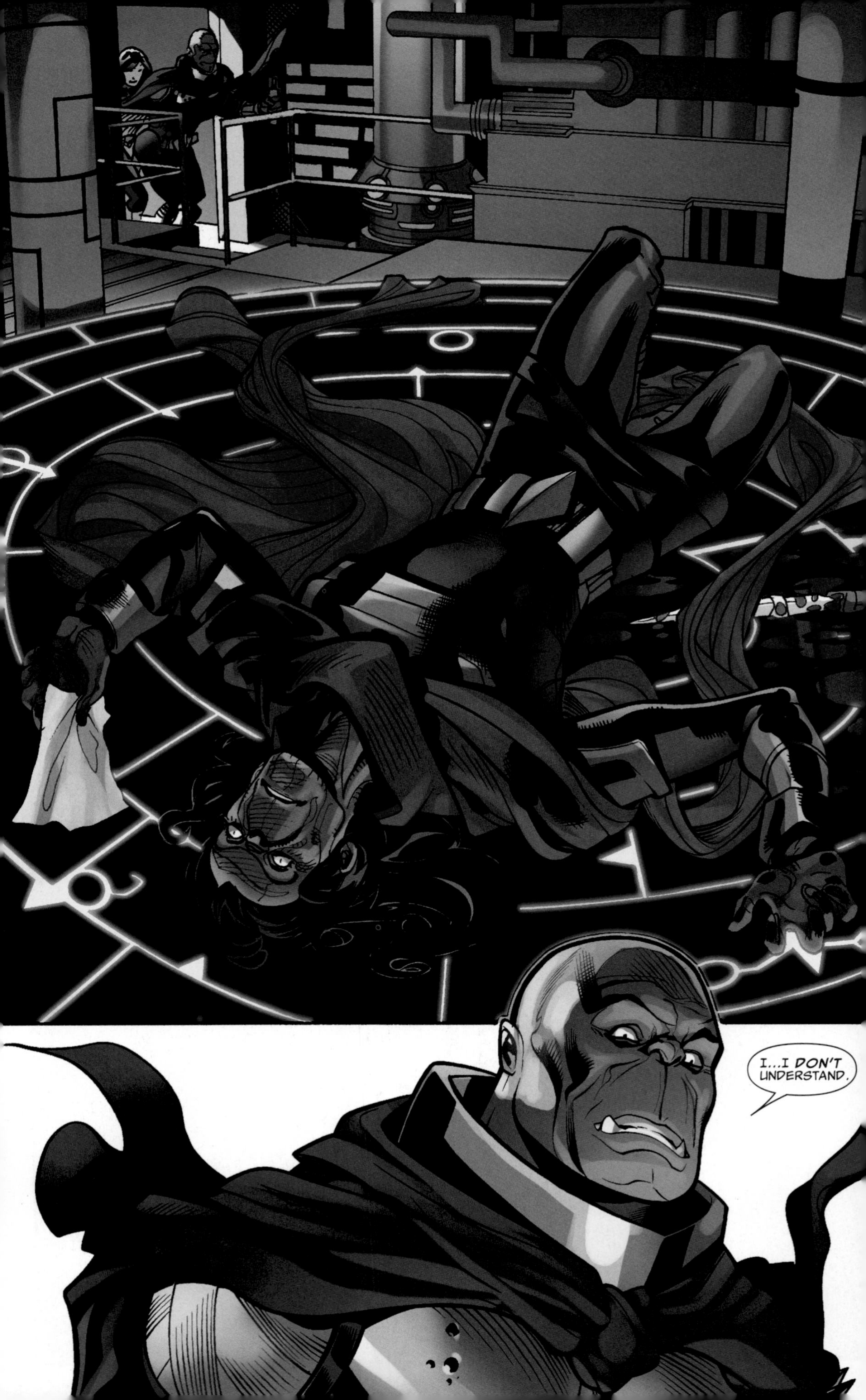
I...I DON'T UNDERSTAND.

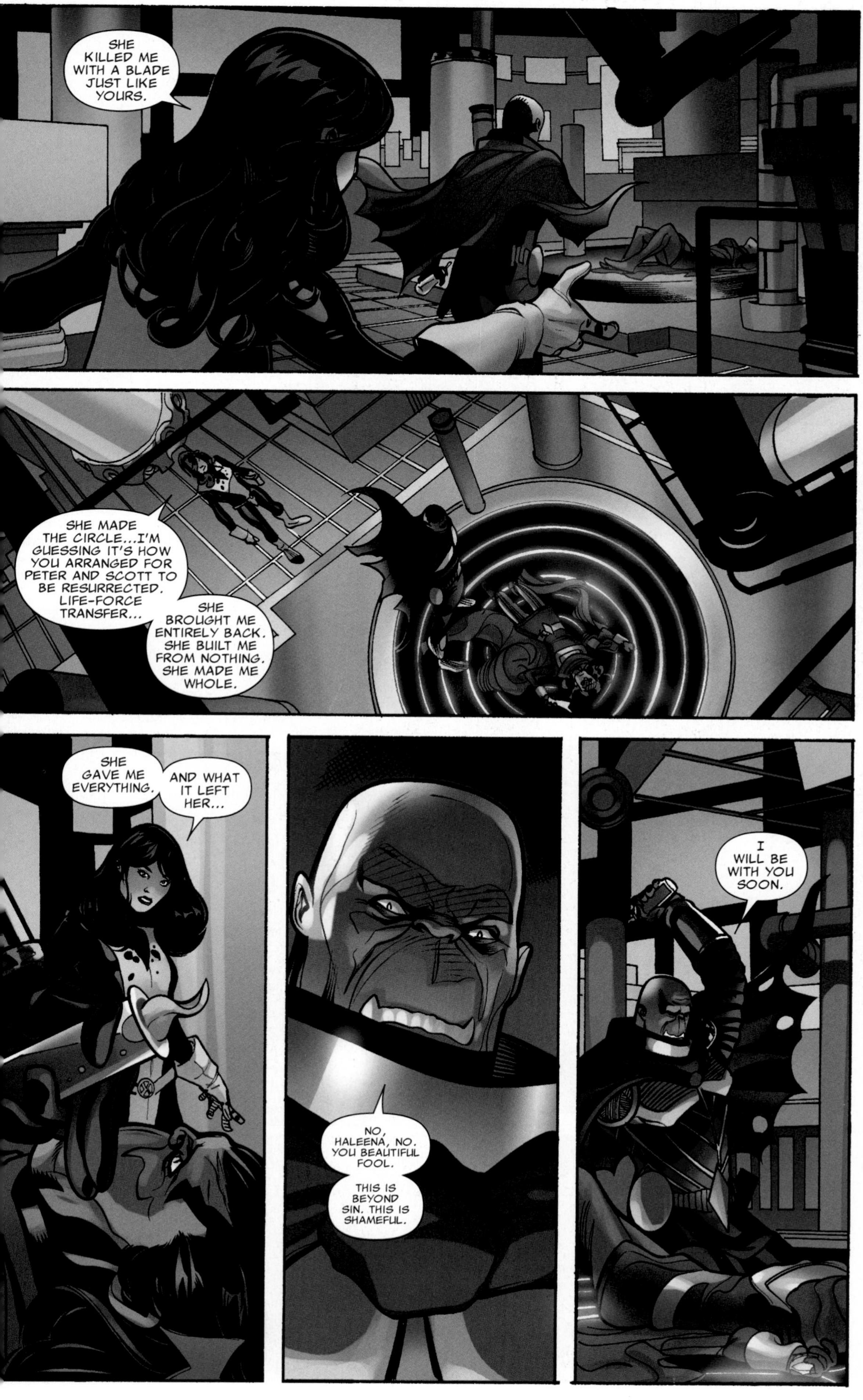
SHE KILLED ME WITH A BLADE JUST LIKE YOURS.
SHE MADE THE CIRCLE...I'M GUESSING IT'S HOW YOU ARRANGED FOR PETER AND SCOTT TO BE RESURRECTED. LIFE-FORCE TRANSFER...
SHE BROUGHT ME ENTIRELY BACK. SHE BUILT ME FROM NOTHING. SHE MADE ME WHOLE.
SHE GAVE ME EVERYTHING.
AND WHAT IT LEFT HER...
NO, HALEENA, NO. YOU BEAUTIFUL FOOL.
THIS IS BEYOND SIN. THIS IS SHAMEFUL.
I WILL BE WITH YOU SOON.

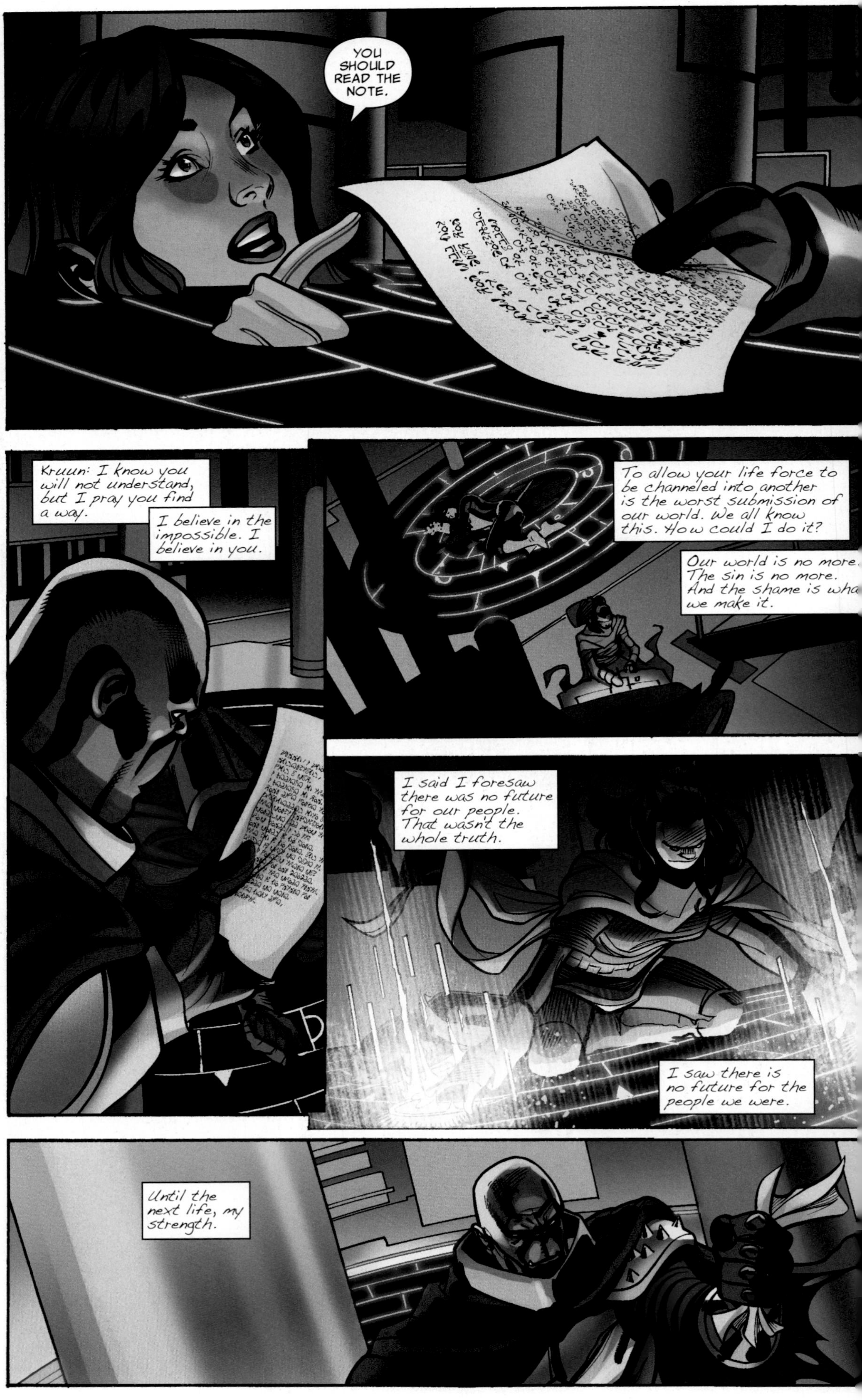
YOU SHOULD READ THE NOTE.
Kruun: I know you will not understand, but I pray you find a way.
I believe in the impossible. I believe in you.
To allow your life force to be channeled into another is the worst submission of our world. We all know this. How could I do it?
Our world is no more. The sin is no more. And the shame is wha we make it.
I said I foresaw there was no future for our people. That wasn't the whole truth.
I saw there is no future for the people we were.
Until the next life, my strength.

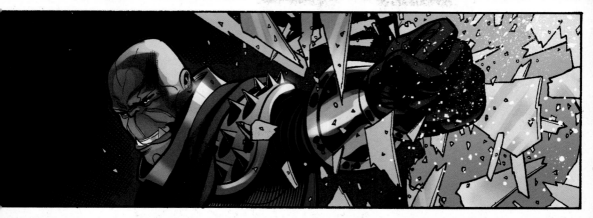

HALEENA. OH, HALEENA. THE ANCIENTS CURSED US JUST BY LETTING US BE BORN.

OH, PRYDE. I WAS WRONG.

KRUUN...

WHAT YOU X-MEN DID WAS NOTHING.

ONLY NOW IS MY WORLD DESTROYED.

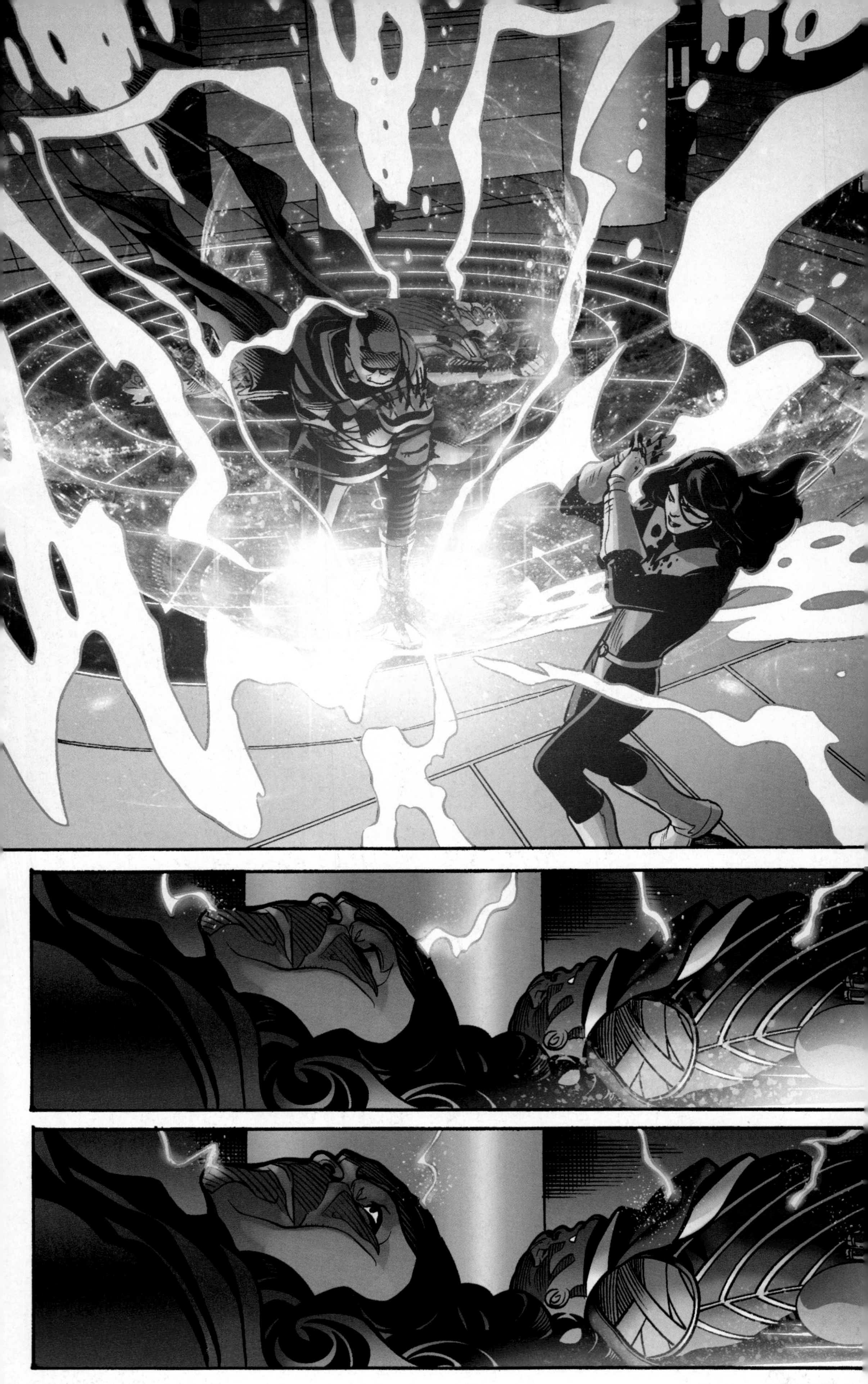

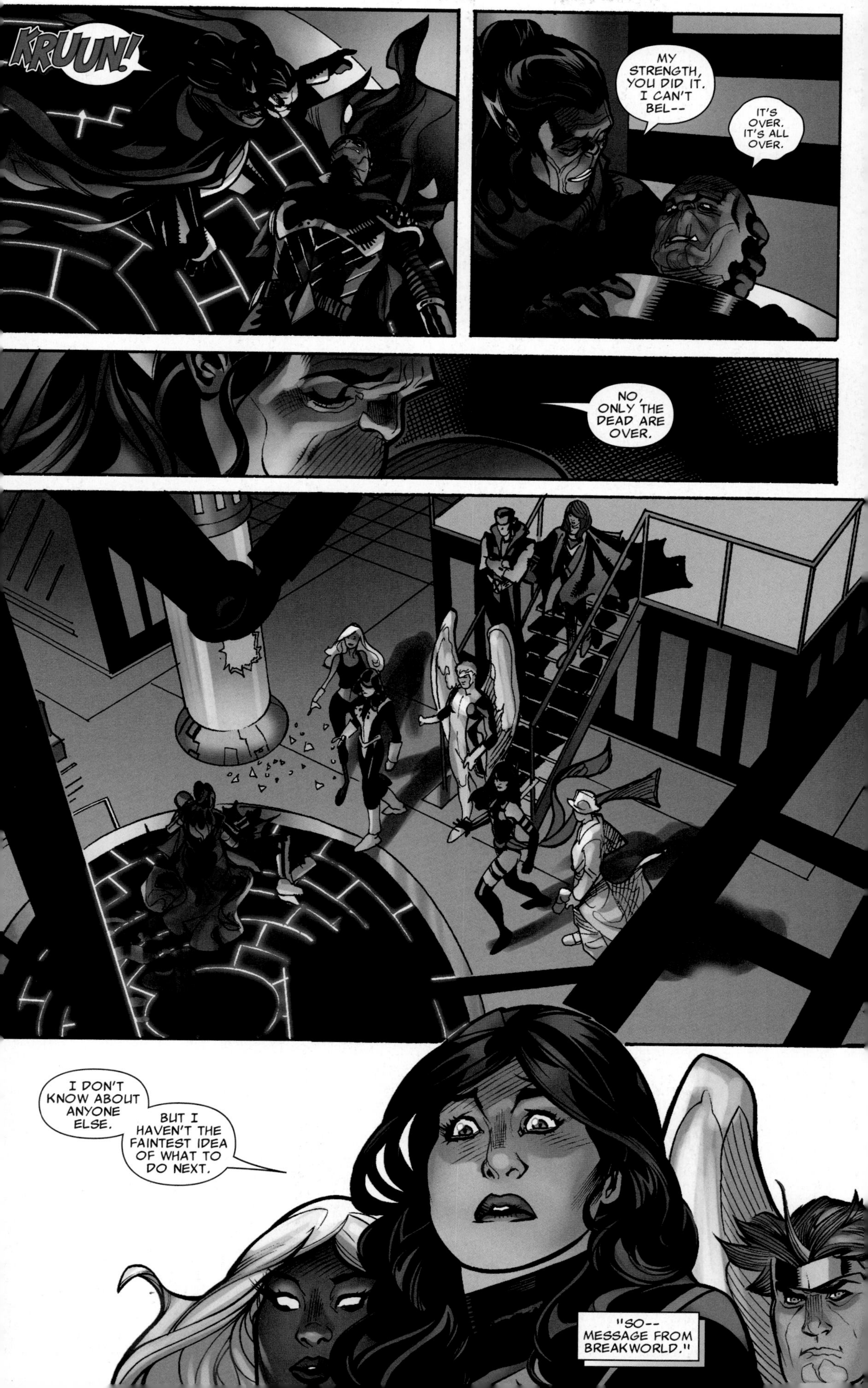
KRUUN!
MY STRENGTH, YOU DID IT. I CAN'T BEL--
IT'S OVER. IT'S ALL OVER.
NO, ONLY THE DEAD ARE OVER.
I DON'T KNOW ABOUT ANYONE ELSE.
BUT I HAVEN'T THE FAINTEST IDEA OF WHAT TO DO NEXT.
"SO-- MESSAGE FROM BREAKWORLD."

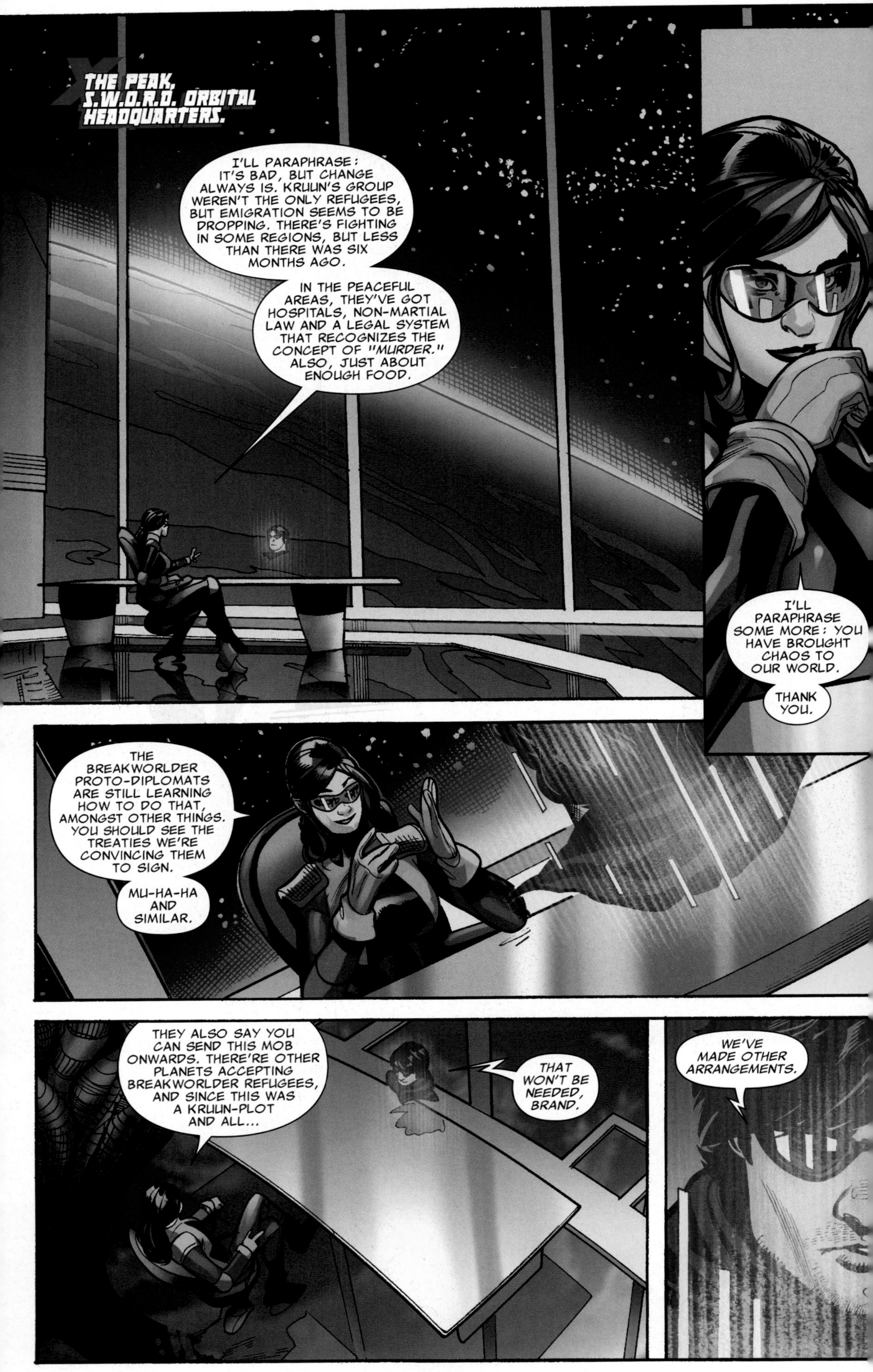
THE PEAK, S.W.O.R.D. ORBITAL HEADQUARTERS.
I'LL PARAPHRASE: IT'S BAD, BUT CHANGE ALWAYS IS. KRUUN'S GROUP WEREN'T THE ONLY REFUGEES, BUT EMIGRATION SEEMS TO BE DROPPING. THERE'S FIGHTING IN SOME REGIONS, BUT LESS THAN THERE WAS SIX MONTHS AGO.
IN THE PEACEFUL AREAS, THEY'VE GOT HOSPITALS, NON-MARTIAL LAW AND A LEGAL SYSTEM THAT RECOGNIZES THE CONCEPT OF "MURDER." ALSO, JUST ABOUT ENOUGH FOOD.
I'LL PARAPHRASE SOME MORE: YOU HAVE BROUGHT CHAOS TO OUR WORLD.
THANK YOU.
THE BREAKWORLDER PROTO-DIPLOMATS ARE STILL LEARNING HOW TO DO THAT, AMONGST OTHER THINGS. YOU SHOULD SEE THE TREATIES WE'RE CONVINCING THEM TO SIGN.
MU-HA-HA AND SIMILAR.
THEY ALSO SAY YOU CAN SEND THIS MOB ONWARDS. THERE'RE OTHER PLANETS ACCEPTING BREAKWORLDER REFUGEES, AND SINCE THIS WAS A KRUUN-PLOT AND ALL...
THAT WON'T BE NEEDED, BRAND.
WE'VE MADE OTHER ARRANGEMENTS.

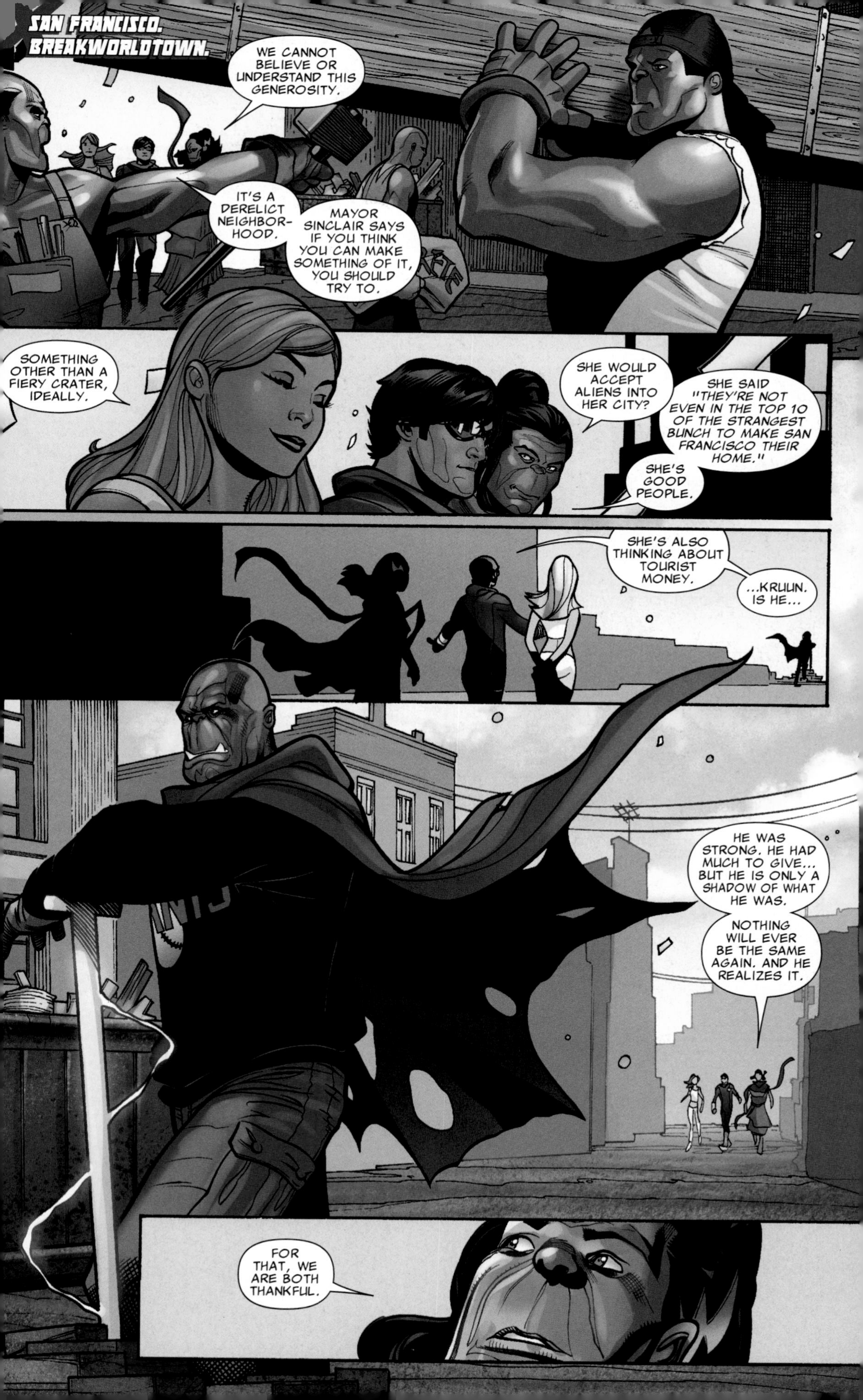
SAN FRANCISCO. BREAKWORLDTOWN.
WE CANNOT BELIEVE OR UNDERSTAND THIS GENEROSITY.
IT'S A DERELICT NEIGHBOR-HOOD.
MAYOR SINCLAIR SAYS IF YOU THINK YOU CAN MAKE SOMETHING OF IT, YOU SHOULD TRY TO.
SOMETHING OTHER THAN A FIERY CRATER, IDEALLY.
SHE WOULD ACCEPT ALIENS INTO HER CITY?
SHE SAID "THEY'RE NOT EVEN IN THE TOP 10 OF THE STRANGEST BUNCH TO MAKE SAN FRANCISCO THEIR HOME."
SHE'S GOOD PEOPLE.
SHE'S ALSO THINKING ABOUT TOURIST MONEY.
...KRUUN. IS HE...
HE WAS STRONG. HE HAD MUCH TO GIVE... BUT HE IS ONLY A SHADOW OF WHAT HE WAS.
NOTHING WILL EVER BE THE SAME AGAIN. AND HE REALIZES IT.
FOR THAT, WE ARE BOTH THANKFUL.

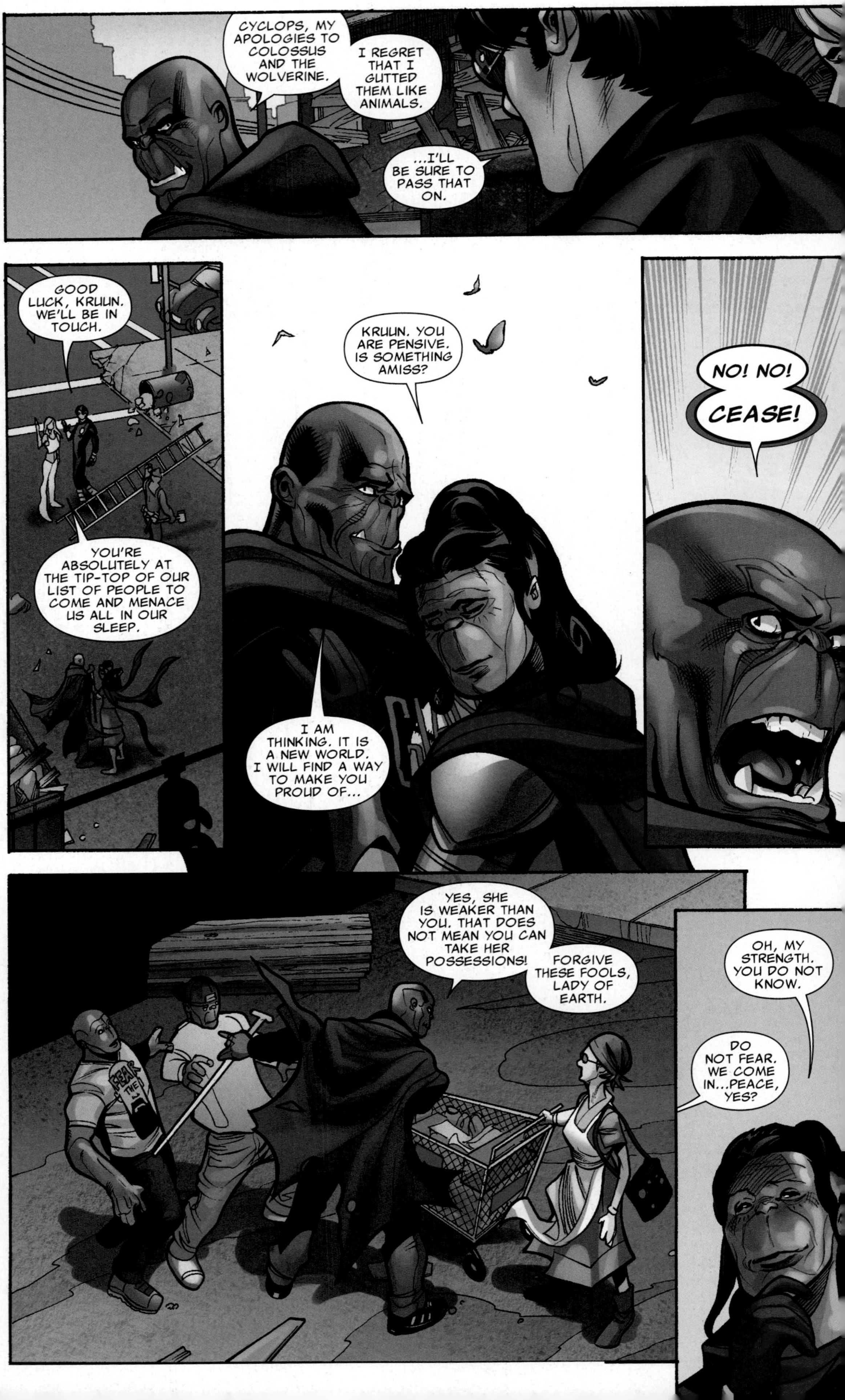
CYCLOPS, MY APOLOGIES TO COLOSSUS AND THE WOLVERINE.
I REGRET THAT I GUTTED THEM LIKE ANIMALS.
...I'LL BE SURE TO PASS THAT ON.
GOOD LUCK, KRUUN. WE'LL BE IN TOUCH.
YOU'RE ABSOLUTELY AT THE TIP-TOP OF OUR LIST OF PEOPLE TO COME AND MENACE US ALL IN OUR SLEEP.
KRUUN. YOU ARE PENSIVE. IS SOMETHING AMISS?
I AM THINKING. IT IS A NEW WORLD. I WILL FIND A WAY TO MAKE YOU PROUD OF...
NO! NO!
CEASE!
YES, SHE IS WEAKER THAN YOU. THAT DOES NOT MEAN YOU CAN TAKE HER POSSESSIONS!
FORGIVE THESE FOOLS, LADY OF EARTH.
OH, MY STRENGTH. YOU DO NOT KNOW.
DO NOT FEAR. WE COME IN...PEACE, YES?

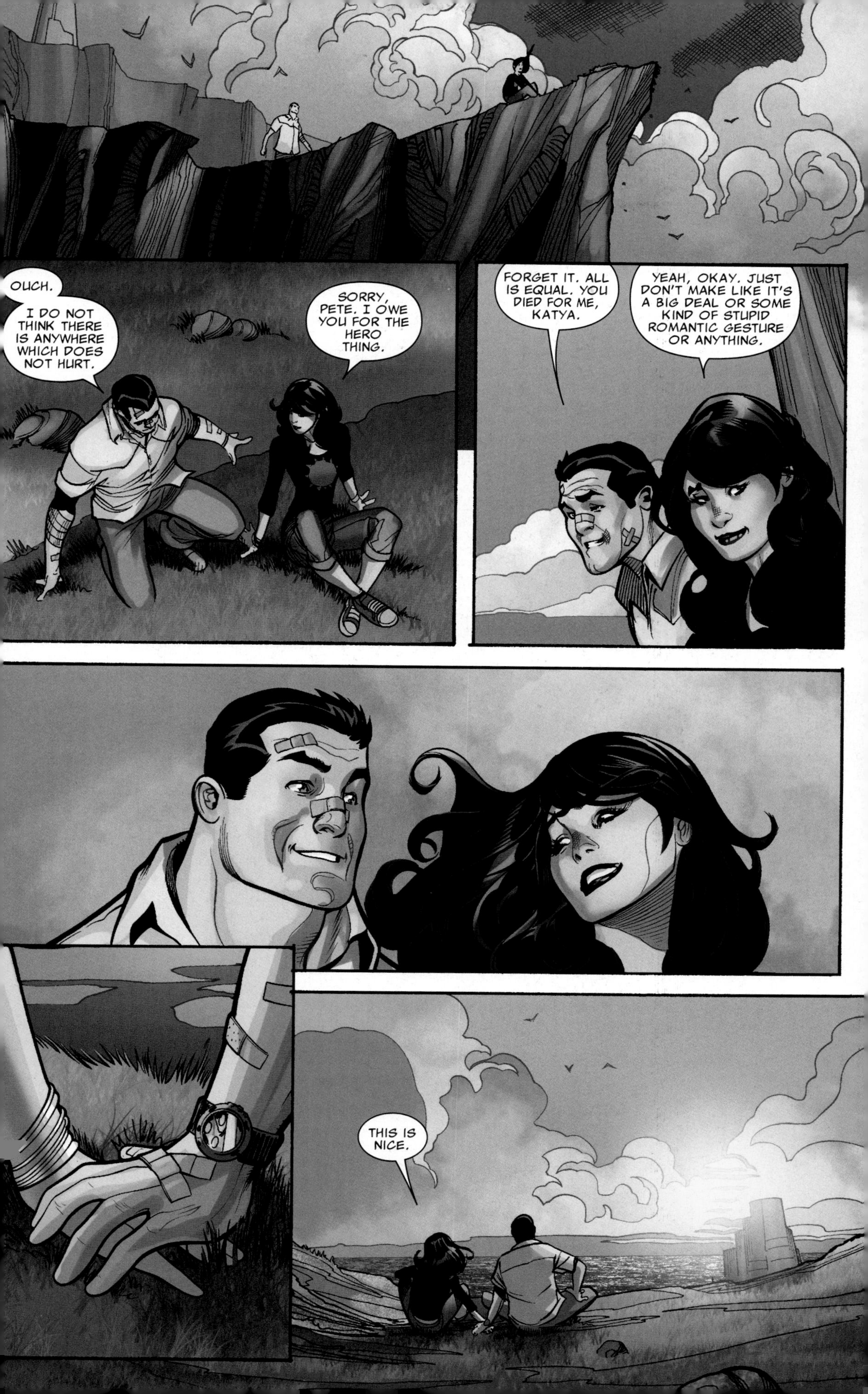
OUCH.
I DO NOT THINK THERE IS ANYWHERE WHICH DOES NOT HURT.
SORRY, PETE. I OWE YOU FOR THE HERO THING.
FORGET IT. ALL IS EQUAL. YOU DIED FOR ME, KATYA.
YEAH, OKAY. JUST DON'T MAKE LIKE IT'S A BIG DEAL OR SOME KIND OF STUPID ROMANTIC GESTURE OR ANYTHING.
THIS IS NICE.

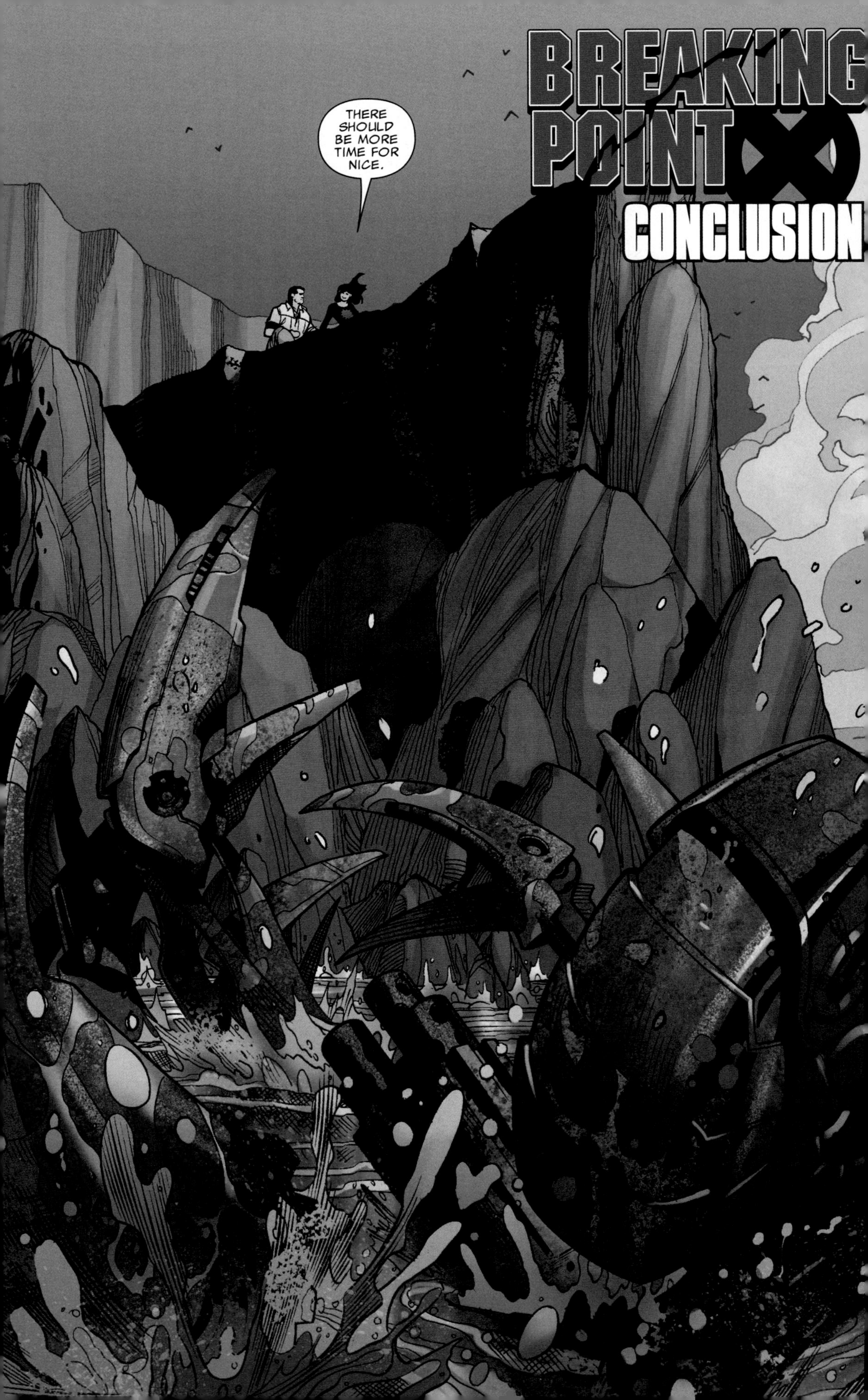
THERE SHOULD BE MORE TIME FOR NICE.
BREAKING POINT
CONCLUSION

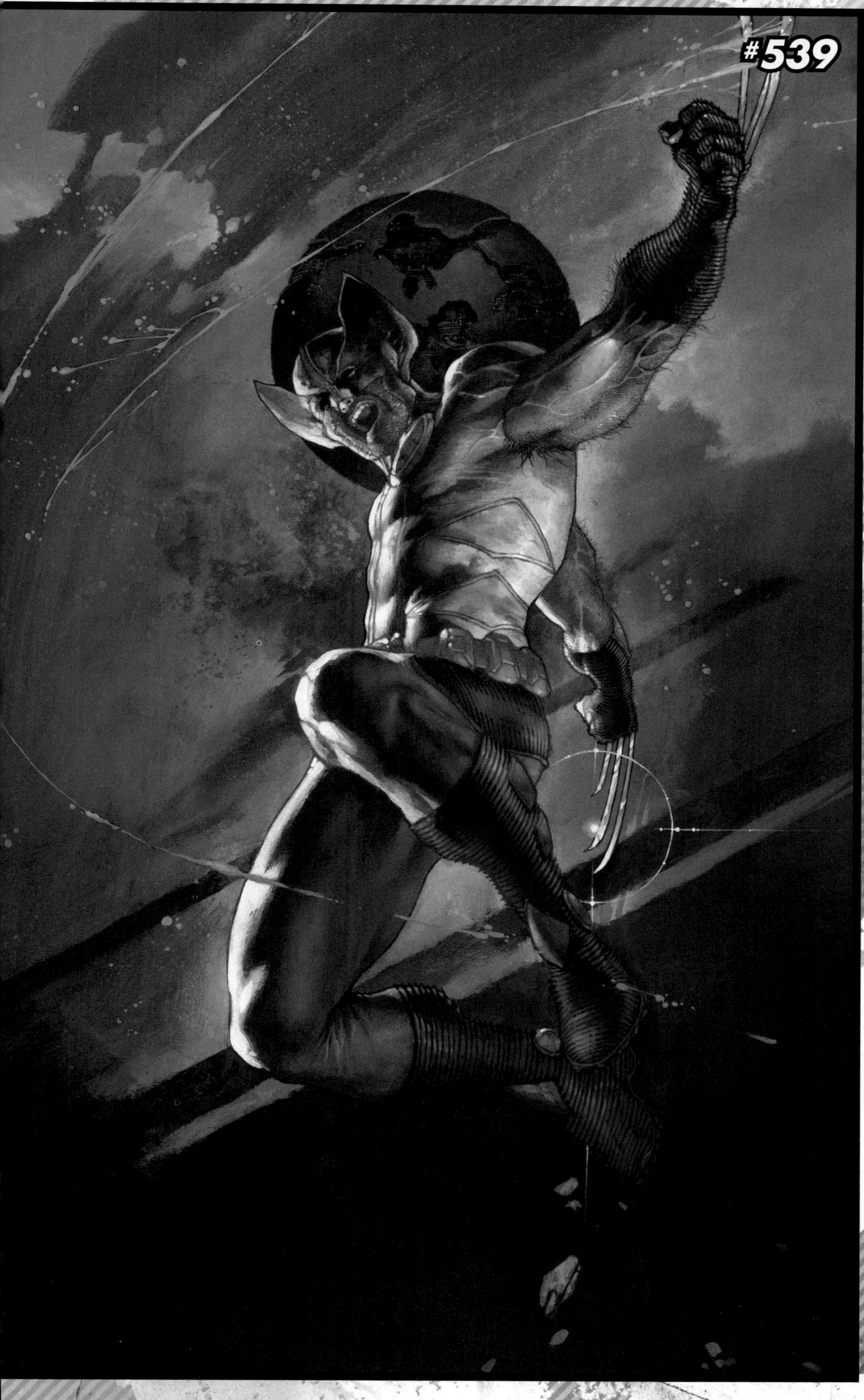
#539

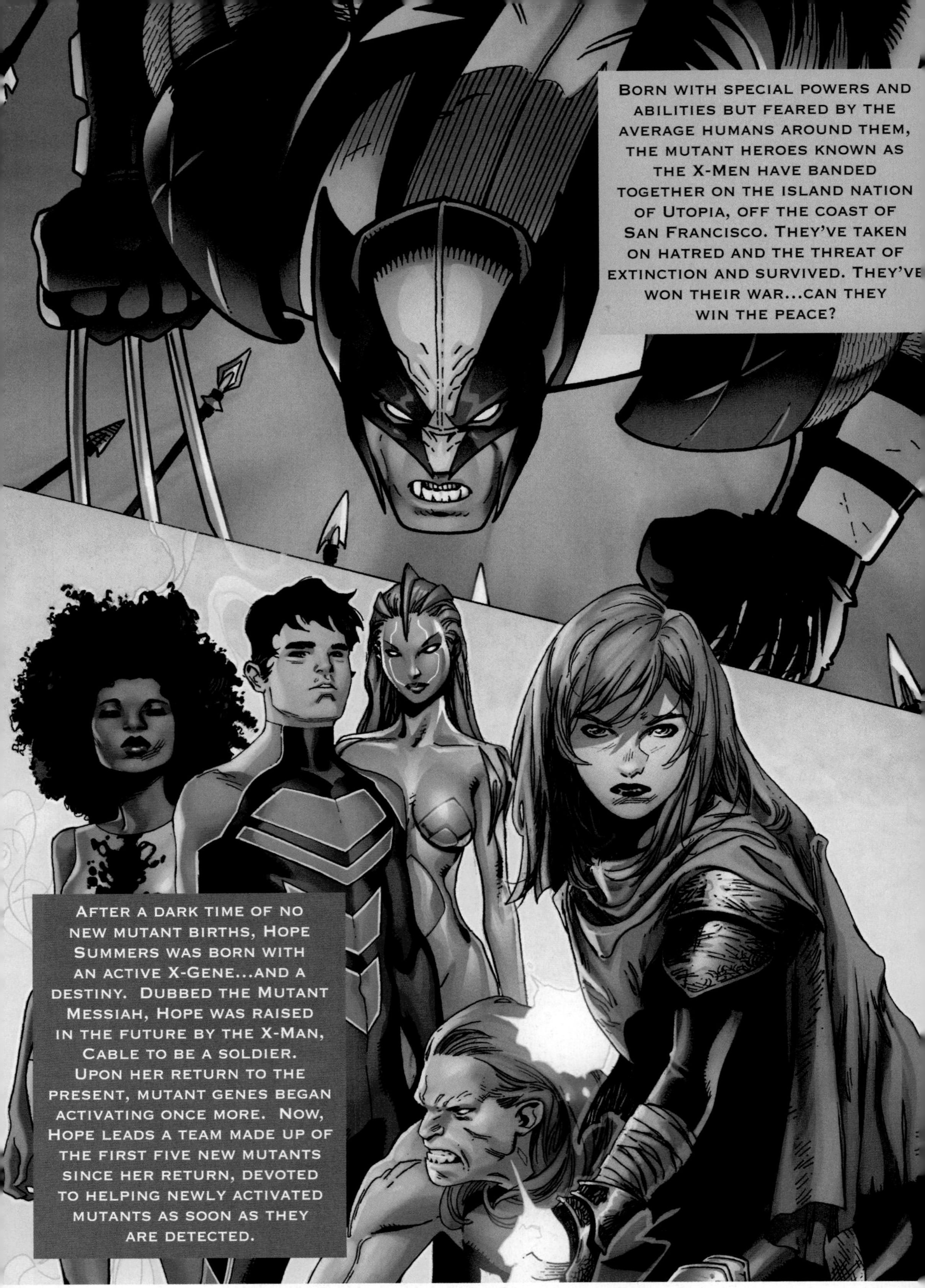
Born with special powers and abilities but feared by the average humans around them, the mutant heroes known as the X-Men have banded together on the island nation of Utopia, off the coast of San Francisco. They've taken on hatred and the threat of extinction and survived. They've won their war...can they win the peace?
After a dark time of no new mutant births, Hope Summers was born with an active X-Gene...and a destiny. Dubbed the Mutant Messiah, Hope was raised in the future by the X-Man, Cable to be a soldier. Upon her return to the present, mutant genes began activating once more. Now, Hope leads a team made up of the first five new mutants since her return, devoted to helping newly activated mutants as soon as they are detected.

LOSING HOPE

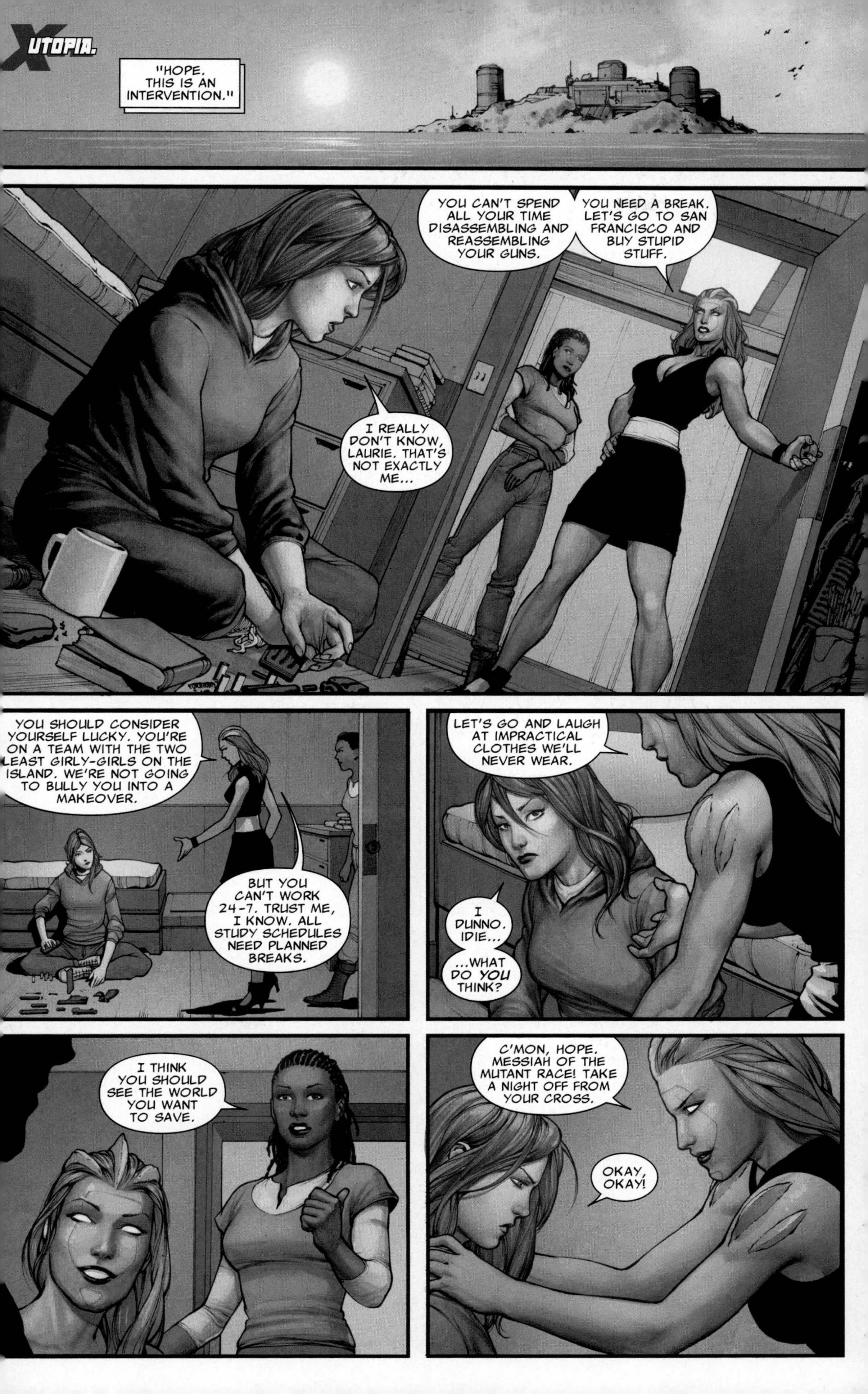
UTOPIA.
"HOPE. THIS IS AN INTERVENTION."
YOU CAN'T SPEND ALL YOUR TIME DISASSEMBLING AND REASSEMBLING YOUR GUNS.
YOU NEED A BREAK. LET'S GO TO SAN FRANCISCO AND BUY STUPID STUFF.
I REALLY DON'T KNOW, LAURIE. THAT'S NOT EXACTLY ME...
YOU SHOULD CONSIDER YOURSELF LUCKY. YOU'RE ON A TEAM WITH THE TWO LEAST GIRLY-GIRLS ON THE ISLAND. WE'RE NOT GOING TO BULLY YOU INTO A MAKEOVER.
BUT YOU CAN'T WORK 24-7. TRUST ME, I KNOW. ALL STUDY SCHEDULES NEED PLANNED BREAKS.
LET'S GO AND LAUGH AT IMPRACTICAL CLOTHES WE'LL NEVER WEAR.
I DUNNO. IDIE...
...WHAT DO *YOU* THINK?
I THINK YOU SHOULD SEE THE WORLD YOU WANT TO SAVE.
C'MON, HOPE. MESSIAH OF THE MUTANT RACE! TAKE A NIGHT OFF FROM YOUR CROSS.
OKAY, OKAY!

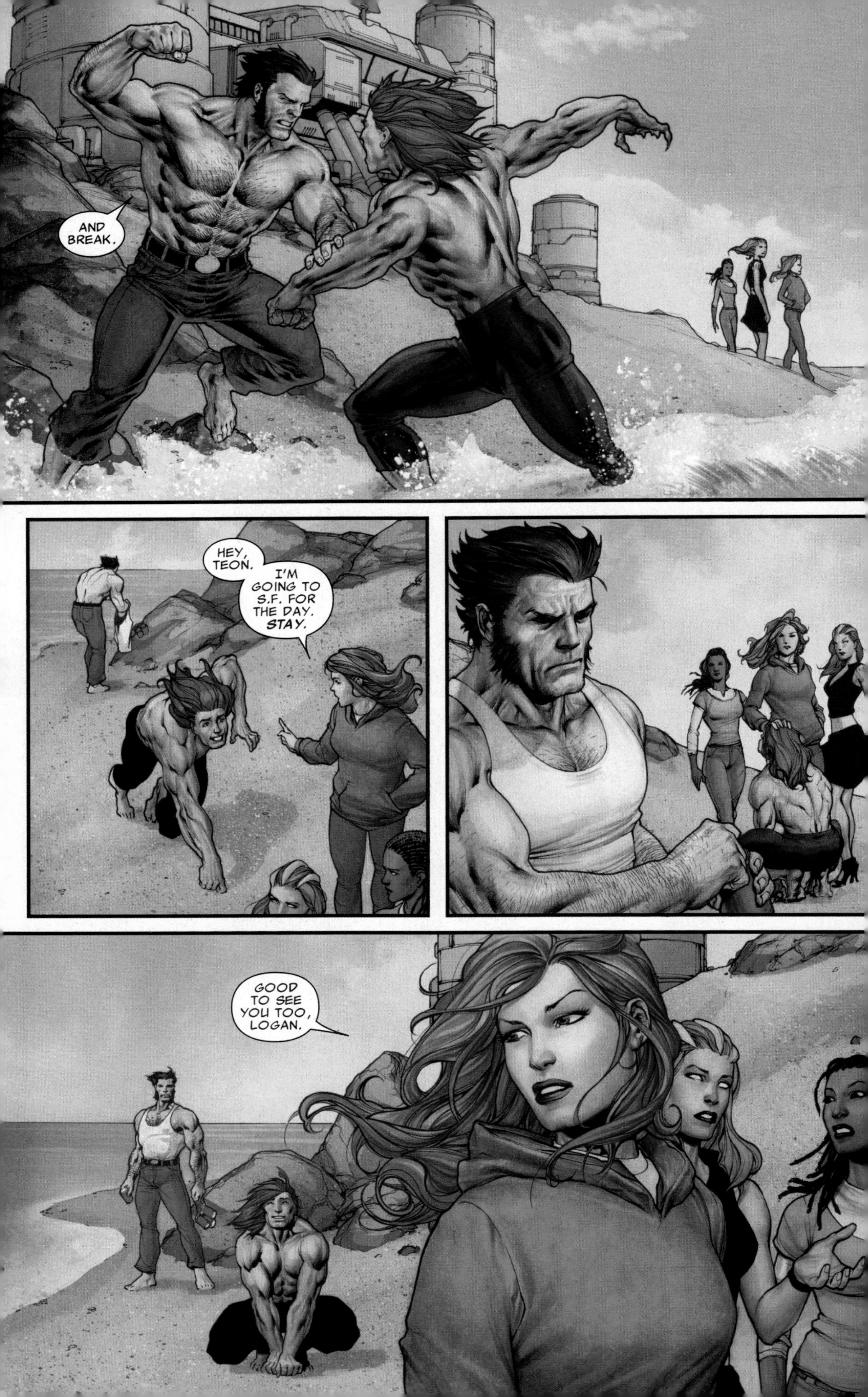
AND BREAK.
HEY, TEON.
I'M GOING TO S.F. FOR THE DAY. STAY.
GOOD TO SEE YOU TOO, LOGAN.

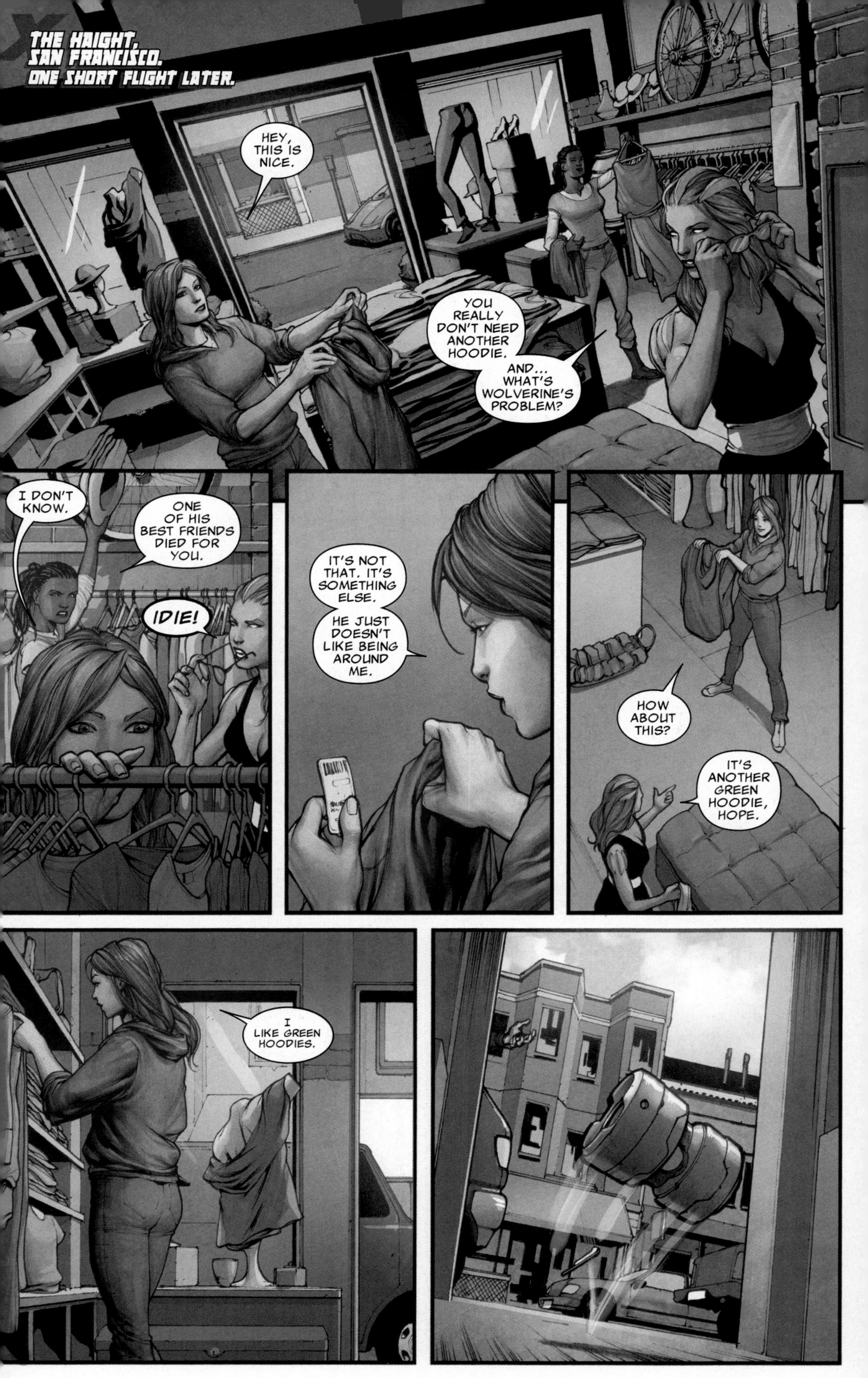
THE HAIGHT, SAN FRANCISCO. ONE SHORT FLIGHT LATER.
HEY, THIS IS NICE.
YOU REALLY DON'T NEED ANOTHER HOODIE.
AND... WHAT'S WOLVERINE'S PROBLEM?
I DON'T KNOW.
ONE OF HIS BEST FRIENDS DIED FOR YOU.
IDIE!
IT'S NOT THAT. IT'S SOMETHING ELSE.
HE JUST DOESN'T LIKE BEING AROUND ME.
HOW ABOUT THIS?
IT'S ANOTHER GREEN HOODIE, HOPE.
I LIKE GREEN HOODIES.

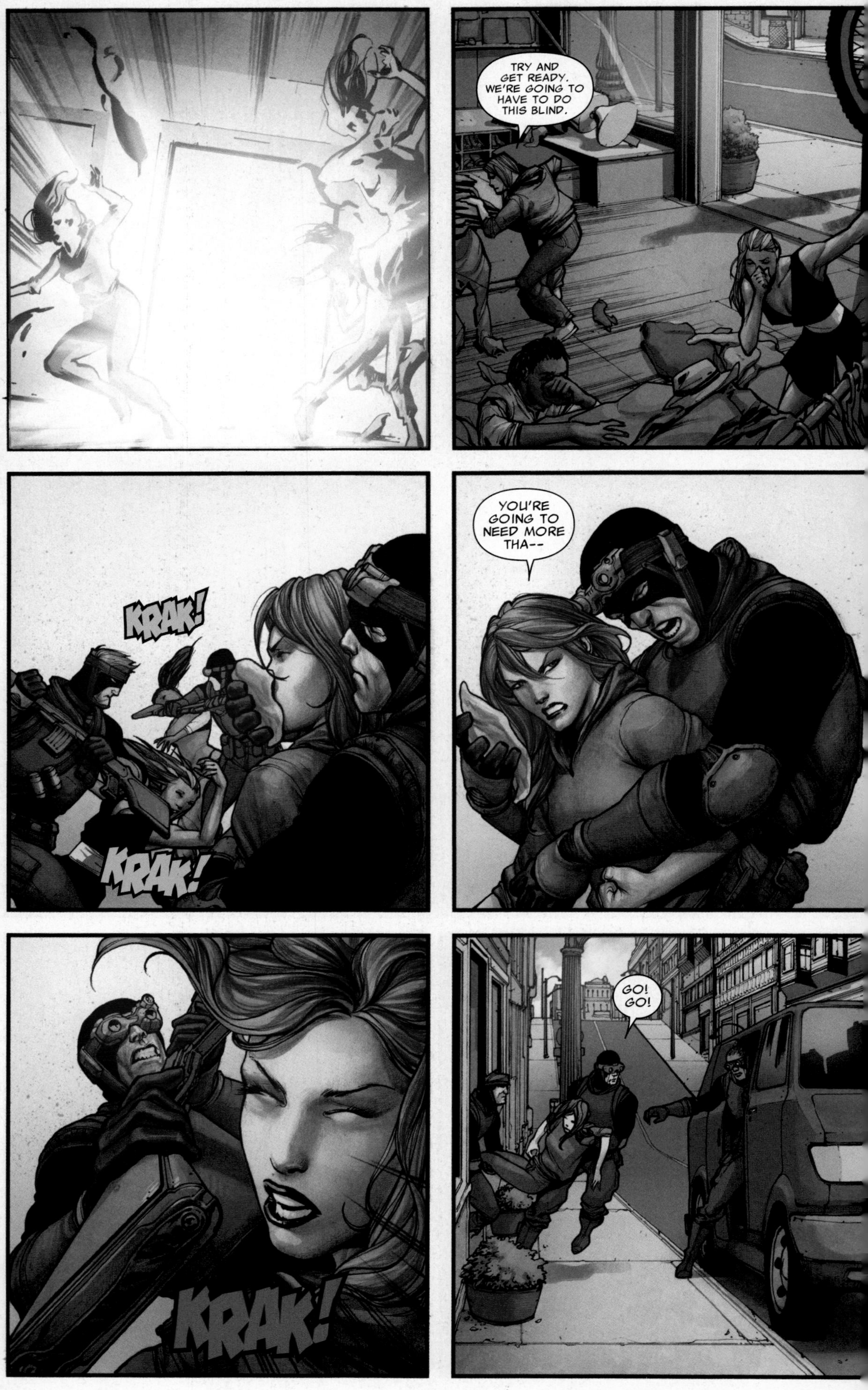
TRY AND GET READY. WE'RE GOING TO HAVE TO DO THIS BLIND.
KRAK!
KRAK!
YOU'RE GOING TO NEED MORE THA--
KRAK!
GO! GO!

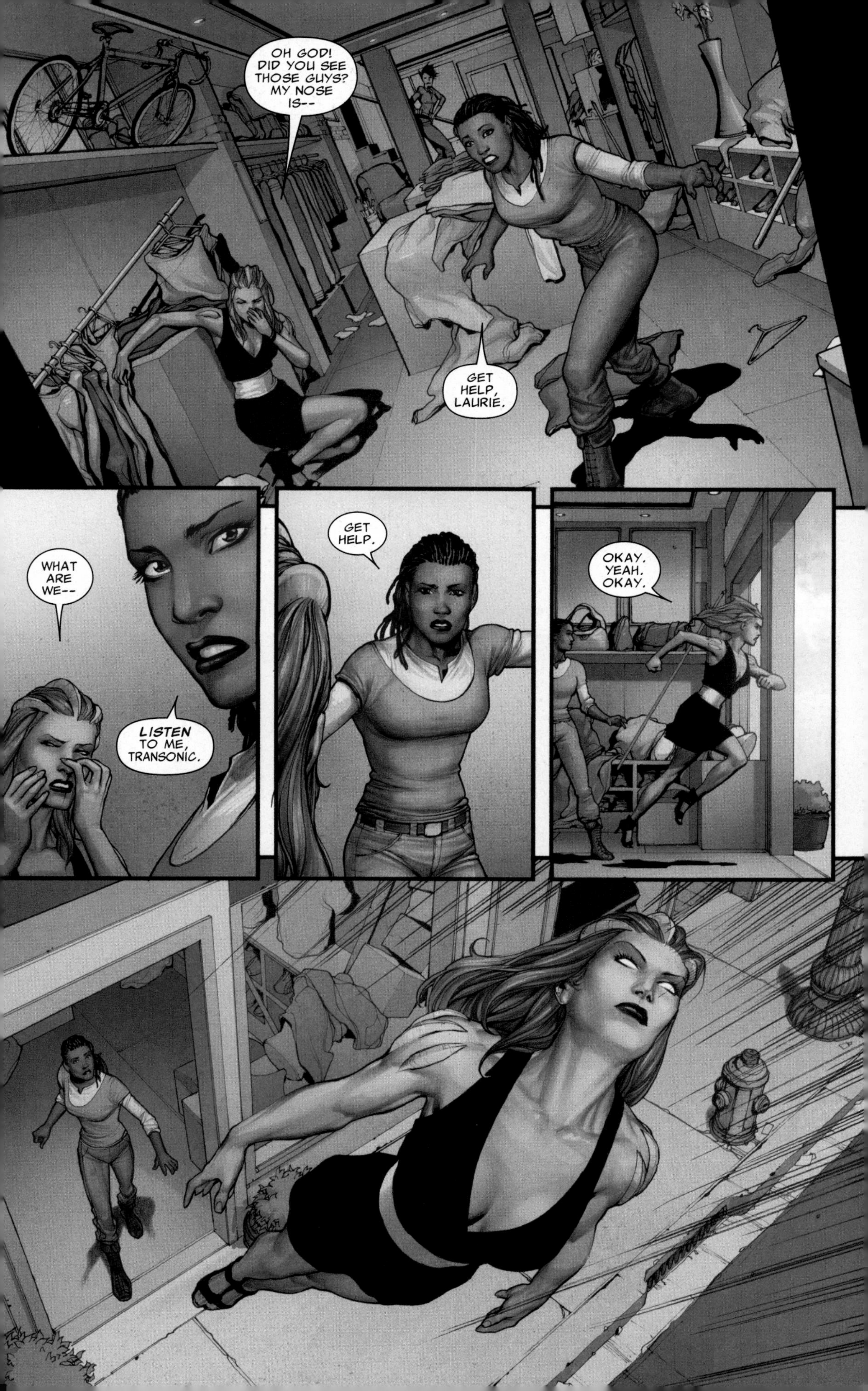
OH GOD! DID YOU SEE THOSE GUYS? MY NOSE IS--
GET HELP, LAURIE.
WHAT ARE WE--
LISTEN TO ME, TRANSONIC.
GET HELP.
OKAY. YEAH. OKAY.

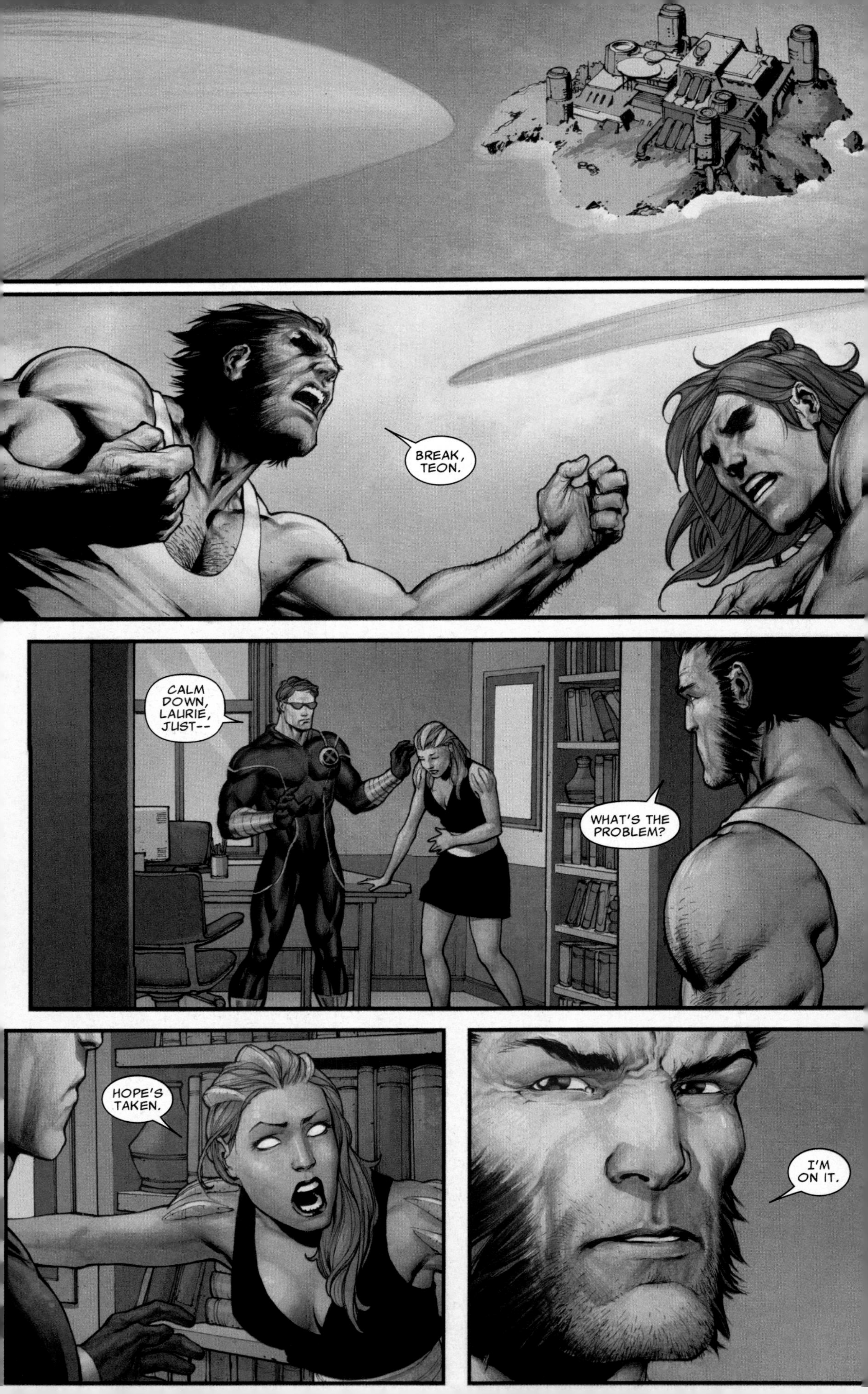
BREAK, TEON.
CALM DOWN, LAURIE, JUST--
WHAT'S THE PROBLEM?
HOPE'S TAKEN.
I'M ON IT.

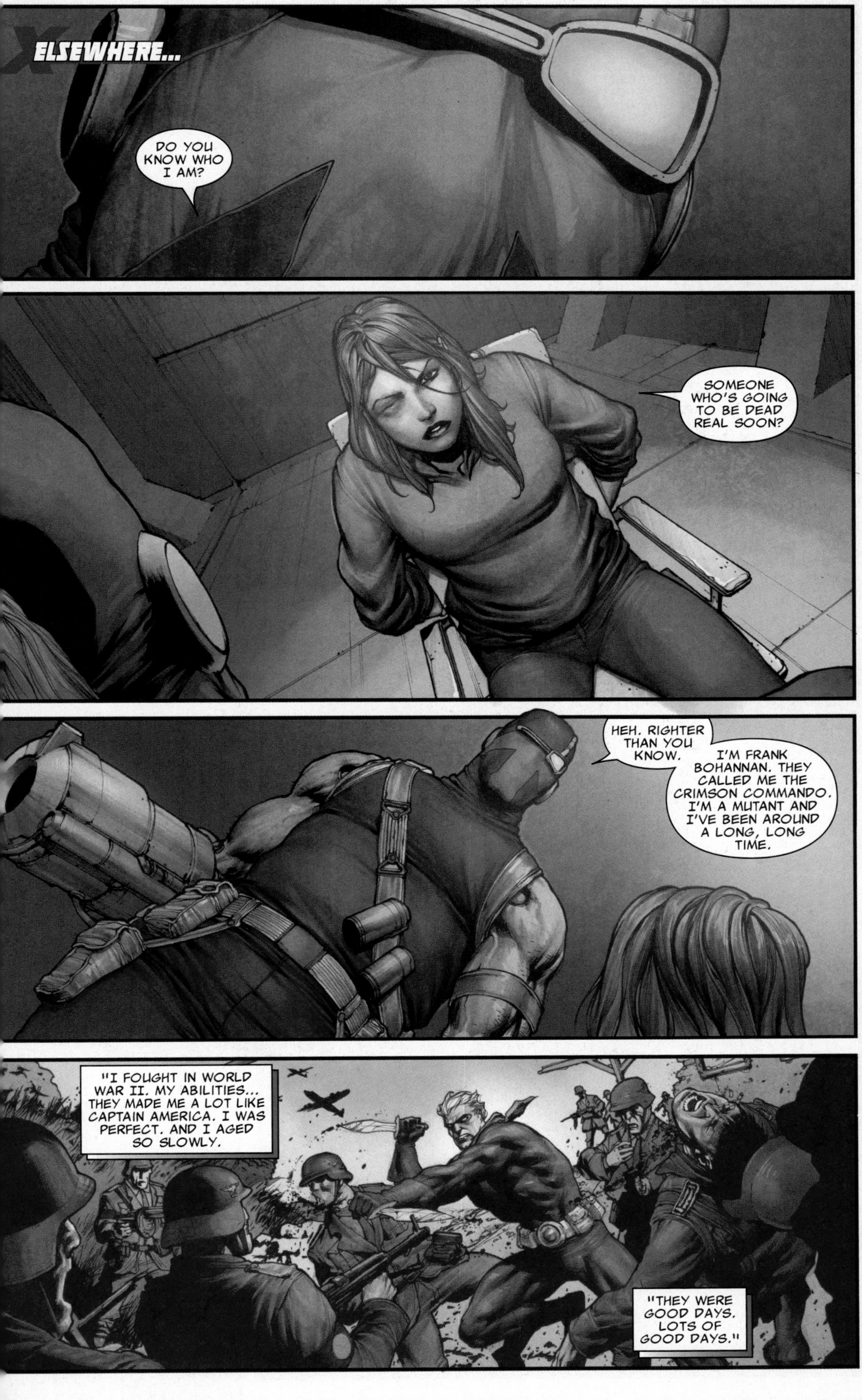
ELSEWHERE...
DO YOU KNOW WHO I AM?
SOMEONE WHO'S GOING TO BE DEAD REAL SOON?
HEH. RIGHTER THAN YOU KNOW.
I'M FRANK BOHANNAN. THEY CALLED ME THE CRIMSON COMMANDO. I'M A MUTANT AND I'VE BEEN AROUND A LONG, LONG TIME.
"I FOUGHT IN WORLD WAR II. MY ABILITIES... THEY MADE ME A LOT LIKE CAPTAIN AMERICA. I WAS PERFECT. AND I AGED SO SLOWLY.
"THEY WERE GOOD DAYS. LOTS OF GOOD DAYS."

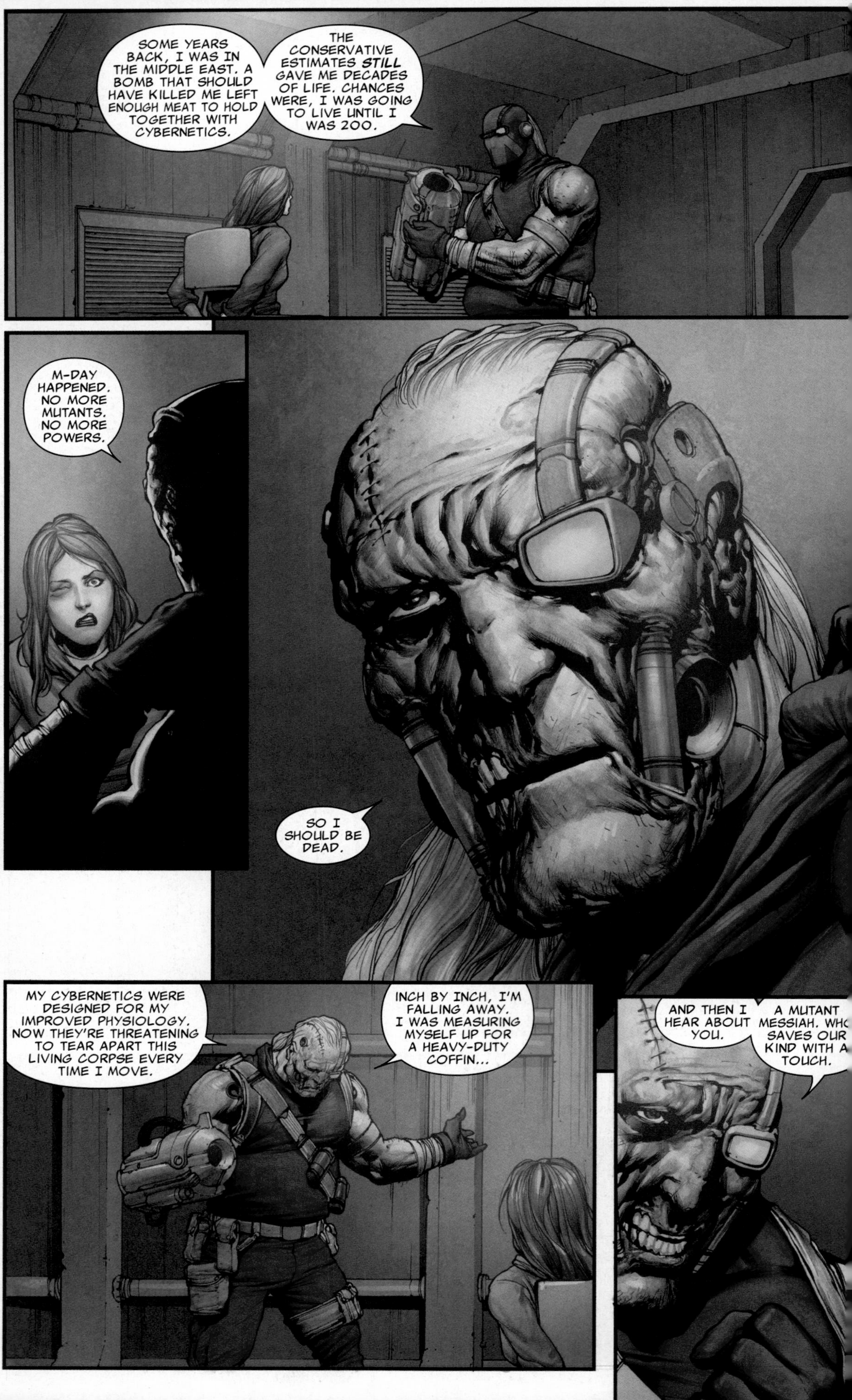
SOME YEARS BACK, I WAS IN THE MIDDLE EAST. A BOMB THAT SHOULD HAVE KILLED ME LEFT ENOUGH MEAT TO HOLD TOGETHER WITH CYBERNETICS.
THE CONSERVATIVE ESTIMATES STILL GAVE ME DECADES OF LIFE. CHANCES WERE, I WAS GOING TO LIVE UNTIL I WAS 200.
M-DAY HAPPENED. NO MORE MUTANTS. NO MORE POWERS.
SO I SHOULD BE DEAD.
MY CYBERNETICS WERE DESIGNED FOR MY IMPROVED PHYSIOLOGY. NOW THEY'RE THREATENING TO TEAR APART THIS LIVING CORPSE EVERY TIME I MOVE.
INCH BY INCH, I'M FALLING AWAY. I WAS MEASURING MYSELF UP FOR A HEAVY-DUTY COFFIN...
AND THEN I HEAR ABOUT YOU.

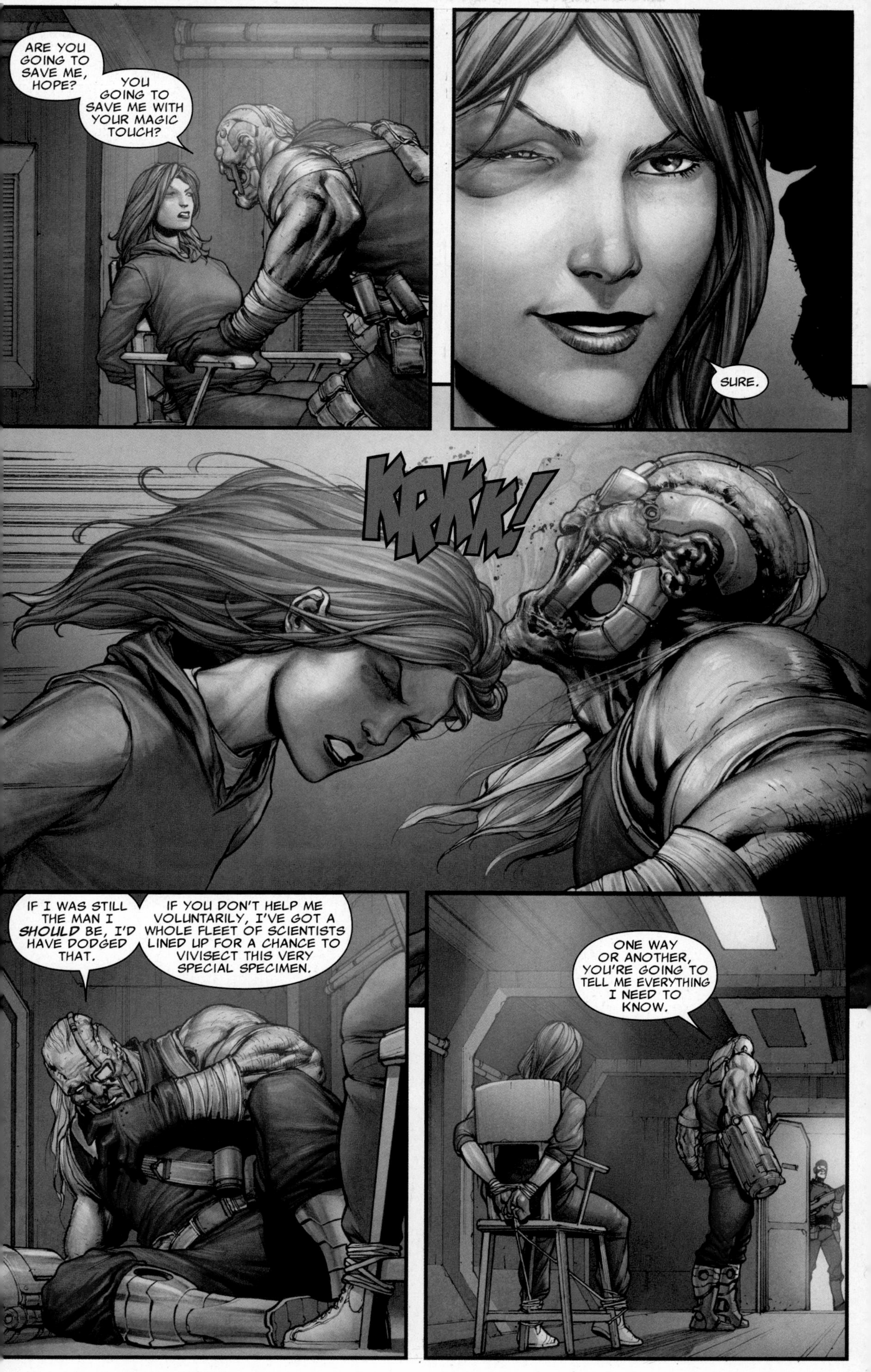
ARE YOU GOING TO SAVE ME, HOPE?
YOU GOING TO SAVE ME WITH YOUR MAGIC TOUCH?
SURE.
KRKK!
IF I WAS STILL THE MAN I SHOULD BE, I'D HAVE DODGED THAT.
IF YOU DON'T HELP ME VOLUNTARILY, I'VE GOT A WHOLE FLEET OF SCIENTISTS LINED UP FOR A CHANCE TO VIVISECT THIS VERY SPECIAL SPECIMEN.
ONE WAY OR ANOTHER, YOU'RE GOING TO TELL ME EVERYTHING I NEED TO KNOW.

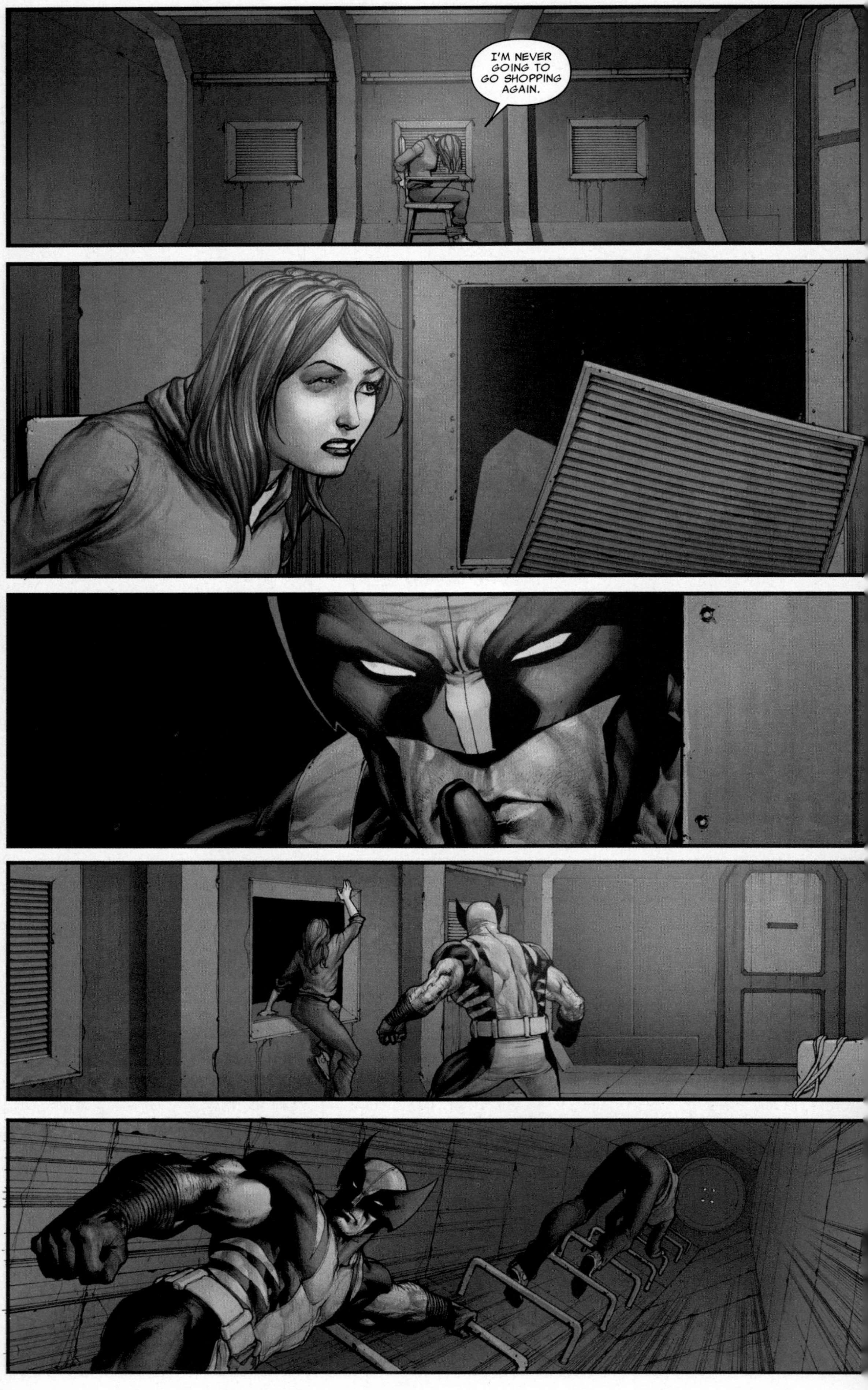
I'M NEVER GOING TO GO SHOPPING AGAIN.

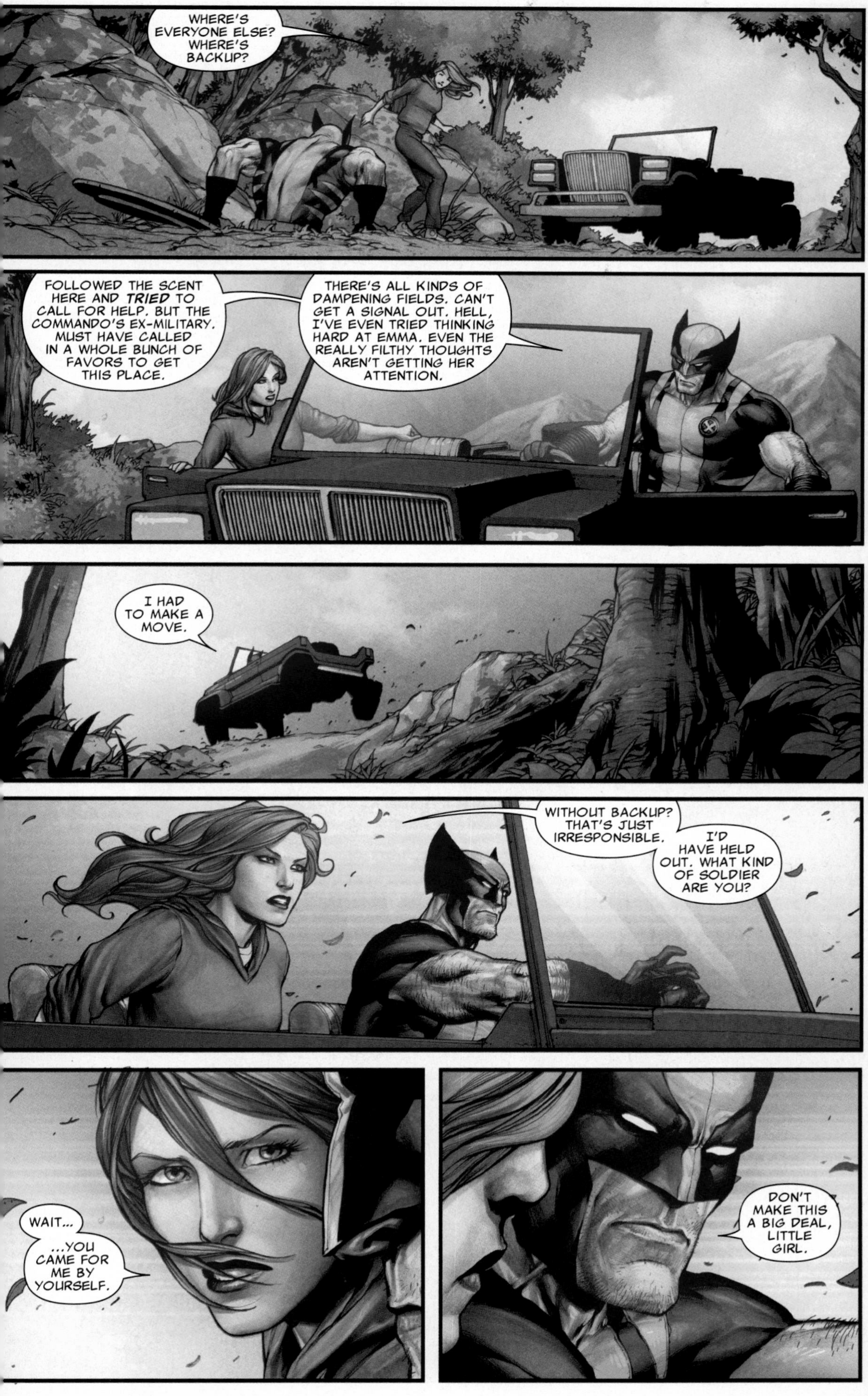
WHERE'S EVERYONE ELSE? WHERE'S BACKUP?
FOLLOWED THE SCENT HERE AND TRIED TO CALL FOR HELP. BUT THE COMMANDO'S EX-MILITARY. MUST HAVE CALLED IN A WHOLE BUNCH OF FAVORS TO GET THIS PLACE.
THERE'S ALL KINDS OF DAMPENING FIELDS. CAN'T GET A SIGNAL OUT. HELL, I'VE EVEN TRIED THINKING HARD AT EMMA. EVEN THE REALLY FILTHY THOUGHTS AREN'T GETTING HER ATTENTION.
I HAD TO MAKE A MOVE.
WITHOUT BACKUP? THAT'S JUST IRRESPONSIBLE.
I'D HAVE HELD OUT. WHAT KIND OF SOLDIER ARE YOU?
WAIT...
...YOU CAME FOR ME BY YOURSELF.
DON'T MAKE THIS A BIG DEAL, LITTLE GIRL.

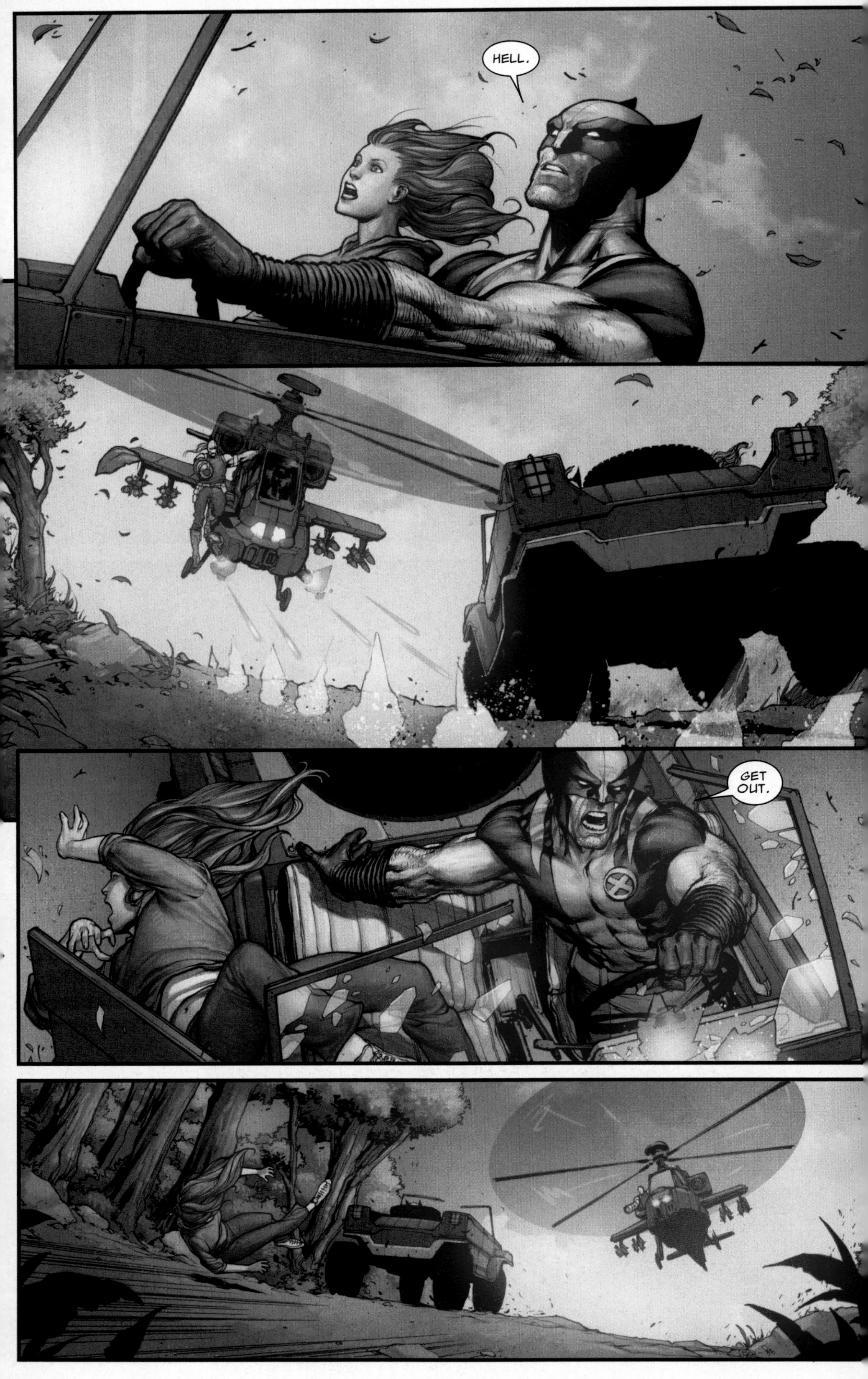
HELL.
GET OUT.

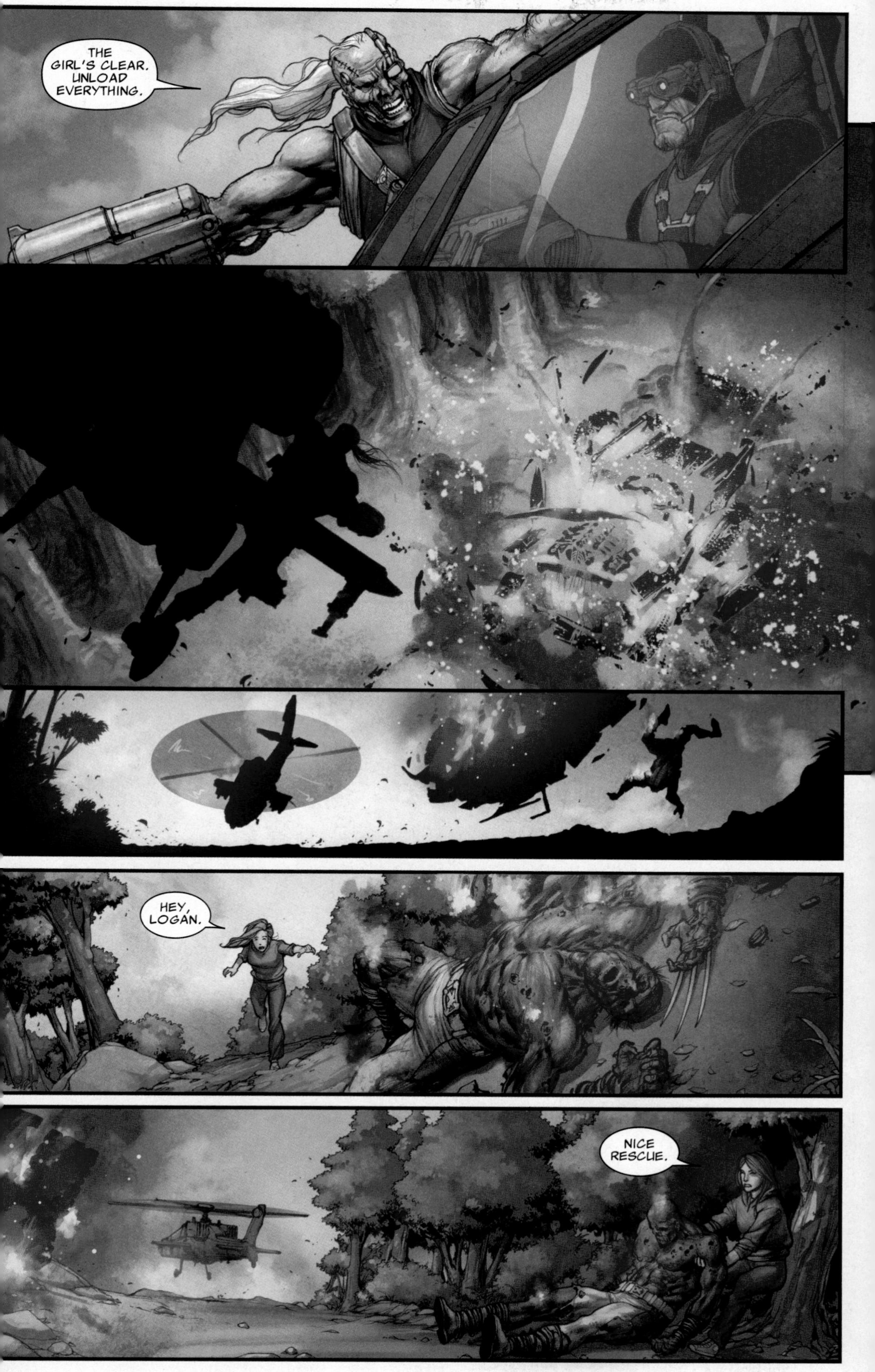
THE GIRL'S CLEAR. UNLOAD EVERYTHING.
HEY, LOGAN.
NICE RESCUE.

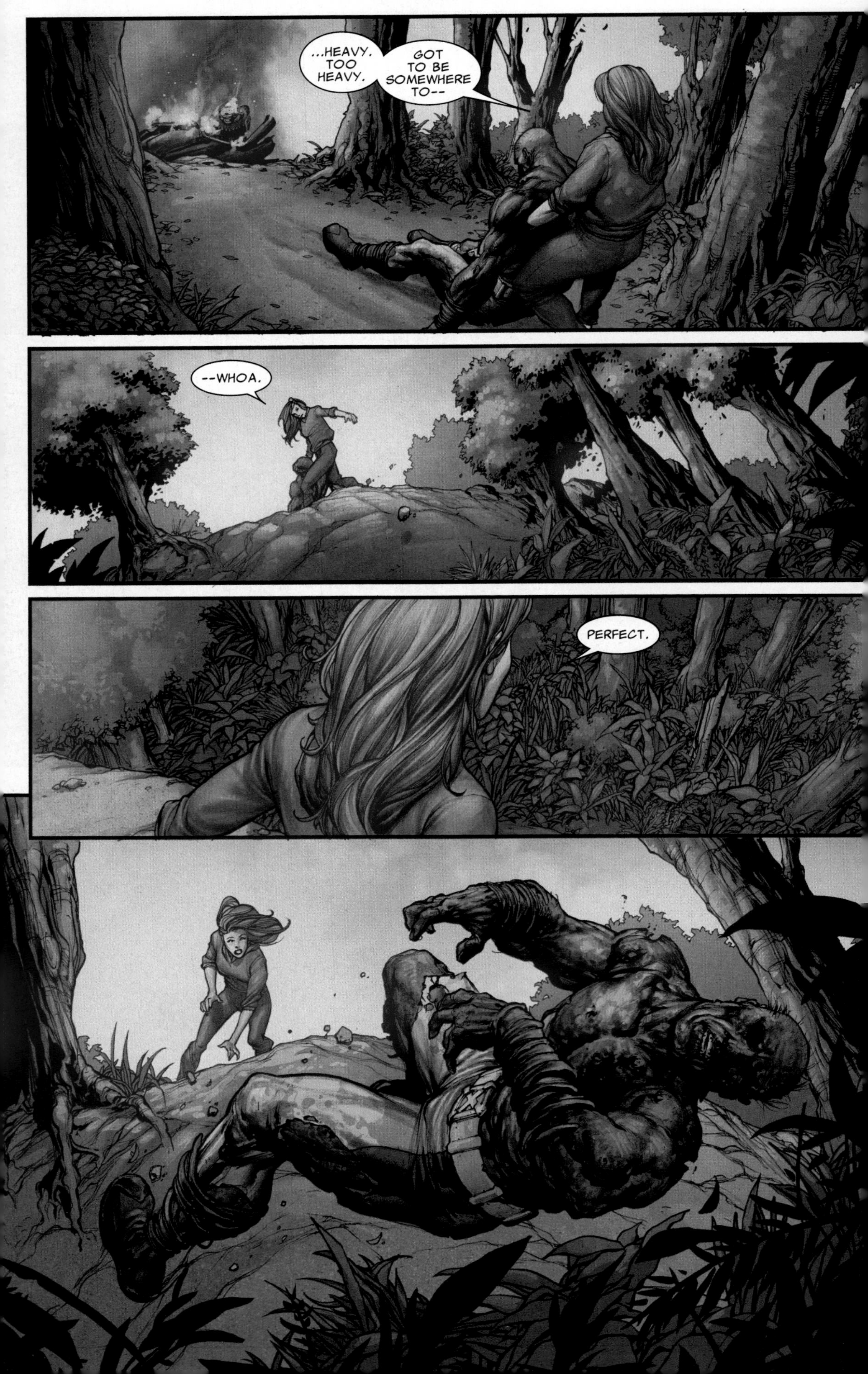
...HEAVY. TOO HEAVY.
GOT TO BE SOMEWHERE TO--
--WHOA.
PERFECT.

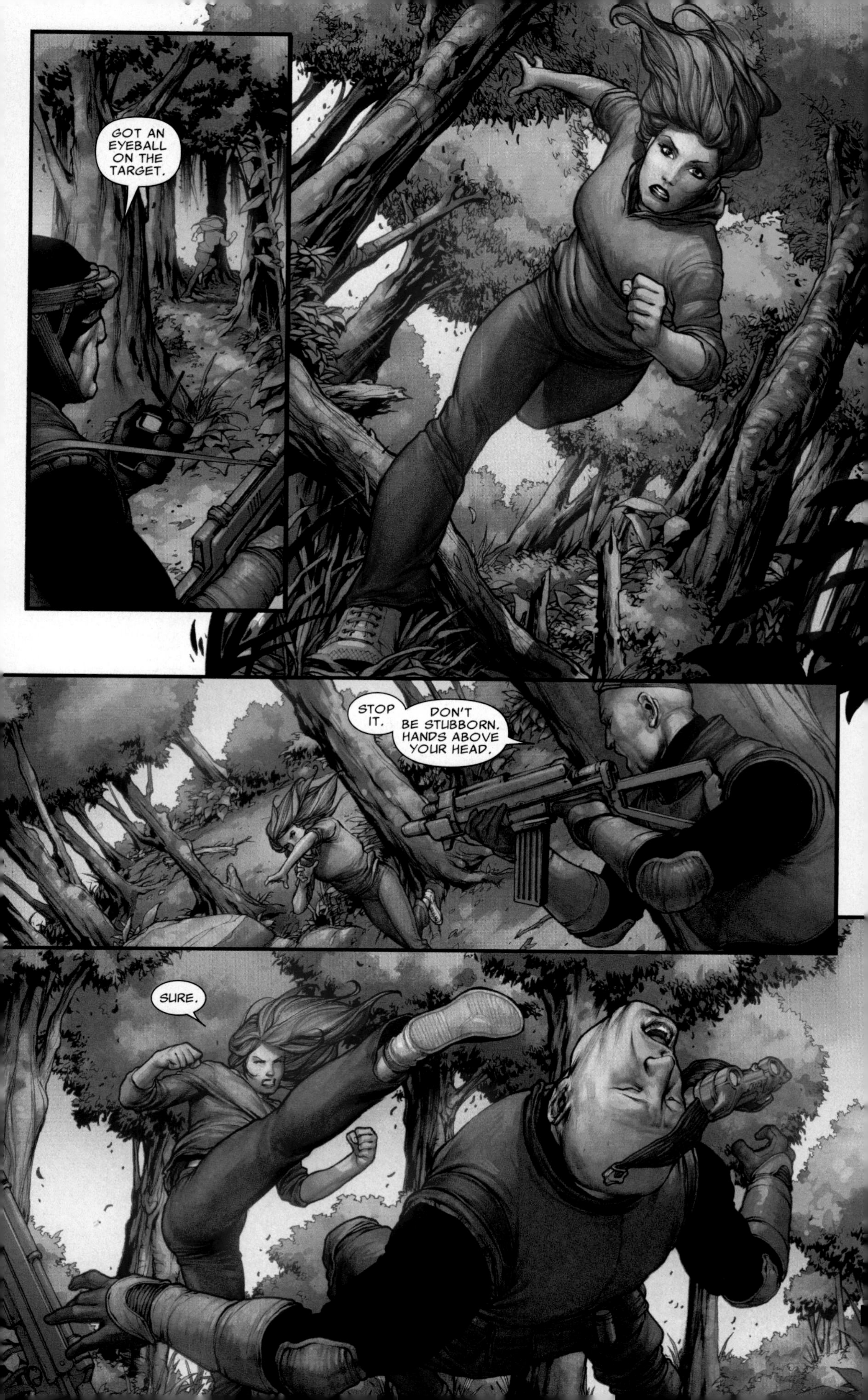
GOT AN EYEBALL ON THE TARGET.
STOP IT.
DON'T BE STUBBORN. HANDS ABOVE YOUR HEAD.
SURE.

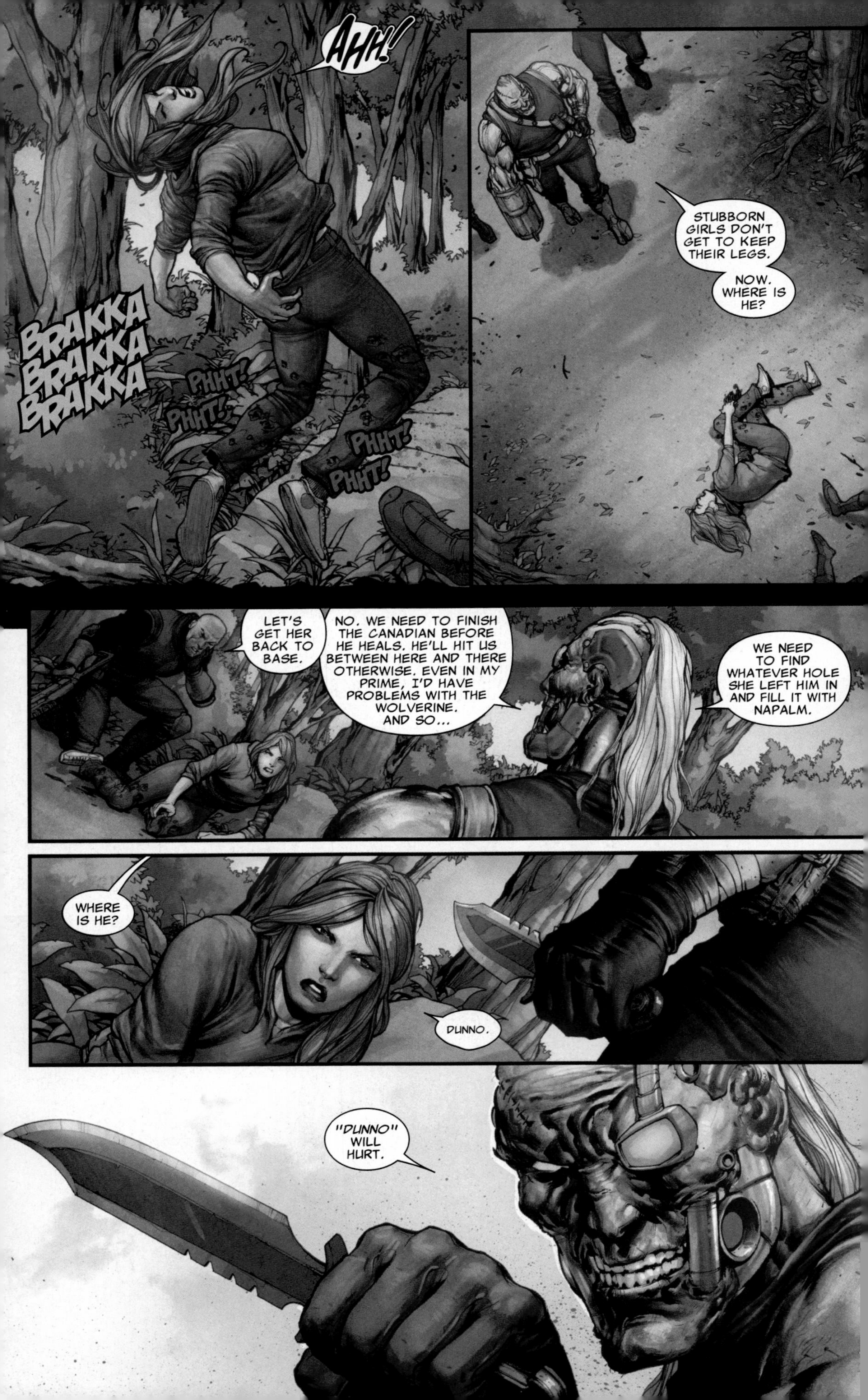
AHH!
BRAKKA BRAKKA BRAKKA
PHHT! PHHT!
PHHT! PHHT!
STUBBORN GIRLS DON'T GET TO KEEP THEIR LEGS.
NOW. WHERE IS HE?
LET'S GET HER BACK TO BASE.
NO. WE NEED TO FINISH THE CANADIAN BEFORE HE HEALS. HE'LL HIT US BETWEEN HERE AND THERE OTHERWISE. EVEN IN MY PRIME, I'D HAVE PROBLEMS WITH THE WOLVERINE. AND SO...
WE NEED TO FIND WHATEVER HOLE SHE LEFT HIM IN AND FILL IT WITH NAPALM.
WHERE IS HE?
DUNNO.
"DUNNO" WILL HURT.

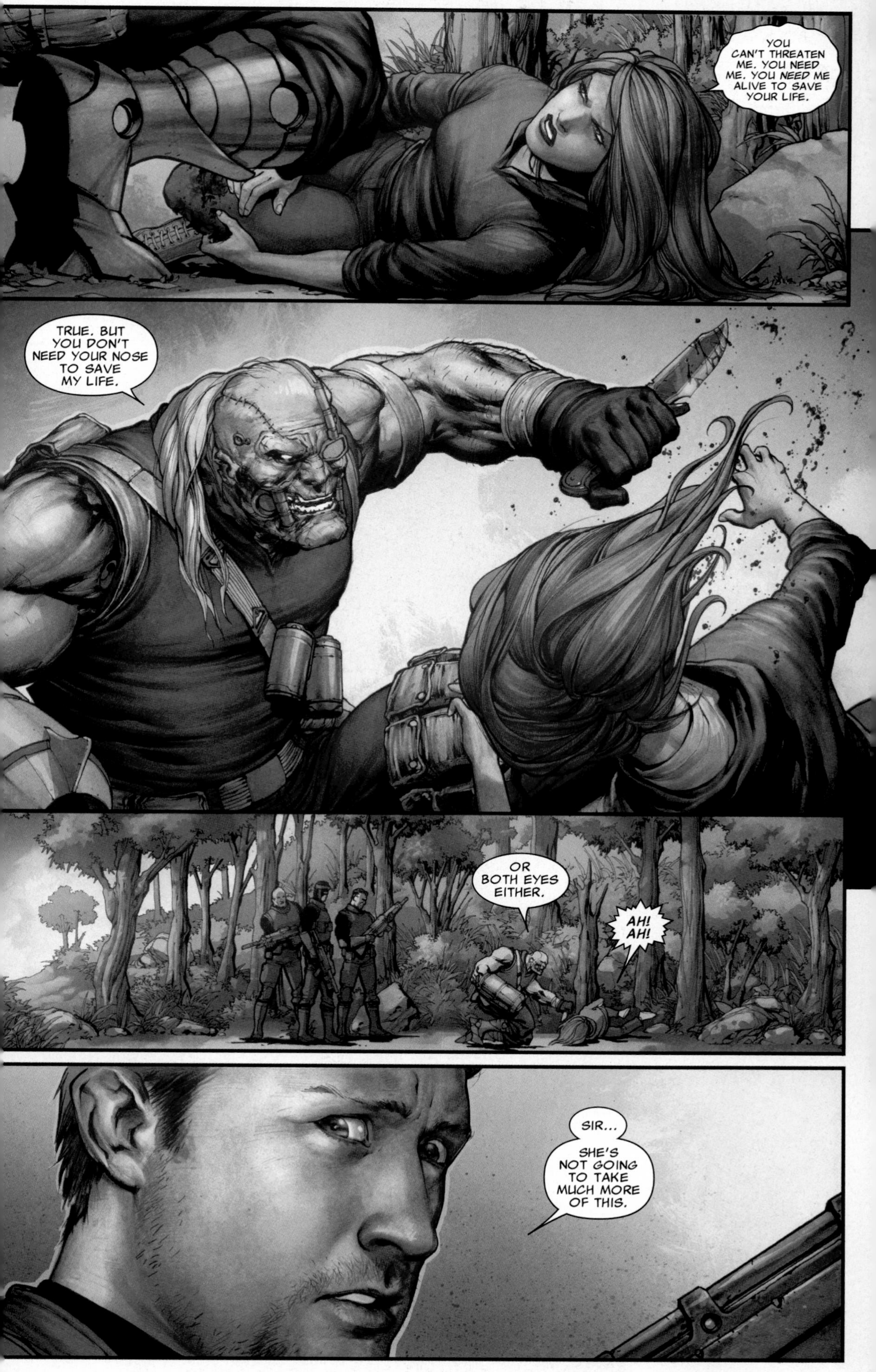
YOU CAN'T THREATEN ME. YOU NEED ME. YOU NEED ME ALIVE TO SAVE YOUR LIFE.
TRUE. BUT YOU DON'T NEED YOUR NOSE TO SAVE MY LIFE.
OR BOTH EYES EITHER.
AH! AH!
SIR...
SHE'S NOT GOING TO TAKE MUCH MORE OF THIS.

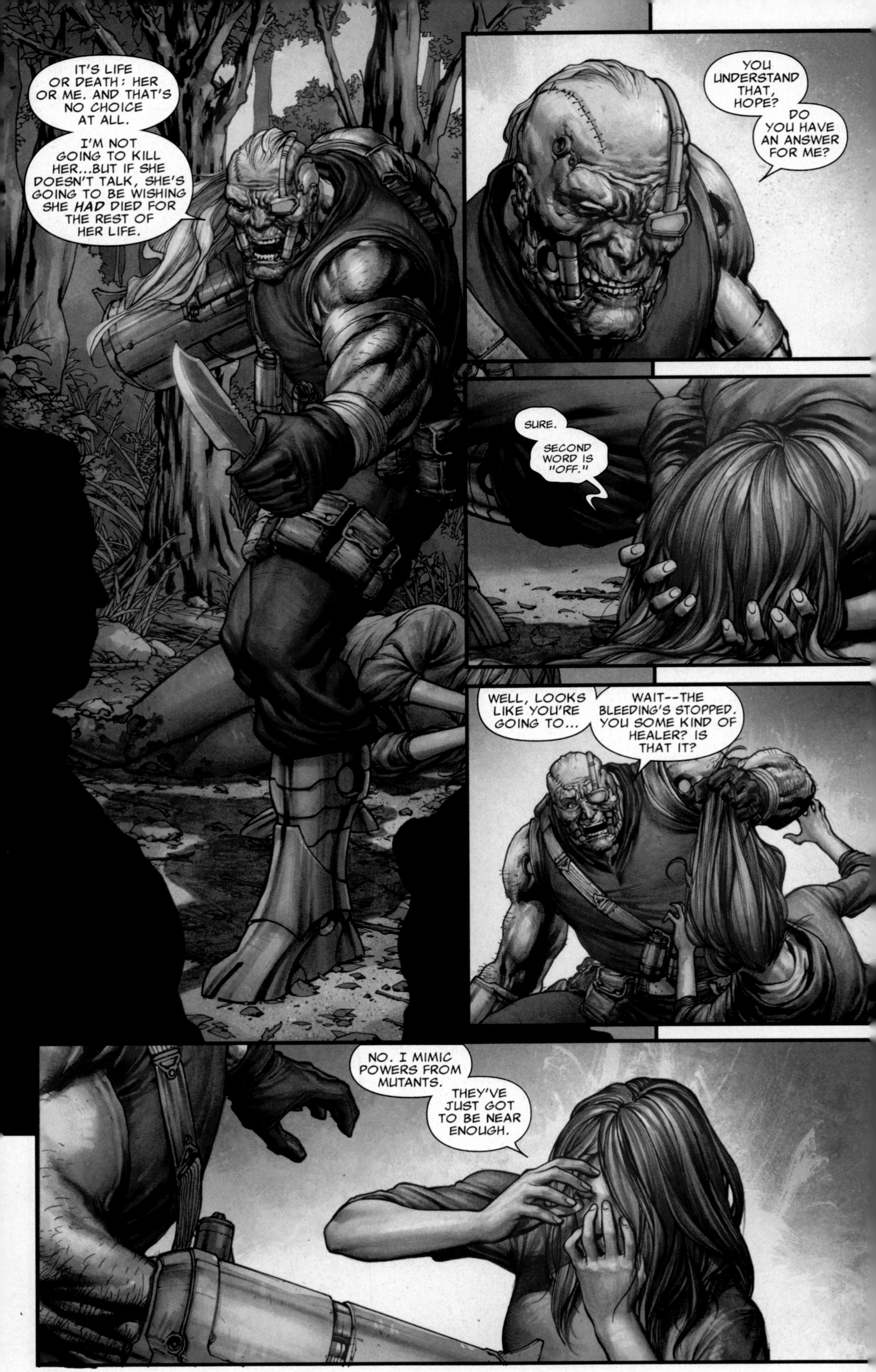
IT'S LIFE OR DEATH: HER OR ME. AND THAT'S NO CHOICE AT ALL.
I'M NOT GOING TO KILL HER...BUT IF SHE DOESN'T TALK, SHE'S GOING TO BE WISHING SHE *HAD* DIED FOR THE REST OF HER LIFE.
YOU UNDERSTAND THAT, HOPE?
DO YOU HAVE AN ANSWER FOR ME?
SURE.
SECOND WORD IS "OFF."
WELL, LOOKS LIKE YOU'RE GOING TO...
WAIT--THE BLEEDING'S STOPPED. YOU SOME KIND OF HEALER? IS THAT IT?
NO. I MIMIC POWERS FROM MUTANTS.
THEY'VE JUST GOT TO BE NEAR ENOUGH.

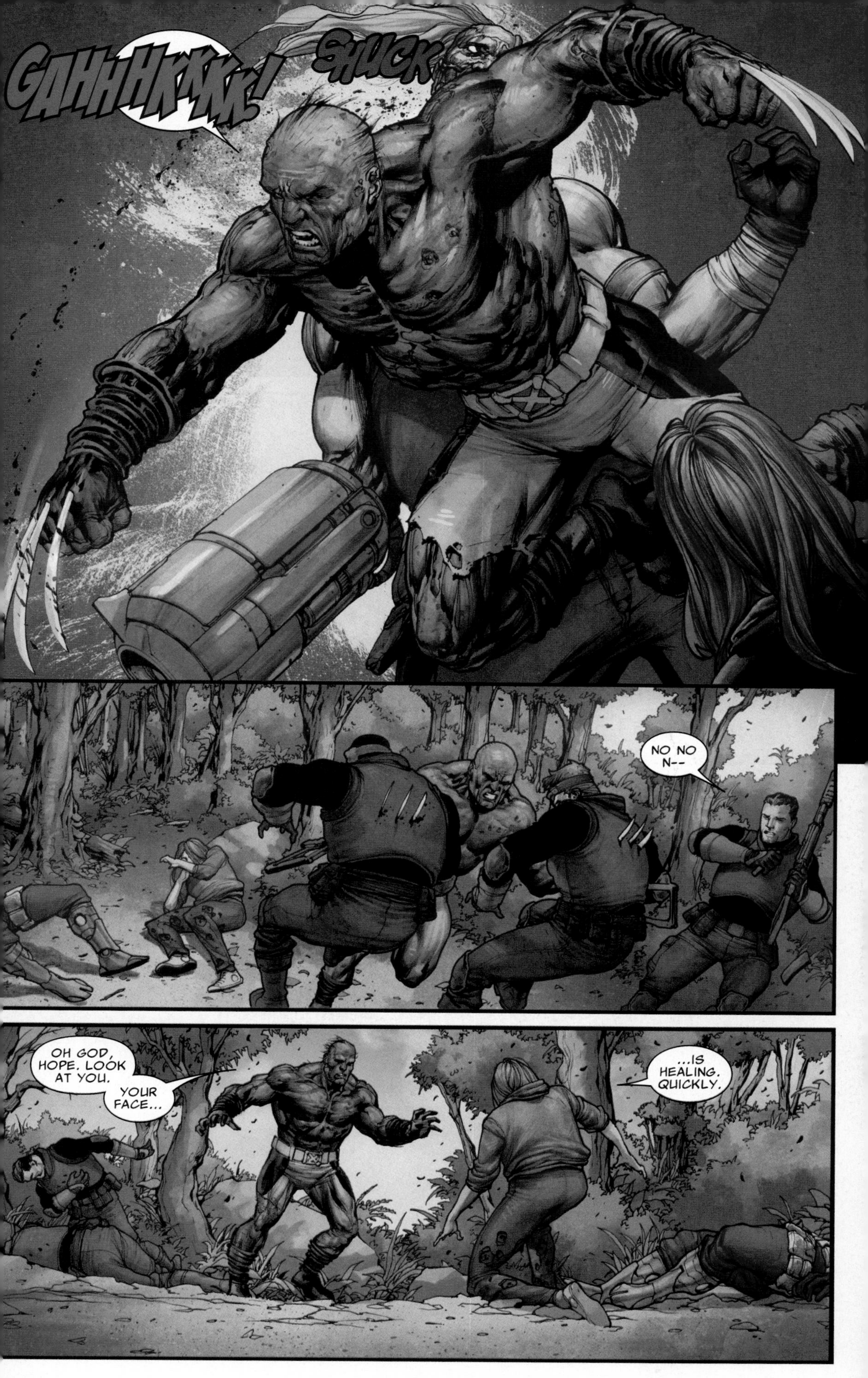
GAHHHKKKK!
SHUCK
NO NO N--
OH GOD, HOPE. LOOK AT YOU.
YOUR FACE...
...IS HEALING. QUICKLY.

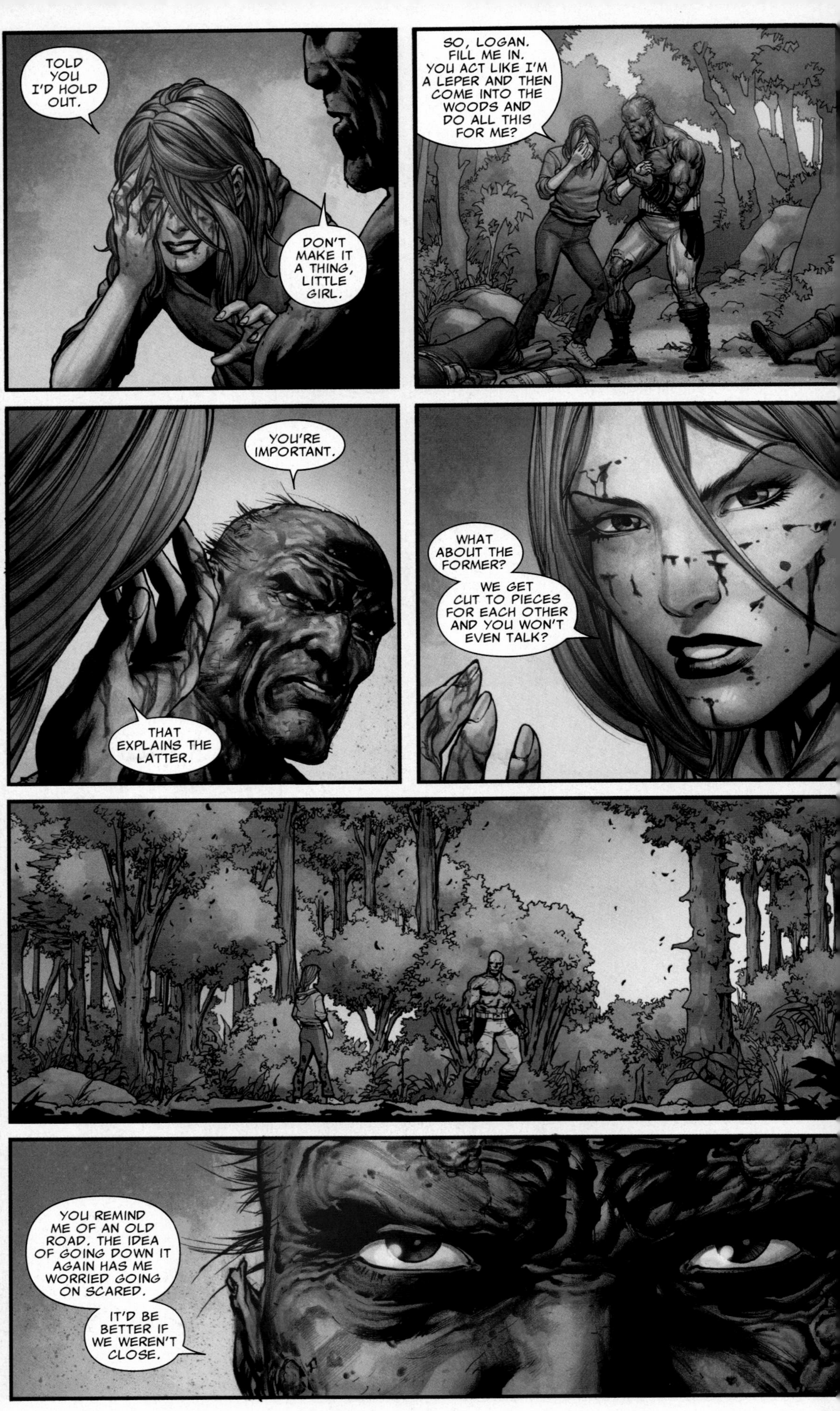
TOLD YOU I'D HOLD OUT.
DON'T MAKE IT A THING, LITTLE GIRL.
SO, LOGAN. FILL ME IN. YOU ACT LIKE I'M A LEPER AND THEN COME INTO THE WOODS AND DO ALL THIS FOR ME?
YOU'RE IMPORTANT.
THAT EXPLAINS THE LATTER.
WHAT ABOUT THE FORMER?
WE GET CUT TO PIECES FOR EACH OTHER AND YOU WON'T EVEN TALK?
YOU REMIND ME OF AN OLD ROAD. THE IDEA OF GOING DOWN IT AGAIN HAS ME WORRIED GOING ON SCARED.
IT'D BE BETTER IF WE WEREN'T CLOSE.

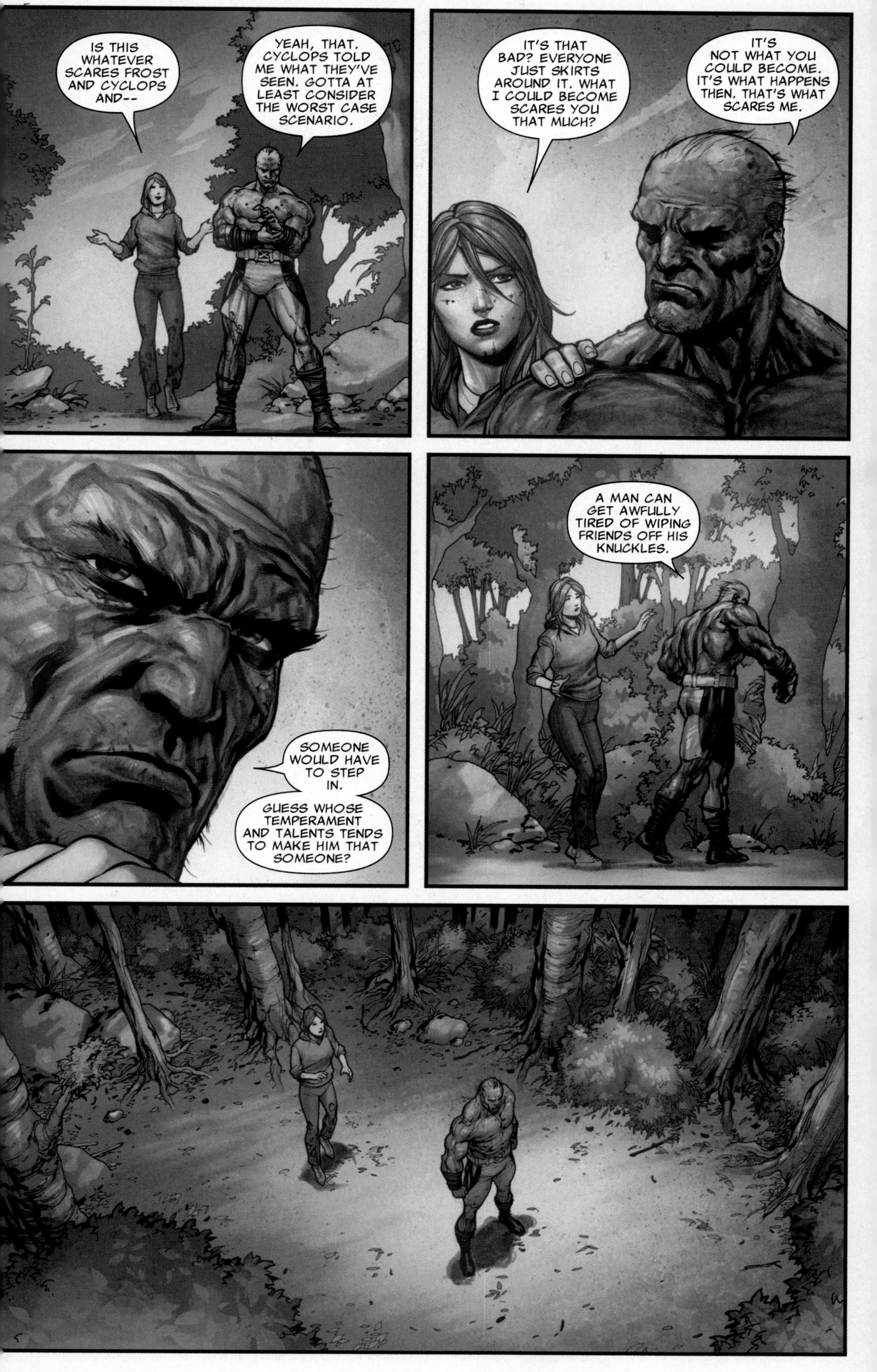
IS THIS WHATEVER SCARES FROST AND CYCLOPS AND--
YEAH, THAT. CYCLOPS TOLD ME WHAT THEY'VE SEEN. GOTTA AT LEAST CONSIDER THE WORST CASE SCENARIO.
IT'S THAT BAD? EVERYONE JUST SKIRTS AROUND IT. WHAT I COULD BECOME SCARES YOU THAT MUCH?
IT'S NOT WHAT YOU COULD BECOME. IT'S WHAT HAPPENS THEN. THAT'S WHAT SCARES ME.
SOMEONE WOULD HAVE TO STEP IN.
GUESS WHOSE TEMPERAMENT AND TALENTS TENDS TO MAKE HIM THAT SOMEONE?
A MAN CAN GET AWFULLY TIRED OF WIPING FRIENDS OFF HIS KNUCKLES.

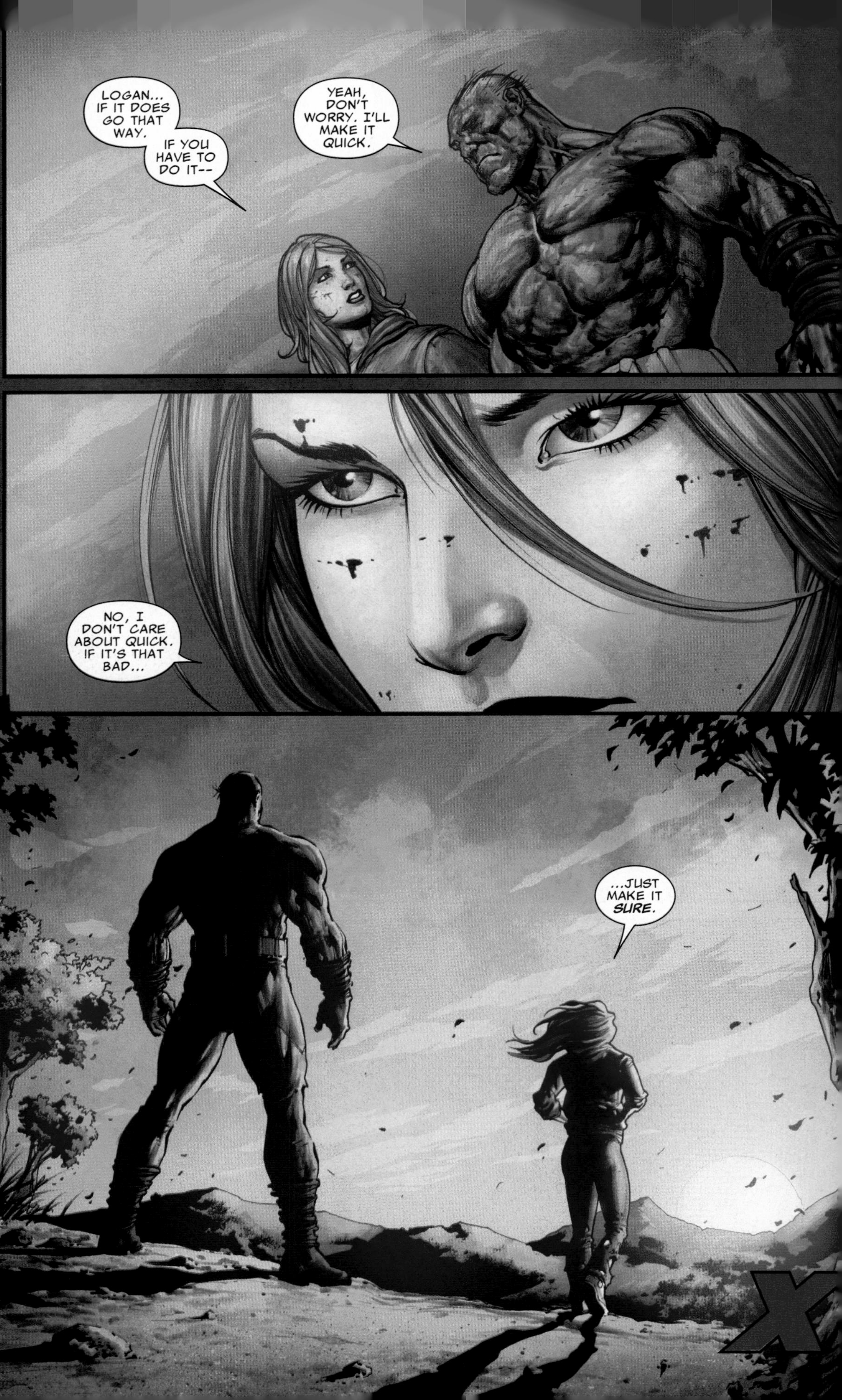
LOGAN... IF IT DOES GO THAT WAY.
IF YOU HAVE TO DO IT--
YEAH, DON'T WORRY. I'LL MAKE IT QUICK.
NO, I DON'T CARE ABOUT QUICK. IF IT'S THAT BAD...
...JUST MAKE IT SURE.

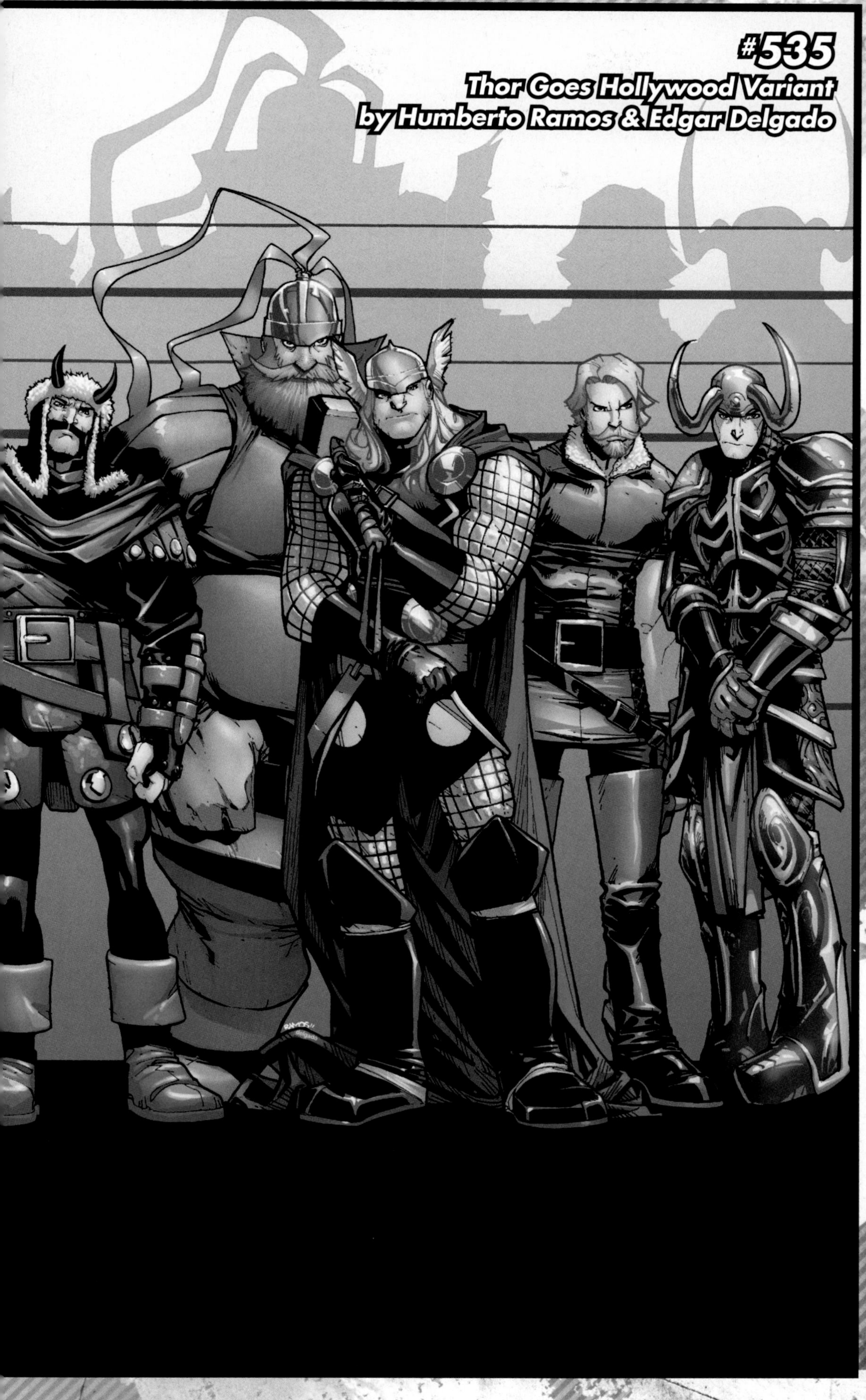

#535
Thor Goes Hollywood Variant
by Humberto Ramos & Edgar Delgado

#539

I Am Captain America Variant by Dave Johnson

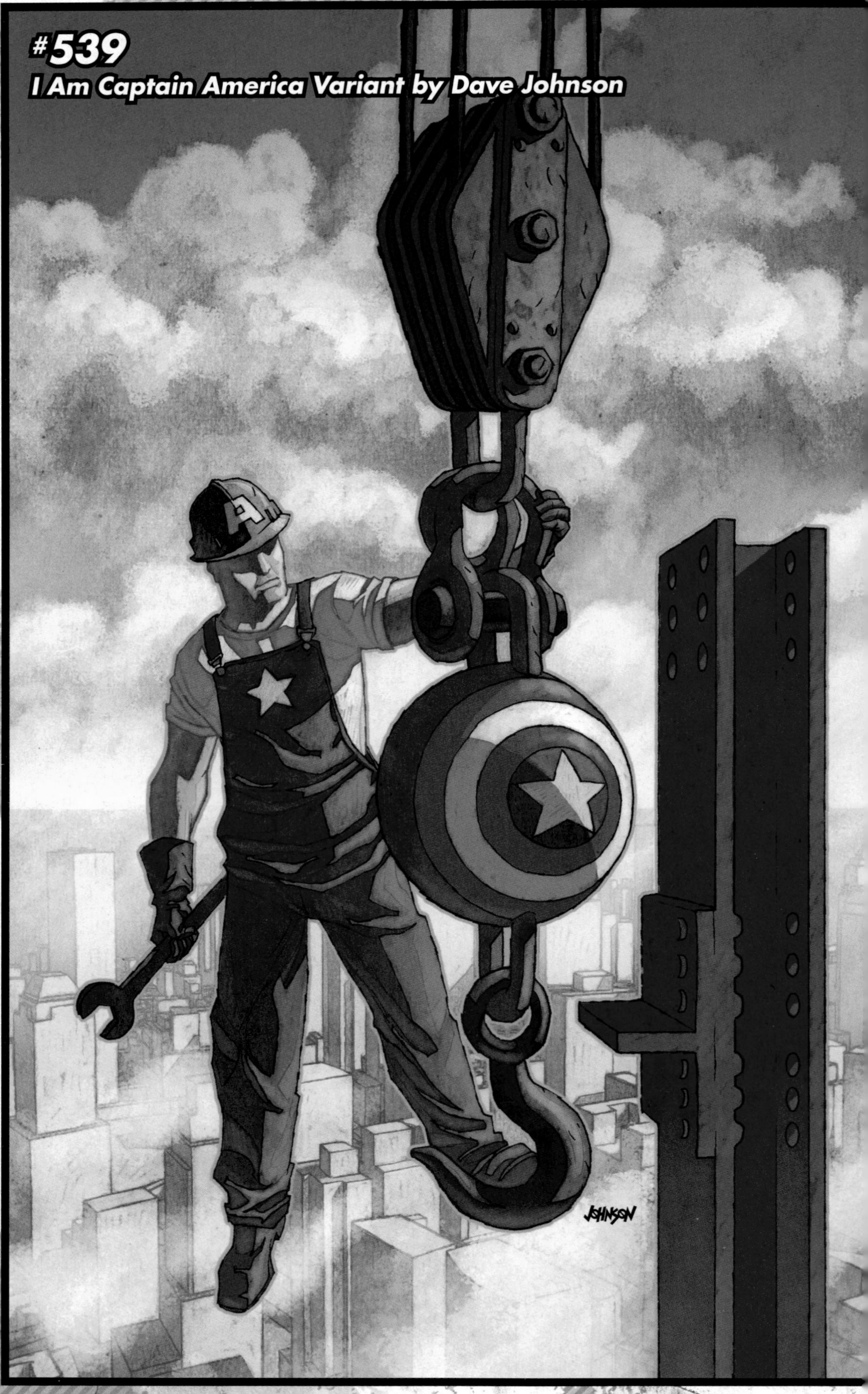
A
JOHNSON